SNOWSHOE TRAILS
IN SOUTHWESTERN
BRITISH COLUMBIA

SNOWSHOE

TRAILS IN SOUTHWESTERN

BRITISH COLUMBIA

AILEEN STALKER
AND TONY KEEN

RMB

RMB | Rocky Mountain Books Ltd.
rmbooks.com
@rmbooks
facebook.com/rmbooks

Cataloguing data available from Library and Archives Canada
ISBN 978-1-77160-188-7 (paperback)
ISBN 978-1-77160-189-4 (electronic)

All photographs are by Tony Keen unless otherwise noted.

Front cover photo: Spring snowshoeing on a North Shore mountain trail

Printed and bound in Canada by Friesens

Distributed in Canada by Heritage Group Distribution and in the U.S. by Publishers Group West

For information on purchasing bulk quantities of this book, or to obtain media excerpts or invite the author to
speak at an event, please visit rmbooks.com and select the "Contact Us" tab.

RMB | Rocky Mountain Books is dedicated to the environment and committed to reducing the destruction of
old-growth forests. Our books are produced with respect for the future and consideration for the past.
We acknowledge the financial support of the Government of Canada through the Canada Book Fund and the
Canada Council for the Arts, and of the province of British Columbia through the British Columbia Arts Council
and the Book Publishing Tax Credit.

Disclaimer

The actions described in this book may be considered inherently dangerous activities. Individuals undertake
these activities at their own risk. The information put forth in this guide has been collected from a variety of
sources and is not guaranteed to be completely accurate or reliable. Many conditions and some information
may change owing to weather and numerous other factors beyond the control of the authors and publishers.
Individuals or groups must determine the risks, use their own judgment, and take full responsibility for their
actions. Do not depend on any information found in this book for your own personal safety. Your safety
depends on your own good judgment based on your skills, education, and experience.

It is up to the users of this guidebook to acquire the necessary skills for safe experiences and to exercise
caution in potentially hazardous areas. The authors and publishers of this guide accept no responsibility for
your actions or the results that occur from another's actions, choices, or judgments. If you have any doubt as to
your safety or your ability to attempt anything described in this guidebook, do not attempt it.

CONTENTS

Acknowledgements   7
Introduction   9

PART 1: GETTING STARTED   13
The History of Snowshoeing   19
Safety First   27
Equipment and Clothing   57
Snowshoeing Is Physical!   67
Snowshoeing Techniques   75
Snowshoeing Is a Sport
   for Everyone   81

PART 2: THE TRAILS   103
Snowshoe Trails in
   Southwestern BC   107
      Coquihalla   107
      Fraser Valley   131
      Manning Park   135
      North Shore   166
      Sea to Sky Corridor   207
      Sunshine Coast   235
      Whistler Interpretive
         Forest Trails   247
      Other Whistler Trails   262
More Snowshoe Adventures in
   British Columbia   281
      South Coastal Mountains   282
      Sunshine Coast   287
      Thompson/Okanagan   289
      Kootenay Rockies   295
      Northern British
         Columbia   306
      Vancouver Island   312
USA Destinations   314

PART 3: SNOWSHOEING
   RESOURCES   315

Appendix A: Navigation   321
Appendix B: Safety   324
Appendix C: Other Useful
   Resources   327
Appendix D: Equipment   329

References   332
Index of Trails   334
About the Authors   336

ACKNOWLEDGEMENTS

This book would not have been possible without the help and support of my family: Tony, Andrew, Stephanie, Danika, Patrick, Debi, Alec (and Joyce, Kevin, Sheila and Anne long-distance and Tony's family as well). A big thanks to friends who did initial editing, came along for many "one more last check" trips and gave encouragement and believed that the book would eventually get finished. Also to the members of the Pathfinders Outdoor Club who patiently (or sometimes impatiently) waited while I made notes and GPS trail markings, and who provided so much company and laughs on this writing adventure. Thanks too to Lynn Sackville for excellent initial editing, and to publisher Don Gorman and the staff at Rocky Mountain Books for helping create this book. A special thanks to RMB's Joe Wilderson, who has to be the best and most thorough editor. Thanks to Jeremy Lindley for reviewing the information about purchasing snowshoes; Nick Hastie for helping with equipment and safety pictures; and Ryan Hill for his exercise expertise. Thank you also to the many individuals who added useful information about the other beautiful locations in BC that have snowshoe trails. Mary Clayton from Avalanche Canada deserves a special thanks for her invaluable help in editing and ensuring the accuracy of the material about avalanche safety. And of course, the book could not have been completed without patient Tony, who volunteered to create the maps and took the majority of the pictures. One thousand thanks, Tony.

INTRODUCTION

In North America snowshoeing is one of the most rapidly increasing winter sports, and no wonder! As a recreational pursuit, whether on well-defined trails or in the backcountry or in organized snowshoe races, the advantages are many. Here are a few:

- Snowshoeing provides a high level of aerobic activity. Snowshoeing at an average speed of 5 km/h (3 mph) compares favorably to running at 10 km/h (6 mph) and to cross-country skiing at 13 km/h (8 mph). An average adult weighing 70 kg burns 289 calories in 30 minutes of snowshoeing.
- Snowshoeing can be enjoyed by any age group and by families.
- Snowshoeing provides a unique wilderness experience. Each trip is different – even on the same trail.
- Snowshoeing can be done on a variety of terrain.
- Snowshoeing trails are generally far away from resorts, noise, crowds and consumerism.
- Snowshoeing helps animals by creating trails that they can use to find food in deep snow.
- Snowshoeing allows you to get up close to nature to identify trees, birds, animal tracks and animals in their winter habitat.
- Snowshoeing is social – you can walk and talk at the same time. People greet you and look you in the eye, give you trail hints or share a treat. (Generally there are fewer electronic devices to distract snowshoers out on the trail.)
- Snowshoeing is inexpensive: reasonable equipment costs or rentals, your own packed lunch, no need for high-fashion clothing. You will have saved a lot and gained a lot by choosing this sport.
- Snowshoe gear does not take up much cargo room in your vehicle.

- Snowshoeing as a winter sport is a green alternative. You may have driven to the trailhead but after that it is your own power that moves you forward.
- Snowshoeing is truly Canadian.

For any author of an outdoor book there comes the inevitable question "How long have you been snowshoeing/kayaking/hiking/skiing?" I first started snowshoeing in Ontario in the 1960s. Cold winters, crisp snow and traditional-style wooden snowshoes with long tails, gut webbing and leather bindings worked well on the relatively flat terrain. When I moved to Vancouver in the early 1970s I brought them along only to discover wet heavy snow, often very steep terrain and a need for a whole different type of snowshoe. So I bought the bearpaw style with the same type of leather bindings and used them for years. But downhill and cross-country skiing captured the interest of my children and myself and so my snowshoes were laid to rest for a while. What a change when I decided to join friends and again go snowshoeing. The lightweight equipment made it so enjoyable and easy that snowshoeing rapidly became one of my favorite winter activities.

My need to have variety in my life led me to find new trails for my friends and me to explore. And in social settings, when people heard that I snowshoed as a winter activity, more and more began to ask, "But where do you go snowshoeing beyond the North Shore?" Then my son Andrew (the same son that suggested I write a kayaking book with him, *Paddling Through History: Vancouver and Victoria*, RMB 2005) said "You know, Mom, what is needed is a book about the snowshoe trails accessible from Vancouver." The rest is, well, this book. Enjoy.

Snowshoeing is truly Canadian

PART 1

GETTING STARTED

This work is intended as a guide to the trails my friends and I have explored and enjoyed during many years of snowshoeing in southwestern British Columbia. "Guide" is the operative word. I have tried to provide enough information to enable you to use the trails safely and learn some of the cultural history or natural history when on the trail. But in winter, travel by snowshoe, foot or skis in the backcountry is an inherently dangerous activity that you need knowledge, physical ability and skills to participate in safely.

As noted frequently throughout, it is the responsibility of each person snowshoeing, and especially the leader of a group, to inform themselves of weather, terrain and avalanche possibility and to be prepared with safety equipment, the Ten Essentials, topographic maps, and clothing appropriate for the trail and time of year. Hopefully, this guidebook will help you have a successful trip, but like any equipment it is an adjunct to your own preparation and knowledge.

Aileen recording GPS readings and making notes

Tony taking pictures

TRAIL MEASURING

Yes, you are right – your measurements of distance, time and elevation will be different from ours. Over the past several years when I was writing this book, we went on the trails numerous times and used one (and sometimes two) Garmin GPS Map 60CSx devices to measure distance and elevation of the trail and calculate the time to snowshoe the route at a moderate pace. We also used a compass and maps, which are the most accurate resources for location and route finding. Landmarks and places requiring special safety consideration were noted, though these may change in each season or be added to because of such factors as weather, fallen trees, bridge washouts and stream divergences. The "tracks" from the Garmin GPS units were entered, with permission from the company, into Garmin's BaseCamp software. The tracks were then overlaid on Government of Canada topographic maps.

Distances

Trail measurements in this book are meant to be guides only, not absolute values. In the text you will see "about" and "approximately" frequently attached to the description of distances. The distances and elevations in this book may vary somewhat from signposts, particularly older BC Parks distances. Repeated measurements indicated that our more recent data was closer to the actual distances and/or elevations. We took into consideration figures given by other guidebook authors, trail mappers posting on recreational websites, and government sources, and those may vary from our numbers and from one another. Frequently guidebook authors give only elevation gain or total distance. Some use only a trail description. After experiencing the struggle to try to record as accurate numbers as possible we understand why they avoided what we attempted!

See **Appendix A: Navigation** for information about NTS maps and where to get them. Also listed there are all the trails covered in this book grouped according to the NTS map they appear on, along with some other useful navigation aids.

Durations

When estimating the time needed to complete a given trail it must be remembered that snowshoeing takes about one-third longer than hiking, and if you are breaking trail even more time is needed. So a 9 km round trip on a tracked trail will feel more like a 12 km trip.

The use of the terms "easy" and "moderate" to describe trail difficulty is based on assessment of both terrain and distance. So the terrain might be easy – generally level ground, few steep sections and with a gradual elevation gain, but the length could be quite long. Moderate trails were ones that were generally long and/or had numerous steep sections or steeper grades overall and required more snowshoeing skill and some possible route finding.

TRAIL MARKING

Summer hikers know how bewildering directions in the forest can get with rainbow coloured flagging going every which way. However, in the summer there is usually a well-defined path to follow for trails described in guidebooks. Not so in winter, and by mid-winter (or if there is early wet snow and/or heavy snowfall) often the orange metal markers visible in summer are covered with snow. Over the years, for our own safety on some confusing winter trails, my outdoor group has marked some trails with orange flagging bearing the words SNOWSHOE TRAIL. These flagging tapes get torn down or blown down or they just wear out in the sun and fade away. In this book I have tried to describe as many permanent landmarks as possible as a guide for directions in a basically white landscape.

Scout knows Aaron should be on a leash when in provincial parks

Please do not add any other flagging tapes. Our outdoor group is presently in discussions with BC Parks to work as volunteers to put up specific snowshoe trail markers for the trails in this book that are located in provincial parks.

DOGS ON THE TRAIL

You love your dog and your dog loves the snow. There are many trails listed in this book that are dog friendly, but please respect the rules where all trails in provincial parks require that your dog be on a leash at all times. In some provincial parks no dogs are allowed at all. And remember: environmentally considerate use of the wilderness with a dog means picking up the poo just like at home.

If one object can be termed a Canadian icon, it's the snowshoe
BC MOUNTAINEERING CLUB ON GROUSE MOUNTAIN CA. 1921; #5682 NVMA

THE HISTORY OF SNOWSHOEING

Long before European settlement of North America, First Nations in eastern Canada created snowshoes using ash frames, skin bindings and rawhide webbing. Although the Vikings who explored the east coast of Canada around 1000 CE made no mention in their sagas of seeing or using snowshoes, it is thought that snowshoeing was a well-established method of travel among Native populations at that time.

Exactly when humans first developed snowshoes is unknown, although archeologists believe the "iceman" found preserved in the Ötz Valley in the northern Alps was wearing relatively sophisticated snowshoes when he died about 5,300 years ago.

Evidence shows that around 4000 BCE, "foot extenders" – modified slabs of wood – were used in Central Asia for travel over snowy terrain. This technology facilitated human migration into Scandinavia, Siberia and eventually North America.

In the Canadian far north, Inuit peoples had less need of snowshoes than did First Nations in more southerly and easterly regions of Canada. High-Arctic snow and ice was easier to travel on than the deep snow found in forests and plains. However, snowshoes developed in Alaska and the Yukon have a unique, very long and slender shape. When French colonists, fur traders, voyageurs and coureurs de bois began to explore eastern Canada in the 1600s, they rapidly adopted many First Nations survival tactics, including snowshoes. While the French settlers dubbed them "raquettes" given their resemblance to the webbed bat used in the French game of tennis, the English adopted the more prosaic name "snowshoe."

In war and peace, exploration and settlement, the snowshoe played an important part in the development of Canada. During the 1757 and 1758 "Battles on Snowshoes" between the French and the English in what is now northern New York State, and in subsequent skirmishes in the Adirondacks and border areas, the use of snowshoes became a key military strategy for movement of troops in winter.

Recreational use of snowshoes evolved around 1840. Prominent English businessmen in Montreal started meeting weekly during the winter to "tramp" using snowshoes on the trails in the region. In 1840 the first club of its kind in the world – the Montreal Snowshoe Club – was formed. Later, clubs were founded in Ottawa, Toronto, Quebec City and as far away as Manitoba and Newfoundland, leading to snowshoe conventions. The clubs were for men only, and the camaraderie and accompanying meals and competitions all contributed to the popularity of the sport. As interest in snowshoeing grew, some women also joined in the recreational activities.

With the founding of American snowshoe clubs, conventions and competitions went international. Snowshoers challenged each other in sprints that ranged from 100 to 880 yards long. They competed over hurdles, usually on a course of 120 yards. They held snowshoeing marathons ranging from one mile up to 10 miles. The Montreal Snowshoe Club established the first winter Mardi Gras Carnival, which took place for a week each year from 1883 to 1889 – a lasting legacy now called the Quebec Winter Carnival.

In the 20th century, interest in snowshoeing declined, overshadowed by the emergence of ice hockey and later skiing. However, by the 1980s, new lightweight, inexpensive and technically superior snowshoes began to draw back fans and attract new participants at both recreational and competitive levels.

The Canadian Snowshoe Union, created in 1907, was initially the governing body for the over 70 clubs in Canada. Now, the organization Snowshoe Canada has as its mission "through fitness, competition and fair play, to provide a safe and friendly environment for all and represent the sport at provincial, national and world championships and ultimately the Olympics."

Today, snowshoeing is the fastest-growing winter sport in North America. For more extensive information about the history of snowshoeing, visit **gvsnowshoes.com/en/snowshoe-history.**

TYPES OF TRADITIONAL WOODEN SNOWSHOES

There are four main kinds of wooden snowshoes, each with its own shape and style to accommodate different terrain and snow conditions. White ash, prized for its strength and pliability, was steamed to form the desired shape. However, location determined what materials were available, and hickory, spruce, birch, elm and larch were also used. Lacing of the deck was done with babiche – untanned caribou, moose or deer hide strips.

The Ojibwe snowshoe was developed by the people of that name, who are one of the largest First Nations groups in eastern and western Canada and the central United States. The design has a narrow frame, curved tip and long, narrow tail. It is one of the oldest types of snowshoe and resembles ones described as being used in Siberia, Scandinavia and Greenland centuries ago.

The long Yukon–Alaskan snowshoe (117 cm or longer) is effective in open, snow-covered terrain in the Northwest. When the wearer is moving forward, the elongated tail helps keep a straight line.

The Huron snowshoe was created by the indigenous people who first lived along the north shore of Lake Ontario and then resettled close to Georgian Bay, where Champlain encountered them. It was probably this style of snowshoe that the early French settlers observed in use by the First Nations. The design provides good flotation in soft snow and general manoeuvrability in wooded areas.

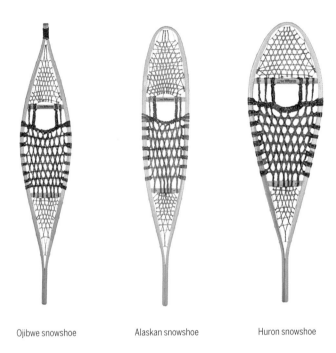

Ojibwe snowshoe   Alaskan snowshoe   Huron snowshoe

The oval-shaped bearpaw snowshoe works well in forests, where manoeuvrability is required. Its width and short length also made it a choice for long-distance travel. The modified bearpaw takes the best of both the bearpaw and the Huron and can be used in many snow conditions.

There are several other styles of snowshoes, including the pickerel, Attikamek, elbow, Green Mountain bearpaw and beavertail.

The shape of the beavertail snowshoe is one of the most interesting. It was developed by the Cree in northern Quebec and

Bearpaw and modified bearpaw snowshoes
THANKS TO GV SNOWSHOES FOR THEIR PICTURES
AND HISTORICAL INFORMATION ABOUT
THE TRADITIONAL SNOWSHOE DESIGNS.

Beavertail snowshoes made by
Jason MacKinnon, Harmony
Custom Woodcraft, Kingston, NS

Labrador. Very wide and flat in shape, it does indeed look like a beaver tail, with a short, rounded back tail (although some of today's manufacturers extend this tail.) The shape works well in soft snow but the wide stance needed for walking could be tiring. The weave of the rawhide decking was denser and more intricate, which increased the flotation capacity of these snowshoes.

A metal snowshoe for a horse
STEWART MUSEUM AND
ARCHIVES, STEWART, BC

SNOWSHOES ON HORSES?

Swedish woodcuts from the 13th century show horses wearing snowshoes. During eastern Canadian winters snowshoes were put on wagon- and log-pulling horses so that timber harvesting could continue throughout the year. If you ever visit the museum in Stewart, BC, you can see pictures and the metal snowshoes that were constructed for pack horses to wear in heavy snow. Weighted down by mining supplies as they went into the Bear Creek Valley during early 1900s mining explorations, these horses would have sunk into the snow without this adapted footwear. It was not an entirely successful invention, though: only about 65 of 300 horses could be trained to use the snowshoes, but they became highly valued (and probably really tired) workers.

A mine pack horse on snowshoes ca. early 1900s
PHOTOGRAPHER UNKNOWN; COURTESY OF STEWART MUSEUM AND ARCHIVES

The Ten Essentials

SAFETY FIRST

Just when you thought you had found the ultimate winter sport (inexpensive, suitable for all ages, social, excellent exercise), the essential subject of snowshoe safety has to be discussed. Perhaps you think a focus on safety may spoil the adventure. Not true – the following information (and more extensive material found in the suggested courses, websites and books) will make you a more thoughtful and aware snowshoer and may even save your life or your friends'.

However, nothing provided in this short section about avalanches, natural winter hazards – and possible medical problems that are more likely to occur in winter conditions – replaces the need to take courses in avalanche awareness, map reading and first aid.

Any time you venture into the wilderness, attention to safety issues should become a primary concern. Although many of the snowshoe trails in this book are close to cities or large ski resorts, they are still considered wilderness trails – the majority are not patrolled, and varied terrain, weather, and snow conditions can create potential challenges. Wherever you snowshoe, you will need to consider many safety aspects both before your trip and while on the trail.

Before you begin your trip

- *Always* check road, weather and avalanche conditions for the road to the trail and for the trail itself. See **Appendix B: Safety** for contact information.
- Tell friends and/or family the location where you will be snowshoeing and the time you plan to return. Indicate the second-choice trail you will take if the first one is closed.
- Ensure you have a topographic map appropriate for the area. See full details in **Appendix A: Navigation**.

- Take along information (map, route description, trail book) about alternative trail possibilities in the area in case the chosen route is unsafe or closed for some reason.
- Check to see that your various device batteries are charged, including your cellphone and, if you are going into terrain where you will use them, a GPS and avalanche beacons. But don't count on cellphones for getting help or saving you – they are not reliable in all backcountry areas; they may run out of power on long trips; and in very cold weather their batteries may stop working altogether.
- Learn how to get GPS coordinates from your cellphone. Useful apps are the iPhone's built-in Compass; MotionX-GPS, also for iOS; and Mapstogo for Android. Remember, however, that map-reading skills, a compass and a printed topographic map provide the most reliable way of identifying your location, and that apps are an adjunct to, not a replacement for, these skills.
- Check that you have complete first aid supplies (see lists below) and that all your safety equipment is in working order (for example, fresh batteries in flashlights, headlamps and other electronic gear; full gas canisters for air horns; avalanche shovels that fold or telescope freely; unclogged whistles).
- Confirm the time of sunset: winter days have fewer daylight hours and snowshoeing back to the trailhead in the dark is dangerous.

SAFETY EQUIPMENT
The Ten Essentials
In the 1930s The Mountaineers, a Seattle group focused on wilderness preservation and enjoyment, developed a list of essential equipment for outdoor adventures. Known as the Ten Essentials, the list has recently been updated and items have been reassigned to different systems of equipment based on

use. See Recreational Equipment Inc. co-op, **rei.com/learn/expert-advice/ten-essentials.html**, for the original version and for an expanded explanation of the following list:

1. navigation (maps and compass)
2. sun protection (sunglasses and sunscreen)
3. insulation (extra clothing)
4. illumination (headlamp/flashlight)
5. first aid supplies (including insect repellent)
6. fire (waterproof matches/lighter/candles)
7. repair kit and tools
8. nutrition (extra food)
9. hydration (extra water)
10. emergency shelter

Although not on the Ten Essentials list, the following equipment is also useful:

- rope and bungee cords (good for carrying snowshoes on your pack if conditions warrant)
- whistle (on the outside of your pack)
- binoculars
- ice cleats/crampons for walking on crusty, icy terrain (lightweight and generally safer and more effective than snowshoes on ice)

Yes, carrying all these items will mean a heavier pack, but should an emergency occur, you will have the equipment to help yourself or members of your party. Share the weight and responsibility of the safety items and first aid equipment among your group members.

First aid supplies
Most people engaging in outdoor activities carry a small first aid

kit for blisters or minor cuts, but for wilderness conditions more extensive supplies are required.

St. John Ambulance first aid kits are available through **sja.ca**. The contents of the Outdoor & Sport Kit, suitable for day trips, are:

- 2 abdominal pads (12.7 × 22.9 cm)
- 6 adhesive fabric bandages (1.9 × 7.5 cm)
- 6 adhesive fabric bandages (5.0 × 10 cm)
- 2 adhesive tape rolls (2.5 cm × 4.5 m)
- 18 antiseptic wipes (benzalkonium chloride/BZK)
- 2 cold packs
- 1 CPR face shield
- 2 elastic bandage rolls (7.5 cm × 4.5 m)
- 6 fingertip fabric bandages
- 3 gauze bandage rolls (7.5 cm × 4.5 m)
- 7 gauze pads (10 × 10 cm)
- 7 gauze pads (7.5 cm × 7.5 cm)
- 6 knuckle fabric bandages
- 2 non-adherent pads (7.5 × 10 cm)
- 1 pair of tweezers
- 1 pair of universal scissors (14 cm)
- 3 pairs of latex-free gloves
- 1 patient info note pad
- 1 pencil
- 1 emergency foil blanket
- 12 safety pins
- 1 first aid pocket guide
- 2 tongue depressors
- 1 trauma dressing
- 2 triangular bandages
- 2 wood splints

Contents of the Outdoor & Sport Kit are included here
with the permission of St. John Ambulance.

The resource books *Wilderness and Remote First Aid Field Guide* and a *First Aid and CPR Manual* as well as first aid kits for various needs are available from the Red Cross at **redcrossproducts.ca**. The contents of the Red Cross All Purpose Kit, suitable for longer trips, are as follows:

- 10 plastic bandages junior (1.0 × 3.8 cm)
- 10 plastic bandages (1.9 × 7.6 cm)
- 6 fabric bandages (2.2 × 7.6 cm)
- 2 fabric bandages, large patch (5.1 × 7.6 cm)
- 3 fabric bandages, knuckle (3.8 × 7.6 cm)
- 2 fabric bandages, fingertip small (4.4 × 5.1 cm)
- 3 fabric bandages, fingertip large (4.4 × 7.6 cm)
- 1 WoundSeal topical powder
- 1 abdominal combine pad (12.7 × 22.9 cm)
- 1 RL conforming stretch bandage (7.6 cm × 3.7 m)
- 2 gauze pads (7.6 × 7.6 cm)
- 2 non-woven sponges, 4-ply 2s (7.6 × 7.6 cm)
- 2 Telfa non-adherent pads (5.1 × 7.6 cm)
- 1 triangular bandage (101.6 × 101.3 × 142.2 cm)
- 2 cotton tipped applicators, 2/pk, STR, single-ended (7.6 cm)
- 2 tongue depressors senior (1.9 × 15.2 cm)
- 1 RL clear plastic tape (1.9 × 90 cm)
- 1 RL elastic support/compression bandage (7.6 cm × 4.6 m)
- 8 alcohol antiseptic swabs
- 9 benzalkonium chloride antiseptic towelettes
- 3 hand-cleansing moist towelettes
- 3 hand-cleansing antimicrobial towelettes
- 2 hand sanitizer antiseptic gel (3.7 ml)
- 2 first aid cream (0.9 g)
- 1 Water-Jel burn dressing (5.1 × 15.2 cm)
- 1 Water-Jel cool jel, 3.5 g
- 1 cold pack, instant, small (10.2 × 15.2 cm)

- 3 after bite treatment swabs
- 1 First Aid & Emergency Care Guide (CRC)
- 1 universal paramedic scissors (15.9 cm)
- 1 pkg Splinter Out, 2s
- 1 pkg safety pins, assorted sizes
- 1 pkg nitrile medical examination gloves, 2s
- 1 infectious-waste bag (15.2 × 22.9 cm)
- 1 CPR face shield w/one-way filtered valve
- 1 foil/mylar emergency blanket (142.2 × 203.2 cm)
- 2 oral/axillary thermometers
- 1 Tempa•DOT instruction insert

Contents of the Red Cross All Purpose Kit are included
here with permission of the Canadian Red Cross.

What is the most important safety issue?

Having all this safety equipment in your backpack is important, but equally vital is the ability to use it appropriately. Learn navigation skills, wilderness first aid and avalanche awareness and rescue skills to be fully prepared for any eventuality.

POSSIBLE WINTER FIRST AID EMERGENCIES

Blisters, bruises, scrapes, cuts, sprains and broken bones might occur on any hike in any season, but certain ailments are more likely to happen during winter activities because of the added factors of cold temperatures and wind chill. Be alert for the following conditions among your snowshoeing companions.

Fatigue

Sometimes people display obvious signs of fatigue – lagging behind or commenting about being tired. Other times they give more subtle clues, such as asking about when lunch is planned or how long it is to the end of the trail. Members of your group may be more vulnerable to fatigue if snowshoeing at a high altitude or if they become cold because they are not appropriately dressed. Help avoid fatigue with regular food and water breaks. If someone is snowshoeing slowly, check that they are dressed warmly and provide extra layers if needed. Inquire whether they have an undisclosed medical condition.

The distance and pace of a snowshoe adventure should match the abilities of all the participants. Know your group – if some participants are new to snowshoeing, anticipate that they may be slower. With a mixed group of different ages and skills, go at the pace of the slowest members. Have a strong snowshoer at the back of the group to accompany and look out for the slowest members.

Be prepared to turn around if the tired person states they cannot make it to the end and back (unless it is a one-way trail with your car at the end point or you are considerably past the midpoint in a loop trip).

Frostbite

Frostbite occurs when blood flow is reduced to exposed body parts, and is most common in the fingers, toes, nose, ears, cheeks and chin. Often others notice frostbite before the affected person, who – beyond the frostnip stage – does not feel it.

The first stage of frostbite is called frostnip. The skin may be cold and turn red or white. If you continue to stay in the cold environment, prickling and numbness may occur in the affected area.

Continued exposure may lead to the second stage, called superficial frostbite. The skin will remain soft but may turn white or pale. Ice crystals may form in the skin, although the affected areas may feel warm. Blisters in the affected areas may appear 24 to 36 hours after warming.

With severe frostbite, the skin may be bluish-white or grayish-yellow and hard or waxy looking. Joints and muscles may feel stiff. Numbness occurs and limits awareness of how severe the condition is. Within 24 to 48 hours after warming, large blisters will occur, followed by blackened, dead hard skin areas.

Prevent frostbite by dressing appropriately. Keep your face warm by wearing a scarf or facemask or a parka with a hood large enough that it will hold warm air around your face. To protect hands, wear waterproof mitts, and for feet, wool socks and waterproof footwear.

To treat surface frostbite on your hands, place them in your armpits or against warm skin to warm up. Find shelter and warm up feet against a partner's warm skin. (Brrrrrr!) Change damp or wet socks. Warm cheeks and face with warm clothing. Use warm (not hot) objects such as a cloth-covered Thermos as a warming tool. **Do not** pour warm or hot water over the affected skin, and do not rub it. When returning to the cold, these areas will freeze again more easily than non-affected skin, so make sure to protect them.

If it's necessary for a group member to walk on or use a frozen part of their body to get back to a vehicle, do not try to thaw the body part. Return immediately with them to the car and seek medical help.

See Environment Canada's page "Wind Chill: The Chilling Facts" (**is.gd/apUiR5**) to understand how wind chill hazards increase the risk of frostbite.

Hypothermia

Hypothermia, a condition in which your body loses heat faster than it can produce it, occurs as your body temperature passes below 35°C (95°F). If this happens, your vital organs (heart, lungs, nervous system) struggle to work efficiently. People who are hypothermic may not be aware of their condition and may exhibit confused thinking that can lead to risk-taking behaviours.

Be alert to the possibility of hypothermia when snowshoeing in very cold temperatures or if there is a high wind chill factor. Wet clothing either from wet snow or rain or from sweating on the inside can also contribute to hypothermia. Hunger, fatigue, anxiety or recent illness or injury may also decrease the body's ability to respond and maintain a normal core temperature. Hypothermia occurs more easily in seniors and children than in young people. Watch for symptoms in an infant – bright red, cold skin, very low energy and a weak cry. Do not take infants snowshoeing in extreme or very cold temperatures, even if you think they will be warm in a snuggly carrier.

Signs and symptoms of hypothermia include:

Mild: shivering, dizziness, hunger, nausea, faster breathing, trouble speaking, slight confusion, lack of coordination, fatigue and increased heart rate

Moderate to severe: shivering (as hypothermia worsens, shivering stops), clumsiness or lack of coordination, muscle stiffness, slurred speech or mumbling, confusion and poor decision-making (such as trying to remove warm clothes), drowsiness or very low energy, lack of concern about one's condition, progressive loss of consciousness, weak pulse, slow and shallow breathing, fruity odour to breath, difficulty controlling urination.

The New Zealand Mountain Safety Council has a clever way of identifying hypothermia. They call it the "umbles":

Grumbles: complains or becomes argumentative
Fumbles: deterioration of eye–hand coordination
Mumbles: mutters and/or speaks unclearly
Stumbles: trips without reason
Tumbles: falls without obvious cause

If someone in your group begins to suffer from hypothermia, find a sheltered place and share enough clothing to warm them up and replace wet clothing. Wrap them in a space blanket. Give the person a warm, sweet drink. When the person is warmed, slowly make your way back to the trailhead.

If the person is severely hypothermic, handle them very gently. To decrease the possibility of irregular heartbeat, do not encourage movement; and to prevent choking, do not give them liquids until they are alert. In warming the person with clothing and foil blanket, ensure their core areas of groin, armpits, neck and trunk are kept warm.

The following tips will help avoid hypothermia:

- Do not snowshoe in extreme conditions and/or if wind chill further decreases an already low temperature.
- Dress warmly in layers and take additional clothing to add to or replace wet clothes. Wear wool and/or wicking polypropylene underclothing and Gore-Tex outer garments.
- Wear a warm hat that repels water and snow. (Heat is lost in proportion to the body area exposed. Our heads are 10 per cent of body area, so 10 per cent of body heat is lost through a head without a hat.)
- Waterproof boots are better than leather, which can become wet and cold. Carry two sturdy plastic bags to put over dry socks if the boots become wet inside. Waterproof mittens keep hands warmer than gloves do.
- To increase circulation throughout your body, swing your arms and keep moving your legs.
- Eat high-energy food containing fats, proteins and carbohydrates, and drink at regular intervals to maintain your energy and hydration.

Leg cramps

Imagine snowshoeing along in a winter wonderland, when suddenly you're grabbed by a cramp! Those involuntary and very painful contractions of your muscles – generally in calves, upper legs and feet during or after snowshoeing – are often a result of dehydration, holding a static position for a long time, or strain or overuse of muscles. To stop the cramp, try stretching the cramping muscle by contracting it against the opposite muscle; for example, stand up on your cramping leg and straighten it as much as you can. If you are sitting down, stretch your upper body gently out over your extended leg towards your feet. Massaging the painful area in a circular motion also decreases the pain. Applying heat (for example, a cloth–covered Thermos) to the painful area should help loosen and relax the muscles. Drink liquids (non-alcoholic) and continue to drink at regular intervals for the rest of the trip.

To avoid leg cramps, do the following:

- Get in shape before participating in any physical activity, and stretch before and after you engage in snowshoeing. (See "Snowshoeing Is Physical.")
- Drink liquids before and throughout your snowshoe activity.

NUTRITION AND HYDRATION

When it's cold outside and you're not sweating as obviously as on a hot summer day, it may seem that you do not need to drink much liquid. As well, you may not feel as hungry as during summer hikes. However, as the temperature decreases, the amount of water vapour in the air also decreases. Increased evaporation of water from the lungs results from breathing cold air and can lead to dehydration in cold temperatures. It takes approximately 20 minutes for liquids to be absorbed and available for your body to use; if you don't drink until you feel thirsty, you have waited too long to rehydrate. Carry at a minimum a litre of water, take along a Thermos (more weight but well worth it on a cold day) of tea, coffee or hot chocolate, hot apple juice or lemonade, and have hydration breaks every half hour. Drinking alcohol is not recommended while hiking in the cold. Eating snow as a means of supplementing water supplies is also not good practice since it cools your insides and may contain bacteria.

Food should have a high-quality protein as a main component. Include energy bars for snacks and as part of an emergency supply. The protein percentage is indicated in the contents list, as is the amount of sugar. While sugar may seem to give you an energy boost, protein will give a sustained increase in energy. It takes about six to eight hours for food to pass out of the stomach and into the small intestine, where absorption speeds up, so eating several smaller snacks as well as lunch will spread out the potential energy you will have available from the food.

MEDICATION

If any participants have a medical condition (such as diabetes or seizures), make sure they inform the group ahead of time. Have them explain the symptoms to watch for and the appropriate response to help them if needed. (Finding out that someone has diabetes only when the individual becomes confused and cannot find orange juice or medication is leaving it rather late!)

People who need medication for aching joints or back pain should take a dose half an hour before starting on the trail, and if it's a short-acting medication, have another dose at lunchtime.

SUNBURN

Snow reflects 80 per cent of UV rays and this reflection of the sun can create a very painful sunburn in twice as fast a time as at the beach. As well, altitude adds to the intensity of UVA rays, with a 10 per cent increase for every 1,000-foot gain in elevation.

Use sunscreen rated 30 SPF or higher on all exposed areas and lips. Apply 30 minutes before going outside and reapply every two hours. Zinc may not look pretty on noses and lips but it provides very good protection from both wind and sunburn. Wear sunglasses to prevent sunburn of your eyes.

If you do get a sunburn, put cooling compresses on the burned areas and use a moisturizer containing aloe or products a pharmacist recommends. If blisters form, do not break them.

AVALANCHES

Snowshoers are often rather cavalier about the possibility of an avalanche in the areas where they snowshoe. While it is unlikely there would be avalanche danger related to using the majority of trails in this book, it could happen, e.g., the trail to the first and second peaks of Mount Seymour and the Poland Lake trail, both of which have avalanche warning signs at the start. Close to urban centres or ski resorts, signs created by Avalanche Canada in conjunction with BC Parks use the Avalanche Danger Rating Scale and Avalanche Terrain Exposure Scale (ATES). These scales are often found posted at the start of backcountry trails. Once away from such centres, in backcountry terrain, there are no posted warnings to help guide decisions, and given specific conditions, an avalanche is possible.

Various smartphone apps are available which provide users with real-time avalanche information. To access this information on the desktop, just click on the mountain icons on the main map at **avalanche.ca**. Backcountry users are encouraged to contribute to the information by submitting photos and text.

As with any technology it is intended to be used by people who can identify avalanche hazard because they have the skill sets, tools and knowledge base from taking an approved avalanche safety course.

Avalanche signage gives life-saving information

On the day of your trip **always consult avalanche.ca for current conditions and avalanche danger ratings for the place where you will be snowshoeing.** Any rating of CONSIDERABLE or higher should alert you to the need for flexibility to choose another destination or for significant caution in snowshoeing in the risky area.

Avalanche basics

The following information is minimal – deliberately. You need to take avalanche danger seriously and sign up for instruction and practice in how to identify and avoid risk when snowshoeing in avalanche terrain, as well as how to rescue buried companions. See **avalanche.ca** for details on courses and materials.

North American Public Avalanche Danger Scale ©Avalanche Canada

Avalanche danger is determined by the likelihood, size and distribution of avalanches.

Danger level	Travel advice	Likelihood of avalanches	Avalanche size and distribution
5 Extreme	Avoid all avalanche terrain.	Natural and human-triggered avalanches certain.	Large to very large avalanches in many areas.
4 High	Very dangerous avalanche conditions. Travel in avalanche terrain not recommended.	Natural avalanches likely; human-triggered avalanches very likely.	Large avalanches in many areas; or very large avalanches in specific areas.
3 Considerable	Dangerous avalanche conditions. Careful snowpack evaluation, cautious route-finding and conservative decision-making essential.	Natural avalanches possible; human-triggered avalanches likely.	Small avalanches in many areas; or large avalanches in specific areas; or very large avalanches in isolated areas.
2 Moderate	Heightened avalanche conditions on specific terrain features. Evaluate snow and terrain carefully; identify features of concern.	Natural avalanches unlikely; human-triggered avalanches possible.	Small avalanches in specific areas; or large avalanches in isolated areas.
1 Low	Generally safe avalanche conditions. Watch for unstable snow on isolated terrain features.	Natural and human-triggered avalanches unlikely.	Small avalanches in isolated areas or extreme terrain.

The basic causes of avalanches can be put under three categories – terrain, weather and people – and each of these factors interacts with the other two. The following information gives you some (but not all) avalanche causes in each category.

Terrain

Open terrain (that is, with few or no trees) at a 30- to 35-degree slope or more has the potential for small and/or large avalanches. Most slab avalanches occur on slopes between 30 and 45 degrees. Even treed slopes may have open areas above or steep areas along the trail and could have runouts of snow from avalanches that start higher up.

Avalanche Canada, in collaboration with Parks Canada, has published ratings of SIMPLE, CHALLENGING and COMPLEX for many backcountry trips. For example, three trips in this book – Mount Seymour Trail, Zoa Peak and Needle Peak West Ridge – are rated as challenging terrain.

Apply the following Avalanche Terrain Exposure Scale (ATES) descriptions to the terrain of your proposed trip. This will help contribute to decisions about the safety of the trail.

Simple terrain has exposure to low-angle or primarily forested terrain. Some forest openings may involve the runout zones of infrequent avalanches, but there are many options to reduce or eliminate exposure. Traversing simple terrain requires common sense, proper equipment, first aid skills and the discipline to respect avalanche warnings. Simple terrain is usually low avalanche risk, and thus ideal for novices gaining backcountry experience. These trips may not be entirely free from avalanche hazards, and on days when avalanche danger is elevated you may want to rethink any backcountry travel that has exposure to avalanches, and stick to tracked snowshoe trails or within the boundaries of a ski resort.

Challenging terrain has exposure to well-defined avalanche paths, starting zones or terrain traps. Options exist to reduce or eliminate exposure with careful route finding. Challenging terrain requires skills to recognize and avoid avalanche-prone terrain. Big slopes exist on these trips. You must also know how to understand the Public Avalanche Bulletin, perform avalanche self-rescue and basic first aid, and be confident in your route-finding skills. You should take an avalanche skills training course prior to travelling in this type of country. If you are unsure of your or your group's ability to navigate through avalanche terrain, consider hiring a professional guide.

Complex terrain has exposure to multiple, overlapping avalanche paths or large expanses of steep, open terrain. There are multiple avalanche starting zones, many terrain traps below the open areas and limited options to reduce exposure. Complex terrain demands a strong group with years of critical decision-making experience in avalanche terrain. There can be no safe options on these trips, as exposure to big slopes is inevitable. It is recommended that at least one person in your group has taken an advanced Avalanche Skills Training (AST 2) course and has several years of backcountry experience. Be prepared! Check the Public Avalanche Bulletin, and ensure everyone is up for the task and aware of the risk. This is serious country and not a place to consider unless you're confident in the skills of your group. If you are uncertain, consider hiring a professional guide.

Although these definitions are useful for general descriptions and broad-scale applications, a more specific breakdown of terrain variables is required to begin to understand the complexities of avalanche terrain – and interact with them. For a printable table of the Avalanche Terrain Exposure Scale, see Parks Canada at **is.gd/NBsJPq**.

Some types of terrain (e.g., gullies, crevasses and cliffs) can also increase the likelihood of being trapped if an avalanche begins, since there is no safe terrain to move towards that is out of the avalanche path. However, terrain alone does not dictate when an avalanche might occur.

Weather

About 90 per cent of avalanches occur within 24 to 48 hours after a storm. Some of the common causes of avalanches attributed to weather are rapid freeze and thaw cycles and then new heavy snow on top of this unstable base; seasonal weather (e.g., warmer spring temperatures and strong sunshine creating slab breakoff in the afternoons); and heavy snowfalls accompanied by high winds causing avalanches on lee slopes. New snow – so wonderful to ski or snowshoe in – can produce dangerous conditions if 30 cm or more falls within 48 hours and then is combined with rain. More than 25 cm of rain in 24 hours contributes to avalanche potential. A wind of more than 25 km/h can form wind slabs. All of these conditions mean that even more conservative decisions than usual should be made about routes.

Social pressure

All the planning and driving and just wanting to "do it" may result in poor choices that lead to individuals (even those who have avalanche training) entering into avalanche terrain. The leader of the group needs to listen to the opinions of those who have avalanche training and also the concerns of anyone in the group. Decisions of where and how far to proceed on any planned trip need to take into account not only knowledge about the potential for avalanche in the area and how to manage this, but also the confidence, goals and skill level of everyone in the group.

If there is any possibility that you and your group will be snowshoeing in avalanche territory, beacons, probes and shovels should be carried and at least several people in the group should know how to use this equipment and perform rescue procedures.

Some important questions you and your group need to ask when assessing the impact of terrain, weather and group dynamics are:

Terrain and weather
- What is the Avalanche Terrain Exposure Scale (ATES) rating for the trail chosen for the day?
- How much new snow has fallen?
- Which direction is the wind coming from and are there deep pockets of snow?
- Is a change of weather predicted for the area?
- Are there signs of recent avalanches or are there shooting cracks underfoot?
- Are there avalanche conditions that can be anticipated because of the season, e.g., spring freeze and thaw cycles or recent past weather such as heavy rain?

Group competence and confidence
- Does everyone in the group feel confident with a decision to snowshoe in the area?
- Are all members able to use a probe and transmitter and locate and rescue a buried companion if the area is designated as Complex or Challenging?

A special thanks to Avalanche Canada for reviewing this information and for the indispensable work they do in providing information for all backcountry users. Canadians are very fortunate to have this valuable resource.

Avalanche skills training

Avalanche Canada has an online avalanche tutorial for an introduction to avalanche safety (click on "Learn" at **avalanche. ca** for more information), and MEC has numerous videos and written information related to staying safe while enjoying snow activities. Avalanche courses in the Lower Mainland are available through various companies: see **Appendix B: Safety** under "Avalanche courses."

OTHER NATURAL HAZARDS

Besides potential avalanches, numerous other natural hazards may occur in the terrain where you are snowshoeing.

Tree wells

Watch out for voids filled with loose snow surrounding the trunks of trees. While generally found in untracked areas, tree wells sometimes develop along the edges of tracked snowshoe trails.

When snow falls in a forest, it accumulates around and under the trees. Many conifers found in British Columbia's coastal and interior forests, such as cedar, hemlock and fir, have long, wide branches with dense needles. These needles prevent the snow from accumulating and consolidating as rapidly under the branches as it does farther out from the trunk. Trees like firs have branches that bow down to meet the snow on the ground and can hide tree wells beneath and behind them. As well, new, soft snow will sometimes fill a tree well and appear to be solid. Small trees can also disguise tree wells, with just their tops showing above the snow and a well surrounding them.

Remember that between trees, the snow is often icy and crusty, especially in the spring. With the change in snow density, you could lose your balance and fall into a tree well. Stay as far away as possible from branches, and use your poles to maintain balance.

Tree well rescue

Digging yourself out from a tree well without help is difficult. Often, someone who falls in ends up head down and is in danger of suffocating if rescue is not started immediately. This frightening fact illustrates another basic safety rule: always snowshoe with at least one buddy and keep each other in sight at all times.

In untracked areas, or in deep new snow even in tracked areas, carry an avalanche shovel and unstrap your poles from your wrists. Strapped-on poles are difficult to remove when you are trapped, and by increasing awkwardness they decrease your ability to clear an airspace for breathing. Flat composite snowshoes can be used as shovels if necessary.

If someone you are with falls into a tree well, first ensure your own stability and safety and then move close to the tree well. Uncover the person's face immediately by digging to the side of their head. Do not try to pull the person out in the same direction they fell in. Continue to enlarge the hole by digging on one side, or on both sides if two of you are there to help with the rescue. Try pulling the trapped person out by grabbing their backpack straps and lifting them back out and upright. This approach often requires two people – one on either side – but is preferable to yanking on a person's arms.

If you fall into a tree well, do not panic. Try to grab branches or the tree trunk on your way down. Yell or use your whistle. If immersed in snow, use your hands to carefully create a space around your face. Struggling will cause more snow to fall into the hole. Try to think about your position and how you may be able to get out. In one successful self-rescue, the snowshoer was able to slowly turn his body and pack down the loose snow surrounding him by carefully rocking as he inched towards upright. He then used branches to pull himself up the tree.

It is easy to avoid being buried in a tree well: stay well away from trees of any size when snowshoeing off tracked trails.

For more about tree wells and rescue techniques, visit **deep-snowsafety.org**. This well-organized website provides information and videos created by a collaboration between the Northwest Avalanche Institute, Mount Baker Ski Area and Crystal Mountain.

A FRIEND'S EXPERIENCE WITH TREE WELLS

Our friend Nicki is a fantastic backcountry skier – Bugaboos, Europe, Japan. While admittedly snowshoeing does not have the speed of skiing, snowshoers too may be moving through tree well terrain once they leave a tracked path. This description of Nicki's experience is terrifying but also illustrates the importance of DO NOT PANIC – you have a chance to get out of this.

"I have been caught in two (tree wells) seriously and they are very hard to get out of, and no one can hear you yelling your face off when you are in one. One, I was caught upside down by my bindings, with my mouth and throat full of snow. I had to wait until the snow melted to breathe. Very scary. And I then released the bindings, fell into the well and had quite a time getting out. I used my poles to distribute my weight while I crawled out on my belly. My buddies were ahead of me and could not hear me calling. It is more of a problem with skiing, as you go a lot faster downhill and can lose one another very easily.

"The second time, I used a whistle but no one heard it. What was disconcerting was that we were buddied up, but you go around one tree and he goes around another … and you don't want to ski in someone's tracks anyway, and that's dangerous too. I was in the tree well, with the whistle, got myself out and they were skinning up to find me but it would have been 10 minutes or so 'til they got to where I was. So if I had been in trouble, I would have been in real trouble. The moral of the story: stay out of tree wells. It is all about prevention."

Tree snow bombs waiting to fall

Getting micro-crampons
on and off sometimes
requires help

Tree snow bombs and falling branches

The snow that rests so beautifully on the branches of trees poses another hazard, especially if combined with crusty ice. On a sunny day, the darker needles beneath and beside the snow on branches may warm up, causing the snow to drop like a small bomb. If you hear the thud of large chunks of falling snow as you walk along, or if you see new, wet lumps of snow under trees, try to snowshoe in clear areas. The snow is most likely to slide from the middle or ends of the branches. Do not walk close to the trunks of trees in an attempt to avoid the falling snow – you may then put yourself in bigger danger from tree wells.

On windy days, not only do you have to cope with blowing snow, but the weight of snow and pressure from wind may cause branches to break off and fall. Be particularly aware of this hazard in forests with a high ratio of trees dead or dying from pine beetle infestation. If the path you are using is not wide enough to safely snowshoe clear of falling branches, turn around, stay in the middle of the trail and return to the start.

Icy conditions

Icy surfaces present their own challenges. Know your snowshoe crampon type and how much grip it gives on packed and loose snow. If you slide a bit on mild snow slopes, then icy surfaces are guaranteed to provide a real challenge.

First, look at the general terrain. If it is fairly flat and the surface is covered in crusty, uneven snow or ice, the teeth on your snowshoes may grip reasonably well. Try to find places with some looser snow or where poles will break the ice and help with balance, such as along the immediate edge of a packed icy trail. Turn around as soon as possible or find a different, safer path around the icy spot. But if it is icy all around, with steep drop-offs in the terrain (e.g., Thunderbird Ridge northeast of Grouse Mountain), stop to think about whether you should be snowshoeing at all in this area with these conditions? Probably NOT.

Warm spring weather can create icy patches as snow shed by trees beside the trail melts and then freezes. If a skiff of snow covers the ground, a small but dangerous ice rink may hide beneath. Carry microspike crampons to ensure you have an alternative means of walking on an icy surface if needed.

Frozen lakes and streams

Do not snowshoe on lakes, rivers or ponds at any time of year. Early and late winter are especially hazardous because snowfalls may cover up thin or rotting ice underneath. Even if you know the area very well, other dangers may lie in wait. For example, running water under ice in creeks or into lakes can cause the ice to become unstable. You may be tempted: "Others are doing it," "It has always been safe," "We've had a really cold winter." But by detouring on solid ground, and forgoing shortcuts over lakes, rivers or ponds, you will be making the safest choice for you and your group.

Bog holes

Bog holes can often be found close to lakes and swampy areas. While generally frozen in the dead of winter, by spring they may be filled with water with just a light skim of ice and a deceptive cover of snow. If you see an unusual depression in otherwise firm snow, it may be a bog hole. Luckily, most are not too deep, but they are wet. Avoid snowshoeing in boggy areas. Select a route that is above the lake or waterway, although bog holes can be found above lakes as well, so be alert and suspicious. The best prevention: test depressed areas in off-track snow with your poles before walking on them.

If you fall into a bog hole, try to get your feet and snowshoes under you. Lean forward onto the edge of the hole. Falling backward may result in most of your body being immersed and require immediate help by members of your group to get you into a position to climb out. Use your arms and upper body to pull yourself forward onto the snow. Find a safe, protected place to replace any wet clothing. If your boots are wet inside (which is almost inevitable), put on dry socks and place your feet in plastic bags in your soggy boots.

A BOG HOLE STORY

I still have "what if" nightmares about the time I fell into a bog hole. Everyone else in the group had walked around on a small elevated area while I saw a shortcut – a short incline and smooth snow to where they were standing. Smooth snow covering a bog hole with a topping of very thin ice, as it turned out. Into the hole I fell and luckily remained upright, as my companions laughed at the expletives that emerged from my mouth! One began taking pictures for our group's blog, others just stood there. I grabbed the snowy side of the hole and was able to crawl out – no thanks to my friends! With soggy, water-filled boots, it was fortunate I had dry socks and lucky that hypothermia was not an issue since it was a fairly warm late March day. We had to snowshoe for over an hour back to the car. But what if I had fallen backwards? With a fairly heavy pack, I could have become submerged totally – but that is only in my nightmares. My suspicion of depressions in snow was heightened considerably, as has been my belief that walking on "frozen" lakes and rivers can often lead to safety problems.

Bridges

On snowshoe trails, you will encounter both man-made bridges and snow bridges. Either one can pose problems for snowshoers.

On man-made bridges, poles are essential for probing where the boards are. Move slowly with poles in front as you assess the safety of each step. Also on man-made bridges, snow often builds up in the middle. A narrow, elevated walkway is created as people track over and more snow falls in a repeated cycle. Many of these bridges do not have sides. Even on those with railings, the snow walkway may be at the height of the railing and just as dangerous. Do not walk on bridges with elevated snow! This is when a lightweight shovel comes in handy. Dig the snow down to create a lower, flatter path. The tail of a flat MSR snowshoe may also work as a shovel to level and reduce the snow.

Natural snow bridges have to be examined carefully. Look at the surrounding area and assess whether the bridge crosses a depression created from low-lying land or from a creek. If the bridge spans a creek, is the water totally frozen or can you see water flowing under the ice? Use your poles to check the density of the snow on the bridge over the depression. Have one person at a time carefully cross, using their poles to help with stability and balance.

Rocks, roots and steep terrain

The majority of the snowshoe trails in this book are also used in summer, thereby ensuring they avoid major obstacles. In the winter, however, snow may alter a trail. The angle may become steeper, the path may be narrower, or rocks and roots covered with ice may need to be avoided.

Before going off a trail (even for a bathroom break), evaluate the immediate terrain and what lies ahead. The coastal mountains have steep, unforgiving cliffs close to well-established trails. Although topographic maps will give you a good idea of the grade of the terrain and many small lakes in the area, you need to be alert to your surroundings and changes in the landscape. Don't rely on the static grip from snowshoes to save you: your

Rainbow Falls Bridge – a
very risky choice

Cornices on Fat Dog Ridge

snowshoes may slide or your foot may slip in the binding, causing movement. Do not stand near the edge of snow-covered cliffs!

Cornices

Cornices are formed when the wind blows snow over sharp edges such as a rocky ridge or the crest of a mountaintop, causing a horizontal buildup of snow that extends outward beyond solid ground. Travelling on or below a cornice is extremely dangerous. When a cornice breaks off, it fractures back in towards the underlying rock. The broken cornice can easily start an avalanche as it plummets down onto snow below. When walking in an area with cornices (e.g., Mount Seymour or at the top of Fat Dog Ridge), follow this mountaineering safety tip: stay back far enough from the edge that you are NOT able to see the drop under the cornice.

Disclaimer: With the exception of Avalanche Canada, whose information each day allows us to make safe decisions while in the backcountry, linking to or referencing safety information in this section is in no way an endorsement by the authors of other sites, other safety information or safety equipment described in such sites.

Peter dressed to go

EQUIPMENT AND CLOTHING

Without snowshoes, boots and a pack, you're just another city resident strolling around a local park in sporty outdoor clothing. But properly outfitted, and after your weekend snowshoe adventure, your Monday morning conversation at coffee break or the parents' meeting or the seniors' centre will make you the centre of admiration and envy.

SNOWSHOES

From traditional wooden snowshoes to high-tech lightweight metal or plastic models, there is a style and material of snowshoe for every size and use. The largest variety are in the recreational category. Consider the following when selecting snowshoes.

Terrain

The type of snowshoe you choose should relate directly to the terrain you'll be crossing. For the soft powder on rolling hills in the Chilcotin region, snowshoes with tails that can be attached will help you float on the snow. For wet or crusty coastal snow, the placement and number of gripping teeth on the bottom are very important. If you will be snowshoeing in bush and treed terrain or on mainly pre-tracked trails, narrower snowshoes are the best choice.

Your weight

Your weight determines the size of your snowshoe. Each manufacturer has a range of weight and size combinations based generally on the following ratio: the area of one snowshoe in square inches equals the person's weight in pounds. Weight should be calculated to include not only your body weight but also all the gear or equipment you'll be wearing or carrying.

Your gender

Adult snowshoes are often offered in both male and female sizes and styles. Snowshoes designed for men are wider and longer to accommodate more weight and bigger boots, while women's snowshoes are narrower and shorter with slimmer bindings for smaller boots and less body weight.

Bindings

Bindings are a critical component of the snowshoe. Freezing fingers and cold, brittle straps make for a frustrating experience that can easily be avoided. Try out the clasps and buckles to see how simple they are to attach and loosen. Make sure the bindings are compatible with the size and type of boots you plan to wear. Rubber or flexible plastic materials bend and cinch-in better than stiff plastic. Before each trip, ensure that all straps and any sliders that hold the ends of straps are intact and adjusted. Flexible swivel bindings that allow your foot to lift up and forward away from the deck of the snowshoe enable a more normal gait and allow the toe of your boot to bite into the snow when going uphill.

Crampon bottom teeth and decking

During the last 10 years, the amount of metal on snowshoes in the form of teeth to grip the snow has increased immensely. There is quite a variation, from simple crampon teeth under the toes and balls of the feet, with a built-in heel crampon or bar to aid braking on the downhill, to serrated metal edges along the length of the snowshoe or as part of the external side rail in the frame that holds the decking. Decking can be of a soft, strong synthetic material attached to the side rails with rivets or it can be a hard composite plastic that is moulded to create the total deck. A snowshoe that provides both toe and heel crampons (sometimes as a raised straight or V-shaped bar beneath the heel) is a good choice

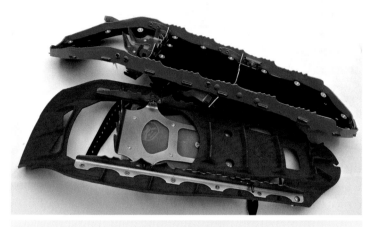

Placement and number of teeth on snowshoes are important

that will allow for braking on downhill slopes. Every additional tooth running the side length of the snowshoe means more grip and stability and less lateral slipping.

Each time you snowshoe, inspect the metal teeth to see that they are all straight. Remember to dry your snowshoes off at the end of each trip to decrease rust on the metal parts.

Heel lifts
The wire loops (televators) mounted towards the tail of the snowshoe deck can be flipped up under your heel for steep ascents. These help decrease stress on the calf muscles and Achilles tendons.

Tail extenders
Extenders can be purchased for some snowshoes. Particularly useful in powder conditions, they provide more surface to "float" on soft snow.

BOOTS

The right boots when snowshoeing can mean the difference between pleasure (cozy, warm) or discomfort and problems (blisters, wet, cold). Choose insulated and waterproof boots with rubber uppers and firm support in the foot and ankle. The boots should come above the ankle in height. A lip on the lower back helps to keep the snowshoe bindings in place. Ensure your boots fit well and do not rub and that your feet don't slide around in them. Wear your new boots inside the house for a few hours with wool socks prior to using them outdoors. This allows you to return them if they're problematic. Before you set out on your first trip, try your boots on with your snowshoes and adjust the snowshoe straps to fit.

POLES

The majority of snowshoers find that poles help with balance and stability when ascending and descending hills. An additional benefit is the aerobic upper body exercise they provide. Poles are especially useful if you plan to carry a heavy pack or a small child in a carrier.

Choose adjustable poles, which you can collapse and attach to your pack when they're not in use. In cold conditions and for weaker or painful hands, poles with joints that adjust using clips rather than twisting work best. Ensure the joints are clean and moveable.

When you finish snowshoeing for the day, dry your poles off while they're extended so the metal does not corrode from dampness. (Warranties are usually not honoured if the pole metal is corroded.) You will also want to choose poles with winter snow baskets on the ends or ones that allow for seasonal change of the basket.

To select the correct size, choose a pole that lets you hold your arm at a right angle as you grasp it just below the basket

In cold weather, clips work the best to alter the height of poles

when the pole is upside down. Keep your arm and hand at a right angle to your body while snowshoeing to help prevent tendonitis from an overextended wrist. The straps on the poles will also allow you to rest your hands at times. To use the straps correctly, put your hands "up through the rabbit hole" made by the looped strap and then "grip the bunny ears" (double strap) and the pole handle.

DAY PACK

Your pack should be made from a waterproof fabric and have an attached waterproof rain/snow cover. Make sure the pack fits well with the maximum layers of clothing you might wear. A firm hip belt and padded shoulder straps mean your back and neck will be comfortable throughout the day. Have your day pack fitted to your height and body shape the same way you would for a larger backpack.

Whether to use a pack that includes a hydration bladder is a personal choice – just be aware that sometimes in very cold weather, the water in the tube freezes. If you're carrying a bottle of water in a pocket on the outside of a pack, turn the bottle upside down so the water freezes in the bottom first.

It's useful if the pack has places to attach poles and snowshoes on the outside using either buckles or bungee cords. People who enjoy spring snowshoe hikes, when the snow line recedes and hikers carry their snowshoes for part of the trip, will find this feature especially important.

The pack should be a minimum of 25 litres in size to be able to accommodate your lunch, water or other liquids, basic first aid equipment, safety equipment, the Ten Essentials and extra clothing.

CLOTHING

One word sums up the type, kind and amount of clothing that will keep you warm, dry and comfortable during snowshoe time on winter trails: LAYERS!

Whether in the depth of winter or for early winter or spring adventures, having the ability to add or decrease the amount of clothes you are wearing enhances comfort throughout the trip. A good part of snowshoeing always seems to include stops to take off or add clothing! As with any vigorous activity, your body temperature changes, from when that first icy blast hits you: "Wow, today is colder than I thought!" to when you've worked up a sweat: "Can we stop for a minute until I take off this vest/coat/sweater?" Then at the lunch break, most of the clothes go back on.

Clothing to wear:

- a base layer of lightweight wool or synthetic wicking top and bottom
- wool socks and wicking liners
- wool or synthetic wicking sweater top
- flexible leggings or pants (wool, fleece or synthetic); no jeans – a killer if they get wet

Fun and warmth combined
PHOTOGRAPHER: TRUDY
VANDERBURG, 2015

- vest (down or synthetic fill) and/or soft-shell jacket
- wool toque (or wide-brimmed hat for sunny spring days)
- waterproof gloves or mittens and liners
- waterproof/windproof (Gore-Tex or other breathable fabric) jacket with a hood
- waterproof/windproof (Gore-Tex or other breathable fabric) over pants with full-length side zippers
- gaiters if your outer pants do not have inner cuffs

Clothing in your backpack

Some of the clothing described above you will end up carrying in your pack until the weather or your body temperature dictates that it needs to be used. Some will serve a layering purpose. For instance, a vest over a soft-shell jacket makes a great combination for spring snowshoe conditions and temperatures, while a vest under a Gore-Tex jacket results in a cozy day during sub-zero temperatures.

Include the following in your backpack:

- an extra pair of socks
- two sturdy plastic bags to cover dry socks if your boots and socks get wet
- an extra pair of waterproof mitts (for really cold hands, mittens warm fingers faster than gloves)
- an extra wool or synthetic sweater
- an extra toque
- a scarf or balaclava
- ski goggles

Wool or synthetics?

Should you choose wool or synthetic fabrics for base layers and outer layers? After years of being convinced by the experts that synthetic fabrics could keep us dry, sweet smelling and warm (or cool) in any type of weather and during any type of activity, many people are re-examining that promise. The emergence of lightweight and washable merino wool clothing has added an alternative that increasing numbers of athletes (recreational or professional) are choosing.

The advantage of wool is it keeps you warm even when wet. Australia's national science agency, CSIRO Textile and Fibre Technology, found that wool absorbs almost 35 per cent of its dry mass at 100 per cent humidity – more drying power than any other fibre. It also has the benefit of not smelling after exercise. In different weights, it can be used for both inner and outer layers. It breathes and the new merino wool is machine washable.

The sheep in Australia and New Zealand have always known that wool is the best outer and inner layer and they want to share that fact with everyone!

ADDITIONAL EQUIPMENT:

- sunglasses
- sunscreen and lip sunscreen or zinc oxide
- binoculars and camera
- Thermos for a hot drink (tea, coffee, hot chocolate, hot apple cider or lemonade)
- Therm-a-Rest or dense foam square for sitting on the snow
- hand warmers (chemical packets)
- the Ten Essentials (see the Safety section)

Ryan loosens up before putting on his snowshoes

SNOWSHOEING IS PHYSICAL!

Snowshoeing can be enjoyed at any pace but it *is* a physical activity. If you have any medical conditions, consult your doctor about the appropriateness of the activity for you. Then, as for any sport, if you want to enjoy the variety of terrain that southwestern British Columbia offers to snowshoers, you will need to begin at least a modest training program. This can be as simple as starting to walk part of the way home from work. Or walking to a grocery store a short distance away and carrying your groceries home in a backpack. Gradually increase the distance and the weight in your backpack. Then find some hills and add that to your route.

Weight training, aerobic exercise and use of gym equipment – any activity that requires movement and increases strength, flexibility and balance should be added to your regime and will help you get strong enough to enjoy your snowshoe adventures. Yoga can also help with flexibility, balance and coordination. Classes and gym facilities are available at moderate cost at many local community centres.

When you start snowshoeing, consider your present physical fitness and match the terrain and length of trip to your ability. Even with conditioning, at first your knees, hips and groin may feel the stretch from the wider stance used for snowshoeing and especially if you lift your knees up very high while breaking trail or moving in powder snow. Trips with little elevation gain often allow for longer distances and are generally suitable for beginners and families with young children. They can offer as much opportunity for enjoyment of the beauty of the wilderness in winter as climbing steeper terrain or going longer distances. As your physical fitness improves, you will find you can gradually add trips that feature elevation gains.

WARM-UP AND COOL-DOWN EXERCISES

Before beginning to snowshoe it is wise to gently warm up the muscles you will be using. Equally important (and exercise physiology suggests even more important) is to do cool-down and stretching exercises at the completion of any physical activity.

The following exercises were provided by sport physiotherapist candidate Ryan Hill, BHK, MPT, and should be tried at home before you use them "in the field." Do not do or hold any position that causes pain. You should start gently and increase the length and amount of stretch over time. If your balance is poor, hold on to something stable (e.g., a vehicle or tree trunk) while doing the exercises.

Before: head to toe dynamic warm-up

This routine can be done in the parking lot or at the trailhead prior to snowshoeing. It is considered a "dynamic warm-up" because it integrates elements of range-of-motion, stretching, balance, posture and functional movement patterns. The purpose is to warm up all the major muscle groups of the body required for snowshoeing, in a short time. Each exercise is cycled through three to five times per side while walking forward and again while walking backward. The walking forward and backward helps with the warm-up. At the finish a snowshoer should be warmed up but not fatigued or feeling pain.

Requirements

- 5–10 minutes
- a few metres of cleared space
- focused attention and intention by the participant

1. Standing Knee-to-Chest
- take a step forward and raise the opposite thigh, pulling that knee towards your shoulder on that side
- focus is on upright posture, shoulders pulled back and slight forward pelvic tilt
- hold the stretch for a few seconds; then lower the raised leg and with it take a step forward and pull up the other leg to repeat

PURPOSE
- stretches glutes, hamstrings and groin
- takes hip and knee into full flexion
- reinforces proper posture
- improves balance on standing leg
- works on upper and lower body coordination

2. Standing Hip Raise
- take a step forward and grasp the ankle or foot of your opposite leg, pulling it up and across the standing leg
- focus is on the hip flexing up and out
- repeat with opposite leg

PURPOSE
- stretches hip, glutes, hamstrings and groin
- puts hip and knee into full flexion/abduction range of motion
- improves posture, balance and coordination

3. Standing Heel-to-Seat
- take a step forward and flex your other leg at the knee until you can grasp that foot with both hands and pull it towards your buttocks
- focus is on the knee bending, the hip extending backward, and the ankle pointing down
- repeat with the opposite leg

PURPOSE
- stretches hip flexors, quads, groin and ankle muscles
- puts knee and ankle into full range of motion
- improves posture, balance and coordination

4. Standing Spinal Twist

- take a step forward and raise your opposite knee so the thigh is at 90° to the hip
- place opposite hand on the outside of the raised knee and twist upper body in the opposite direction from the direction you're pulling the knee
- at the same time, the free shoulder is opened up sideways, with the thumb pointing upwards
- repeat with the opposite leg as above

PURPOSE

- stretches torso, elbow and wrist flexors
- puts body into full spinal rotation and shoulder/elbow range of motion
- improves posture, balance and coordination

5. Walking Squat to Toe Raise

- squat low and touch the ground, with your arms between your knees
- stand back up and reach overhead while rising up on toes
- turn body 90° to the left and repeat sequence 3–5 times
- return to your starting position, then rotate 90° to the right and again repeat 3–5 times

PURPOSE

- provides upper and lower body warm-up
- replicates functional movement patterns
- stretches upper back and shoulders
- improves posture, balance and coordination

6. Walking Lunge-to-Side Bend

- take a large step forward to assume a lunge position
- reach overhead with opposite arm while other arm reaches towards the ground
- lean sideways toward the outside of the forward leg to do a spinal side bend
- repeat for the opposite side

PURPOSE

- provides upper and lower body warm-up
- replicates functional movement patterns
- stretches upper back, shoulder blades and hip flexors
- improves posture, balance and coordination

7. Walking Toe-Touches

- take a step forward and reach toward forward foot with opposite hand
- move the rear leg backward and upward into the air until you are leaning forward on the front leg alone, with your back leg parallel to the ground
- return to starting position by using your hip muscles and keeping your back straight
- repeat for the opposite side

PURPOSE
- provides upper and lower body warm-up
- replicates functional movement patterns
- improves posture, balance and coordination

After: standing cool-down

These exercises are a condensed static-stretch routine to keep fatigued muscles loose. Each stretch is held for 30–60 seconds and repeated until the snowshoer no longer feels a significant stretch sensation.

Requirements

- 5–10 minutes
- a large, stable object for support such as a rock, log or vehicle
- focused attention and intention by the participant

Calves, forearms
- step left leg slightly back and bend the right knee while putting body weight on the right leg
- stretch the back of the left forearm at the same time by holding left arm out in front of body and, with the right hand, bending the left wrist downward and backward and twisting it away from the midline
- repeat for the opposite side

Calves, forearms
- take a larger step back with left leg, straighten the back knee and lean forward
- stretch the front of the left forearm at the same time by holding the left arm out in front of body and, with the right hand, bending the left wrist down and backward and twisting it towards the midline
- repeat for the opposite side

Ankle, hip, torso, upper back, shoulders
- take a large step forward with left leg
- extend right foot leftward behind the front leg so that you are leaning on the outside edge of the rear (right) foot
- hand in hand, reach overhead and bend the body leftward, making a C shape
- repeat for the opposite side

Quads, hip flexors, chest, torso
- place right foot on a stable object behind body to stretch out quads
- balance right leg on the toes with ankle flexed; tilt pelvis back and extend hip to increase the stretch
- twist torso leftward, away from the stretching leg, and reach left arm out as in Standing Spinal Twist, exercise 4 on page 70
- twist can be progressed by pulling on pelvis with free hand
- repeat for opposite side

Hamstrings, groin, upper back, shoulders, neck
- while standing on one leg, place your opposite heel on a stable object such as a large rock, log or vehicle bumper
- keeping back straight, tilt pelvis forward and lean hips back
- rotate the elevated leg 45° inward to bias the outer hamstring
- place behind your back the arm opposite to the forward leg; pull that arm with your other hand and bend neck away from the direction of the pull

Hamstrings, groin, upper back, shoulders, neck
- rotate the elevated leg 45° outward to bias the inner hamstring
- place behind your back the arm opposite to the forward leg and pull with your other hand; place ear to shoulder and look upward in direction of raised shoulder

Hamstrings, groin, upper back, shoulders, neck
- turn whole body 90° to the right relative to the stable support object, and place left heel on the object to further stretch groin
- place right hand behind neck and look downward and around left shoulder
- repeat for opposite side

Walking backwards on snowshoes requires skill – think safety

MAN WEARING SNOWSHOES ON GOAT MOUNTAIN CA. EARLY 1900s;
10109 NVMA NORTH VANCOUVER MUSEUM AND ARCHIVES

SNOWSHOEING TECHNIQUES

Most people would agree that if you can walk, you can snowshoe. However, due to variable terrain and weather in southwestern British Columbia, knowledge of a range of techniques is useful. Steep inclines, rocks, fallen trees and the heavy, crusty or icy snow found at times in this region create challenges even for experienced snowshoers. By starting on flat terrain and gradually adding trails with increasing grade and elevation, you can develop the skills you need.

This book is for recreational snowshoers, so the techniques described here relate to the type of activity and terrain they may encounter. Racing and mountaineering snowshoers have their own specific techniques.

For weblinks to snowshoeing videos, see "How-to videos" in **Appendix C**.

ON LEVEL GROUND

Flat terrain provides an easy surface and snowshoeing should be as simple as walking. The width of the snowshoe, though, may require that you walk with a wider stance. Poles can offer upper extremity and torso exercise as well as aiding balance. If you are moving quickly on flat terrain or the snow is icy or crusty, lead with alternate poles and watch where your feet are about to land. When snowshoeing in deep powder, tail extensions sold with some snowshoes provide the extra flotation needed to walk on the soft snow. Lifting your knees up high with each step also helps and is useful too if you are breaking trail.

TURNS

To make a turn, move the snowshoes like two hands going around on a clock. Alternatively, you can place one snowshoe at a right angle to the other to make a T and then lift and move the second one around to take the lead step forward.

UPHILL

Uphill snowshoeing requires a good grip. Using the metal teeth under your toe and instep, dig the toe teeth into the snow with each step to create a base, using the side teeth to augment the grip. The snowshoe itself will lie at the same angle as the snow while the swivel toe crampons bite down into the snow through the open space in the decking. Some snowshoes have metal "televators" that can be flipped up under your heels to keep the feet at right angles to the hill as you ascend, which decreases the stretch on your Achilles tendon.

Poles help maintain balance while climbing up the hill. Some snowshoers choose to shorten their poles when leaning into and climbing directly up a hill. If the snow is crusty and kicking your toe crampons into it is difficult, make use of all the bottom and side crampons to grip the snow, and push yourself up and forward with your poles. If you still can't get a grip, take a different route.

On modest slopes, try the herringbone, or "duck walk," that cross-country skiers use to climb hills. Place the snowshoes slightly outward on each step as you make your way up.

DOWNHILL

Downhill snowshoeing technique depends on the angle of the slope and the type of snowshoe crampons you have. Hills with a grade of 20 per cent or more are commonly thought to pose a challenge for snowshoers because of the increased possibility of inadvertently sliding rather than walking down.

For steep hills, consider traversing the slope. If travelling straight down is unavoidable and your snowshoes do not have heel crampons, bend your knees loosely, keep your weight over your heels and dig in the toe teeth with each step. If your snowshoes

Snowshoeing uphill – kick toe crampons in, traverse if necessary
PHOTOGRAPHER: PATRICK NOLAN, 2016

Snowshoeing downhill: bend your knees, kick heel crampons into the snow
PHOTOGRAPHER: PATRICK NOLAN, 2016

do have heel teeth, centre yourself over the heel, bend your knees and lean slightly backward while kicking the heel teeth into the snow with each step. Side teeth really show their benefit on steep hills, providing extra grip to keep you from sliding. For lateral balance as you descend, hold your poles at the side and slightly forward, angled into the hill.

Beware of leaning too far back, which can put you and your snowshoes into a position where you start sliding down the hill. If you do begin to slip, sit down and try to stay away from trees or cliffs. Stop as soon as possible by making your body as wide as you can. If you are headed towards rocks or a cliff or gaining speed, use the mountaineering technique of flipping yourself over onto your stomach facing uphill and digging into the snow with your hands and your snowshoes as well as with your poles if you can grab them close to the baskets.

Traversing across hills requires that you kick-step a flat base into the side of the hill as you angle across it. Point the toes of the snowshoes slightly uphill to maintain a grip. Using a long downhill pole and a shortened uphill pole may help with balance. Keep your weight on the uphill snowshoe. Make sure each step is flat and stable before putting down your full weight. To turn at corners, kick a platform by moving the snowshoes around like the hands of a clock until facing the other way.

ON ICE

Snowshoeing on icy surfaces presents its own challenges. First, look at the general terrain. If it is fairly flat and the surface is covered in crusty, uneven snow or ice, the teeth on your snowshoes may grip reasonably well. Try to find places with some looser snow or where poles will break the ice and provide help for balance, such as along the edge of a packed icy trail. Alternatively, you could choose to carry your snowshoes on your pack and use micro-crampons that grip on ice. If all of the surfaces of the terrain are icy, change your plans and find another trail.

WALKING BACKWARDS

There usually is little need to walk backwards on snowshoes but if that requirement does arise, having poles to help balance is very handy. Lift your knees up high, use a wide gait and move slowly, one foot firmly positioned before the other one is lifted. The main problem often is stepping on your own snowshoes and tripping, so try to keep the snowshoe line in a straight path on each side.

FALLING DOWN, GETTING UP

While you may not fall down very often when snowshoeing, at the very least you will have to get up from sitting down for lunch. It is easier to rise if you do not have your backpack on. Age and

Fall down, get up. This 80-year-old can still use
a deep knee bend to get up. Can you?
PHOTOGRAPHER: ALAN TOON, 2016

fitness will determine your choice of technique for getting up.

- **young and fit:** rise as though from a deep knee bend.
- **a little help from your friends:** have a friend stand in front
  of you and grab both of your hands to pull you up.
- **using leverage:** from a sitting position, plant your poles on
  either side, lean forward and push upward.
- **roll over:** from a sitting position, roll over to kneel on the
  snow. Place one bent leg forward, pressing on that knee with
  your hand as you rise, and bring your other leg and snowshoe under your trunk.

If a fellow snowshoer falls face forward and needs help getting up,
one method is to lift both shoulder straps of their backpack rather
than tugging on their arms. If trying to get up by yourself after falling forward, use the rollover and kneel technique described above.

If you fall while on a hill, move your poles and arms so they face
uphill and position your knees underneath you and pointing into
the slope, with your snowshoes behind. Kick your toe crampons
into the snow to grip as you rise. Grasp the poles partway along
their shaft and use them to push yourself up and keep your balance.

Happy family on a warm day in early winter

SNOWSHOEING IS A SPORT FOR EVERYONE

SNOWSHOEING WITH CHILDREN

As other family winter sporting activities escalate in cost (downhill skiing being the obvious example), participation by families in snowshoeing adventures is increasing. No more expensive lessons and days spent wondering if your children are safe on the hill – they and you can spend quality time together starting when they are infants. In a backpack, warmly dressed and as long as temperatures are mild, small children enjoy the scenery and wildlife or contentedly sleep. Preschoolers respond well to travelling in a carrier or being pulled in a toboggan behind a parent or family friend. Soon they will want their own snowshoes, and while this leads to shorter trips it is worth the effort to encourage their interest.

If you are planning to take a young baby in a backpack, remember that they cannot yet regulate their own warmth, so frequent monitoring is needed for hands, feet and body. Mittens pull off, snowsuits shift up and toques slide over children's eyes, so enlist a friend or the other parent to walk beside or behind the baby to check on and fix these aspects while you are carrying the baby. Infants inevitably poop, pee and want to eat a lot and this does present the problem of how to change or feed them while keeping baby (and mother) warm. Preplan the possible responses to the feeding and changing challenges so you have the necessary equipment (e.g., a warm surrounding fleece for mom and child) when you need it.

For toddlers, make sure they have warm, waterproof mittens (attached to their sleeves), a toque that ties under the chin, waterproof boots and a snowsuit that unzips for toilet events. A scarf for windy days and sunglasses and sunscreen lotion for sunny days are important for all children. As well, try to encourage your stronger friends to come along – they can spell you when you get tired carrying a heavy toddler in the backpack.

It's best to select short trails for snowshoeing with young children, and children may need encouragement with rewards, both during the adventure (e.g., fruit jellies, count the birds and give them sunflower seeds) and at the end of the trail (sliding down a hill on the toboggan, say, or a treat at the lodge).

For school-aged children, select short routes on mainly flat terrain and build up to slightly longer trips with elevation gain. Trips that have an interesting destination such as Hollyburn Lodge or a warming hut will persuade children to walk on to the end of the trail.

Include special lunch food – treats for the adults as well as "special" food for the children to make lunch part of the whole adventure. Baguettes or croissants and special cheeses anyone?

Bringing same-age friends along is an effective strategy at any age and ensuring that your children are warm and dry and well fed with high-energy food and liquids (and a few strategic treats) makes for happy junior snowshoers.

Take along an alternative means of travel such as a light-weight toboggan – it will be easier to pull that than trying to carry a tired child. This can also serve as a reward for your child at lunchtime or at the end of the trip, when the whole family can go tobogganing together.

Carry dry socks and gloves for children who love to make snowballs and snowmen, or who enjoy making snow angels. Have fleecy blankets in your vehicle so that children can snuggle down and perhaps nap on the way home.

Preparing your child for snowshoeing

Include your child in the planning of the snowshoe trip. Show them a map and where you will be going. If pictures are available

A tired girl gets a ride back to the car

on the Internet, show these to increase interest and familiarity. For school-aged children print a copy of the map and let them help follow the trail. Discuss how to recognize the intersections and rivers if shown on the map and how to follow the coloured tapes or metal markers on trails marked in this way. Talk about and show pictures of the animals and birds or footprints in the snow that they might see. If there is a lodge or pictures of warming huts on the trail available on a website, show them the pictures so they have an idea of where they will be heading. Get your child to help lay out their winter clothes and talk about why they need warm and waterproof clothes, mittens, toque and boots.

Have your school-aged child carry an age-appropriate backpack with a small amount of their needed supplies in it.

Encourage your child to participate in selecting the types of sandwiches, energy bars, drinks and healthy treats you include. Hot chocolate on the trail provides warmth, energy and an incentive for any age of snowshoer. Allow school-aged children to carry their own treats and choose when to eat them. Bring same-age friends along when snowshoeing with teenagers.

Ensure your child has had a good night's sleep before the snowshoe trip.

Preparing yourself for snowshoeing with small children

You're a parent so you already know about the need to be flexible. As parents find out, even when the baby is in a carry-pack the trips sometimes have to be shortened or changed to accommodate the child. With active toddlers in a carrier, do not expect to go the same distances or to the same places as when a younger baby was able to peacefully sleep in a carry-pack.

In truth there may be an age range when your child is too heavy (or big) to carry and yet not strong enough or old enough to use snowshoes. This is where loving aunties or grandmothers hopefully can be encouraged to babysit to allow you and your partner to still have some snowshoe time together.

Selecting snowshoes for children

Considerations for selecting snowshoes for children are similar to several of the factors to weigh when choosing for teens and adults.

- **anticipated use:** With young children snowshoeing, it is unlikely you will be going on steep terrain or for long trips, so use will probably be on flat or mildly rolling terrain.
- **the child's weight:** Snowshoes for children, like those for adults, are sized for the weight of the child. Also consider the length of the snowshoe relative to the size of the individual, since a short, heavy child might struggle with long snowshoes even though their weight might indicate that the size and length are correct.
- **weight and material of the snowshoe:** Lightweight construction is essential to decrease the overall weight

the child will be lifting with each stride. Several companies make plastic snowshoes for very young children that make a design (e.g., a bear paw) on the snow. However, they do not provide an effective grip for forward movement. Our preference is to put children on snowshoes that are made of lightweight tubular metal or polymer that have a good grip on the bottom of the snowshoe. There is no reason to think that just because a child is closer to the snow, sliding and falling from lack of grip is fun for children. Purchase snowshoes that have metal claws under the ball of the feet or, even better, serrated metal or plastic teeth along the sides as well.

- **bindings:** Select quality, easy to use bindings that an older child can at least sometimes manage independently. Have your child do them up and undo them in the store to see how much help they will need.
- **poles:** Poles may not be necessary but if the particular child has problems with balance then they will be helpful. Try them out and see if they are needed. Downhill or cross-country ski poles may work effectively.

SNOWSHOEING WITH TEENAGERS

The struggle to get a teenager away from their electronic devices or their downhill skis is worth it for all the family – a time for talk, laughter and fun if all goes well. But what can you do to engage the teen in the adventure? If they have snowshoed with the family as younger children they may already have enjoyed the slower pace and the joy of walking along a forest trail. For any teenager, food and friends are the answers. Bring along one or more friends. (Make sure the friends have adequate clothing and equipment.) Have a continuous source of food and drink available throughout the trip. Take pictures of the adventure. Let them

Bring friends and food along
with your teenagers

take pictures to post on their Facebook if they have one. Give
them the map or the GPS and let them be the leader of the group.
Encourage races in the snow. Have a snowball fight or as a family
do some of the snow games listed below. Make snow designs in
open areas away from tree wells. Stop for a pizza or other favourite food on the way home. Say thanks for coming and how much
you enjoyed the family outing.

SNOW FUN ACTIVITIES FOR FAMILIES

Have a repertoire of snow-related activities to do as you snowshoe
along. This will encourage forward movement on the trail and
positive memories for everyone.

- "I spy with my little eye" encourages children to be visually
  aware in the winter landscape.

- Take pictures to record the great moments: a Whiskey Jack feeding from your child's hand; the big smiles when everyone arrives at the warming hut; making panini on a wood stove in a warming hut etc.
- Learn songs and poems to say and sing (e.g., The Grand Old Duke of York, Frosty the Snowman, The Teddy Bears' Picnic, Winter Wonderland – lyrics are on websites) and review your favourite children's stories so you can tell them along the way. Stories that have a phrase for repetition where everyone can join in are always good choices.
- Learn the different shapes of animal tracks common to your snowshoeing area. Encourage your children to identify any of the prints you see in the snow. Learn the different kinds of birds and coniferous trees along the trail area and share this knowledge with your children.
- Think of as many words as possible that have the word snow in them, e.g., snowball, snowberries, snowblower, snowboarder, snowmobile, snowplow, snowshoe, snowcapped, snowdrift, snowfield, snowflake, snowmakers, snowscapes, snowslide, snowstorm, snowball, snowbanks, snowbell, snowbird, snowbound, Snow White, snowdrop, snowfall, snowpack, snowshed, snowslide, snowsuit, snowpants, snowline, snow shovel, snowman, snowy owl, snow goose, snow leopard.
- Name animals and birds that have snowshoe-like feet to help them walk on snow, e.g., red fox, ptarmigan, snowshoe hare, lynx, caribou, mountain lions, pumas and cougars.

Some games that will add more fun to the snowshoe trip and provide a break from snowshoeing are:
- Follow the Leader, making new tracks in wide flat areas away from trees (and possible tree wells) and creeks

- Snowshoe Slalom around day packs placed along a racecourse
- Spell words by stamping the letters in a flat stretch of new snow
- Fox and Geese requires four or more players. Stamp a circle in new snow with two intersecting paths going through the middle. At the middle, stamp a small circle – the safe zone. A designated fox chases the others – the geese – and tries to tag them. Geese run only on the paths and cannot be tagged when in the safe zone. Once a fox catches a goose, that goose becomes the next fox.
- Scavenger hunts can involve the children by getting them to develop a list of things they want to see or find on the trail, before they leave home. Write the ideas down and see how many can be found. Even if the suggestions seem impossible to find, such as, say, a fish, usually something like a piece of moss or a stick can be seen to have (or be made to have, with a bit of parental help) the desired shape. Variations such as an alphabet hunt, e.g., Apple in our lunch for A, bunny footprints for B, chocolate Smarties for C, down jacket for D etc., are fun.
- Tic-tac-toe requires a 3 × 3 grid on the snow and pinecones and sticks as the symbols.
- Target practice – make a horizontal circular target on the snow or define a spot on a large tree trunk and throw snowballs at it.
- Frozen tag needs a safe area, away from tree wells and wet spots, for running. One person is chosen as the tagger. Once a child or adult is tagged they have to remain frozen until a free person tags them to unfreeze them. Change taggers frequently.
- Snow bowling makes use of the family water bottles. Line them in a triangle and use snowballs to try to knock them down.

Playing in the snow is part of the fun of snowshoeing

- Snow art. Before you start the trip, show the children pictures on the Internet of the snowshoe art made by Simon Beck (**snowart.gallery**). Even the adults will want to try making artful designs in the snow after they see these wonderful creations.

Your children *will* grow up, and these early years of gentle encouragement will result in people that respect and enjoy the outdoors for a lifetime (and soon they will be wearing racing snowshoes and beating you up the hill!).

TRAIL TREATS

There is nothing like a hot drink and a healthy sweet treat when snowshoeing on a cold day. Warm up apple juice or lemonade and put it in your Thermos as an alternative to tea, coffee or hot chocolate. If milk allergies create a challenge, use a delicious chocolate almond or coconut drink that can be heated.

Hot chocolate

For each cup of hot chocolate, combine until smooth 15 ml (1 tbsp.) of cocoa, 30 ml (2 tbsp. of sugar), 30 ml (2 tbsp.) of water, 2.5 ml (½ tsp.) of vanilla. Add 250 ml (1 cup) of milk or soya milk and heat to desired temperature. Remember, the liquid will cool down somewhat in the Thermos as you snowshoe.

Chocolate fondue

While there are commercial opportunities to partake in a chocolate fondue snowshoe party during the day or at night, why not create your own event? Sporting headlights and very warm clothes and going on a simple, well-known trail in good weather allows flexibility in timing and group membership. Save the money it would cost for a commercially sponsored outing for new snowshoes and outdoor equipment.

Remember to bring along a small non-stick pot and a stirring spoon as well as a camping/backpacking propane stove, propane canisters, matches and fondue forks.

Prepare the ingredients at home before leaving. Melt 8 oz. (230 g) of good quality chocolate. Combine 90 ml (3 oz.) of heavy cream and (optional and for adults only) 30 ml (1 oz.) of liqueur (e.g., Kahlúa, crème de cacao, framboise) with the chocolate. Place in a wide-mouth unbreakable container with a good seal. Reheat at the snow site, stirring frequently to prevent burning. Use firm fruit (e.g., mandarin orange pieces, apple slices, grapes, bananas) and chunks of angelfood cake or banana loaf to dip into the fondue.

Energy bars and cookies
Energy filled snacks are important for everyone when burning the extra energy needed to both snowshoe and keep warm.

Sweet and salty granola bars
These bars can be gluten-free if the oats and chocolate chips are certified gluten-free.

- 750 ml (3 cups) rolled oats
- 250 ml (1 cup) toasted almonds, coarsely chopped
- 250 ml (1 cup) sunflower and/or pumpkin seeds
- 250 ml (1 cup) raisins or craisins or dried blueberries or any dried fruit
- 300 ml (1 small can) sweetened condensed milk – regular or low fat
- 125 ml (½ cup) vegetable shortening melted
- 16 ml (1 tbsp.) kosher salt or coarse sea salt (must be coarse or it will be too salty)

and for the topping:

- 200 ml (1 cup) semi-sweet chocolate chips melted
- 1.5 ml (⅛ tsp.) kosher salt

Preheat oven to 160°C (350°F) Line a 380 × 250 mm (15" × 10") jelly roll pan or cookie sheet with parchment paper or aluminum foil, leaving an edge all around.

Combine all ingredients for bars in a large bowl. Mix well. Press evenly into prepared pan.

Bake in preheated oven 25–30 minutes or until golden brown. Cool slightly.

Topping

Combine the melted chocolate and kosher salt. Drizzle over bars. Allow chocolate to harden. Cut into bars. These bars freeze well.

Milk allergy? Substitute the following for the sweetened condensed milk:

- 1 can (approximately 400 ml) of unsweetened coconut milk
- 80–125 ml (⅓–½ cup) granulated sugar, honey or light agave syrup
- 15 ml (1 tbsp.) brown sugar (optional but adds good flavour)

Place the coconut milk, sweetener of choice and brown sugar (if using) into a saucepan and whisk gently over medium heat for 2–3 minutes. This will help the solid bits of coconut milk melt and incorporate with the sugar.

When the mixture is just beginning to bubble around the edges, reduce heat to the lowest flame or setting. Set a timer for one hour (you may need to go a bit longer depending on your stove) and simmer uncovered, whisking every 5–10 minutes to release steam and aid evaporation. The mixture will reduce by about half and should be quite thick. You will also notice it is a darker colour.

Remove from heat, stir thoroughly and pour into a glass jar or container. Cool in the refrigerator. It will continue to thicken as it cools. Use as needed in recipes or to stir into coffee or tea.

Courtesy of freeeatsfood.com.

Chocolate cashew bliss balls

Soak eight dates for 4 hours, then chop.

Blend 250 ml (1 cup) of cashews until smooth.

Add 30 ml (2 tbsp.) of honey and 10 ml (2 tsp.) of vanilla extract.

Mix in 30 ml (2 tbsp.) of cacao powder.

Blend all ingredients well and form into small balls.

Roll in desiccated coconut and refrigerate until firm. If packing in layers, put foil or parchment paper between layers.

Date squares

A family favourite, these bars are filled with energy and healthy ingredients. Dates contain iron, calcium, manganese, potassium and copper. As well, they supply dietary fibre, tannins and vitamins A, B-complex and K. What is there not to like about dates?

Mix the following ingredients with a pastry blender or two knives until they are in small crumbles. If the mixture appears too dry, add a beaten egg, although this makes the oatmeal mixture a bit firm when cooked. Gluten-free oats and flour can be used.

- 625 ml (2½ cups) rolled oats
- 375 ml (1½ cups) all-purpose flour
- 250 ml (1 cup) packed brown sugar
- 15 ml (3 tsp.) cinnamon
- 250 ml (1 cup) butter or margarine softened for the filling
- 375 g (one package) pitted dates (check carefully – sometimes there are still pits in pitted dates). If you like a really date-filled bar, increase quantities for the filling.
- 30 ml or more (2 tbsp. or more) each of lemon and orange juice
- 15 ml or more (1 tbsp. or more) of grated orange rind

Mix the ingredients together and cook until well blended and soft.

Press half of the oatmeal mixture into a 200 mm square (8") pan greased or lined with parchment paper.

Spread the date mixture evenly over the base. Top with the remaining oat mixture and press down lightly.

Danika enjoys a rest and a treat along the trail

Bake at 180°C (350°F) for about 40 minutes until light golden brown. Cool and cut into squares. These squares freeze well.

Adapted from "Sweet Treats," with permission from *Canadian Living* magazine.

Rice Krispie squares

These are an all-time favourite and so easy to make that your children can help create their own.

- 50 ml (¼ cup) of butter or margarine
- 1.25 L (5 cups) miniature or 40 regular (250 g package) marshmallows
- 2 ml (½ tsp. vanilla extract (optional)
- 1.5 L (6 cups) of Rice Krispies cereal

In a large saucepan over low heat, melt margarine. Add marshmallows; stir until melted and well blended. Remove from heat.

Stir in vanilla. Add cereal, stirring until coated.

Using lightly buttered spatula, press into buttered 3.5 L (13" × 9") pan. Cool. Cut into bars.

Step up the flavour and energy by adding dried cranberries, raisins, chopped nuts or other dried fruits. Add a few more marshmallows for extra stickiness to accommodate the added ingredients.

Recipe courtesy of Kellogg's.

One-bowl chocolate brownies

Traditional chocolate brownies can't be improved upon and these are simple enough for children to help make them. Allergy alert for nuts and gluten. Cranberries can be used instead of nuts and you can substitute gluten-free flour.

- 4 oz. Baker's unsweetened chocolate, chopped
- 180 ml (¾ cup) butter
- 500 ml (2 cups) sugar
- 3 eggs
- 5 ml (1 tsp.) vanilla
- 250 ml (1 cup) flour
- 250 ml (1 cup) chopped pecans (dried cranberries can be substituted, although they are not in the original recipe)

and for the glaze:

- 4 oz. Baker's semi-sweet chocolate
- 15 ml (3 tsp.) butter
- 15 ml (3 tsp.) water

Melt unsweetened chocolate and butter in microwave in large bowl on medium power for 2 minutes until butter is melted. Stir until chocolate is completely melted.

Add eggs; beat until well blended. Stir in sugar and flour until well blended. Add nuts or dried cranberries.

Spread in greased 33 × 23 cm (13 × 9 inch) pan. Bake at 180°C (350°F) for 35 or 40 minutes or until toothpick inserted in centre comes out almost clean. Cool brownie and cut into squares.

NOTE: Using either the glaze or the rocky road topping may make the brownies more difficult to carry in a backpack, but you decide.

Glaze
Melt semi-sweet chocolate squares with butter and water in microwave; blend until smooth and spread over cooled brownie

Rocky road
Prepare as directed, topping with 250 ml (1 cup) each of jet-puffed miniature marshmallows and Baker's Semi-sweet Chocolate Chips for the last 5 minutes of the baking time.

Courtesy of kraftrecipes.com.

Gorp/trail mix
Choose your own combination of nuts, cereals such as Chex or Cheerios, large-flake dried coconut, dried fruits such as dates, raisins, cranberries, papaya or apple and maybe Smarties and pretzels for a tasty energy boost. By making your own mix you can also avoid any allergies family or friends may have.

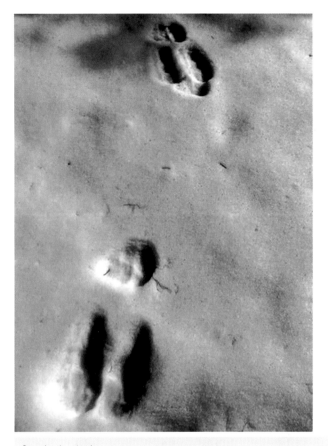

Snowshoe hare tracks   PHOTOGRAPHER: DOUG FARENHOLTZ

TRAIL TRACKS

While snowshoeing, one of the interesting activities everyone can participate in is to identify bird and animal tracks found in the snow. The following images are not to scale but will give a silhouette of some of the different animal and bird tracks you might see during the winter throughout BC.

Weasel

Deer mouse

Grey squirrel

Chipmunk

Bald eagle

Raven

Moose

Elk

Mule deer

Bobcat

Coyote

Cougar

Wolf

Grey fox

Black bear

Grizzly bear

Snowshoe hare

Raccoon

Steller's Jay

Gray Jay/Whiskey Jack

Pine Grosbeak
PHOTOGRAPHER: PETER CANDIDO, 2015

Raven

Chickadee

BIRDS IN WINTER

As well as tracks in the snow you may see birds perched in the trees or flying in your vicinity. Children and adults alike are always delighted with the cheeky antics of the Gray Jay/Whiskey Jack, and the startling sapphire blue of the Steller's Jay adds colour to a white landscape.

Wind snowball shapes made us feel hungry

WIND SNOWBALLS

Another interesting natural track and formation is that made by wind pushing snow down a slope and making natural "wind snowballs." To make these kinds of forms, a wet snowfall that is good for packing and strong winds blowing continuously are needed so the snow gathers more layers as it rolls down the hill.

These different shapes were seen on the Fat Dog Ridge trail in late winter and reminded us of cinnamon buns, croissants and other pastry delights – we must have been hungry after a long day of snowshoeing!

PART 2:

THE TRAILS

COQUIHALLA   107
Falls Lake Trail   107
Mount Henning Cabin Loop Trail   110
Mount Ottomite Trail   115
Needle Peak Ridge Trail   118
Portia to Iago Station Trail   123
Zoa Peak Trail   127

FRASER VALLEY   131
Burke Ridge via Old Harper Road
     Trail   131

MANNING PARK   135
Cambie Creek Loop Trail   135
Fat Dog Ridge Trail   139
Lightning Lake Loop Trail   142
Flash Lake Loop Trail   145
Monument 78 Trail   147
Poland Lake Trail   151
Skagit River Trail   155
Windy Joe Trail   160

NORTH SHORE   166
Black Mountain Loop Trail   166
Eagle Bluffs   171
Bowen Lookout Trail   174
Dog Mountain and First Lake Loop
     Trail   179
Hollyburn Mountain Trail   184
Howe Sound Crest East Trail Loop   190
Mount Seymour First Peak Trail   195
Thunderbird Ridge Trail   201

SEA TO SKY CORRIDOR   207
Cal-Cheak Recreation Site to
     Brandywine Falls   207
Cheakamus Crossing Loop Trail   212
Cheakamus Crossing to Cal-Cheak
     Recreation Site Trail   217

Garibaldi Lake and Taylor Meadows
     Trails   222
Lava Lake Loop Trail   226
Red Heather Meadows   231
Elfin Lakes Trail   233

SUNSHINE COAST   235
Tetrahedron Provincial Park: Edwards
     Cabin Trail   235
Tetrahedron Provincial Park: Batchelor
     Cabin Trail   239
Knuckleheads Winter Recreation Area:
     E Branch Cabin   240

WHISTLER INTERPRETIVE
     FOREST TRAILS   247
Black Tusk Microwave Tower Road
     Trail   248
Cheakamus Lake Trail   252
Highline Loop Trail   255
Logger's Lake and Ridge Loop Trail   259

OTHER WHISTLER TRAILS   262
Ancient Cedars Grove Trail   262
Mid-Flank Trail   266
Rainbow Falls Loop   271
Parkhurst Ghost Town Loop   273

SOUTH COASTAL
     MOUNTAINS   282
Mount Seymour   282
Hollyburn Mountain   282
Grouse Mountain   283
Squamish Sea to Sky Gondola   283
Whistler/Blackcomb   284
Whistler Olympic Park   285
Callaghan Country   285
Hemlock Ski Resort   286

SUNSHINE COAST   287
Dakota Ridge   287
Knuckleheads Winter Recreation
      Area   287
Tetrahedron Provincial Park   288

THOMPSON/OKANAGAN   289
Big White Ski Resort   289
McCulloch Nordic Area   289
Crystal Mountain   290
Silver Star Mountain Resort   290
Sovereign Lake Nordic Centre   291
Nickel Plate Nordic Centre   291
Sun Peaks (Kamloops)   292
Stake Lake   292
Kane Valley   293
Mount Baldy   293
Wells Gray Provincial Park
      (Info Centre)   294
Larch Hills   294
Logan Lake   295

KOOTENAY ROCKIES   295
Kimberley Alpine Resort   295
Kimberley Nordic Centre   296
Panorama Mountain   296
Mount Macpherson   297
Paulson Nordic Ski Area   298
Fernie Trails   298
Fernie Alpine Resort   299
Red Mountain Resort   299
Jack Rabbit Trail (Nakusp Community
      Forest Trail)   300
Summit Lake Ski & Snowboard
      Area   300
Whitewater Winter Resort   301
Creston Valley Wildlife Management
      Area   301
Kicking Horse Mountain Resort   302

Emerald Lake Lodge in Yoho National
      Park   303
Nipika Mountain Resort   303
99 Mile Ski Trails and Nordic Day
      Lodge   304
Spruce Hills Resort & Spa at 108 Mile
      House   304
Wells/Barkerville Mountain Trails   305
Williams Lake Bull Mountain
      Trails   305
Tweedsmuir Provincial Park South,
      East Branch   306

NORTHERN BRITISH
      COLUMBIA   306
Smithers and Burns Lake   306
Babine Mountains Provincial
      Park   307
Howson Hut Wilderness Retreats
      (privately owned)   308
Eskers Provincial Park   308
Powder King Resort   309
Otway Nordic Ski Centre   309
Giscome Portage Trail
      Protected Area   310
Bear Mountain Ski Hill   310
Tumbler Ridge   311
Beatton Provincial Park   311
Onion Lake Ski Trails   312

VANCOUVER ISLAND   312
Mount Cain   312
Mount Washington Alpine Resort   313

Amy on the Edwards Cabin trail in Tetrahedron Provincial Park
PHOTOGRAPHER: PATRICK NOLAN, 2016

SNOWSHOE TRAILS IN SOUTHWESTERN BC

COQUIHALLA

Falls Lake Trail

ACCESS: Drive Highway 5 (Coquihalla) to Falls Lake Exit 221.
Turn left after exiting and go through the underpass; then
turn left and park on the side of the road.

RATING: easy terrain, short distance

SEASON: December to early April

MAP: 92H11 Spuzzum

BEGINNING ALTITUDE: 1190 m

DESTINATION ALTITUDE: 1300 m

DISTANCE: 4.1 km loop

TIME: 1½–2 hours round trip

CELL-PHONE ACCESS: intermittent

FOOD AND DRINK: Hope

WASHROOMS: environmentally considerate use of the forest

DOGS: yes

AVALANCHE CONDITIONS: **avalanche.ca**

*This short trail is excellent for families and also provides an exercise
opportunity when heading into the Okanagan to snowshoe or ski at
the resorts or snowshoe areas in the Interior. Because the Coquihalla
area receives so much yearly snowfall, it may continue to have snow
long into spring.*

Directions

The trail begins at the roadside with a track that intersects after approximately 1.1 km with the old Coldwater Road and the

Falls Lake from Mount Zoa PHOTOGRAPHER: JIM PEARSON

pipeline right-of-way that leads to the Zoa Ridge trail. The area at the base of the hill is the summer parking lot. Cross the bridge and look to the left and slightly uphill. There is usually a small cornice of snow at the forest edge (sometimes with dirt showing below it) that marks the beginning of the trail to Falls Lake. Walk along the narrow trail for approximately 300 m to an intersection with a trail leading to the right (the return trail option). Take the left trail and follow it for about 500 m to where another choice can be made, with either route arriving at the lake. Travelling left and uphill and then down to the lake for approximately 100 m results in arrival at the lake campsite, as does choosing the right branch

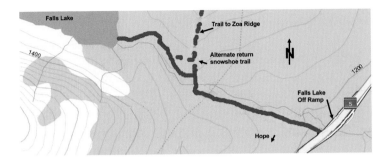

and looping round to the campsite. There is no trail around the lake and ice conditions can be variable, so walking on the lake is not advisable, enticing though it is.

To provide some variation on the return trip, at the intersection where the trail leads to the right to regain the entrance used at the beginning of the trail, take the trail to the left, which will lead to an upper exit along the pipeline cut. Descent is fairly rapid, and if there are no protruding bushes or rocks, this hill is a safe spot to practise modest stride and slide technique (glissading) to the bottom and then snowshoe back to the bridge and the track out to the parking lot.

ACCESS: Drive north on Highway 5 (Coquihalla) to Coquihalla Lakes Exit 228. Turn right on Old Coquihalla Road, going towards Coquihalla Lodge. Then turn left onto the gravel Tulameen Forest Service Road, which leads on the left to the parking lot of the Coquihalla Summit Snowmobile Club.

RATING: easy with long slopes for elevation gain; avalanche terrain

SEASON: December to March

MAPS: 92H10 Tulameen; 92H11 Spuzzum

BEGINNING ALTITUDE: 1125 m

DESTINATION ALTITUDE: 1630 m at Mt. Henning cabin

DISTANCE: 9.1 km for the loop

TIME: 4½–5 hours for the loop

CELLPHONE ACCESS: yes

FOOD AND DRINK: Hope

WASHROOMS: outhouses in parking lot and at Mt. Henning cabin, provided by the snowmobile club; Britton Creek rest area

DOGS: yes, but be aware that snowmobiles may be on any trail at any time on any day, so keeping your dog on leash is advised

AVALANCHE CONDITIONS: **avalanche.ca**

The trail to the lower reaches of Mount Henning provides an easy snowshoe in deep snow at most times of the winter. Once elevation is gained there are panoramic views of the Coquihalla corridor and the surrounding mountains. The downside is that this is a favourite and designated recreational area for the Coquihalla Summit Snowmobile Club, so there may be snowmobiles on the trails even during the week. Weekends are best avoided, and checking the club

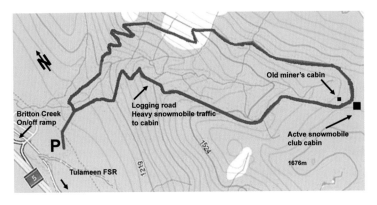

website, **coqsnow.com**, is essential to see whether there are any big get-togethers or rallies planned for the day you have in mind.

NOTE: *This is a high-risk avalanche area, and although most of this trail is in treed alpine terrain, there are some wide, long, open slopes with steep grades above and below, so make sure you check and heed the avalanche conditions on the day of your snowshoe adventure.*

Directions

After parking in the snowmobile club lot, begin the trail by climbing up the bank out of the parking area and walking to the left along the pipeline right-of-way. Within about 200 m there is an opening in the forest on the right and a sign saying MOUNT HENNING. There also is a map showing the snowmobile routes in the area. (Maps of these routes are also available at the Mount Henning Hut or online.) Take this trail and very soon there is a narrow path leading to the left. While this branch path is used by ATV riders in the summer and therefore the brush is cleared out regularly, it seems to hold little interest for snowmobilers. Walk along the path, soon crossing a shallow creek. Follow the trail in a northeasterly direction along its many switchbacks, gradually gaining elevation and viewpoints from about 1300 m and after

Old mining cabin on Mount Henning

about 1.4 km of snowshoeing. To the south the Coquihalla Lakes and Coquihalla Lodge and cabins come into view. To the west there is the Coldwater Valley and the road to Little Douglas Lake, with road maintenance sheds in the valley. Opposite is Zoa Ridge and the deep, avalanche-prone valley.

The views gradually disappear as the trail levels out and winds around the side of the mountain in an easterly direction. After about 3.4 km and 2½ hours of snowshoeing, a junction occurs where the trail intersects with a snowmobile route.

The left turn leads to a viewpoint overlooking the same vistas seen on the way up. As well, the left trail accesses the ridge to Mount Henning. (The snowmobile club map shows this area towards the ridge as challenging terrain with a high risk of avalanche.) A right turn taken on this trail continues for about another 1.4 km to the snowmobile club's Mount Henning Hut, at about 1630 m elevation. The abandoned ruins of an old log cabin seen on the right in the meadow are reputed to be the remains of buildings constructed for a minerals exploration project called the Independence Prospect claims.

There are two choices for the return route, both about the same length. One is to return on the ascent trail (about 4.9 km). The other is to descend alongside the most direct snowmobile route that comes up from the parking lot to Mount Henning Cabin (about 4.2 km). This latter route requires the ability to anticipate and avoid any snowmobilers going up or down – it is, after all, part of their playground. If the snowmobile trail is chosen, it can be found by walking past the outhouse and heading to the left to intersect with a wide, well-used trail.

As the trail descends the sounds of the highway gradually return, and after about 60 to 90 minutes of snowshoeing an exit from the same entrance where the morning snowshoe trail began can be made. Turn left and return to the parking lot.

MOUNT HENNING PROSPECTING

No mine was ever developed on Mount Henning, although prospectors first staked it in 1901 to explore copper–molybdenum deposits. Between 1906 and 1908 the Granby Mining, Smelting and Power company completed 300 m of tunnelling. Between 1951 and 1981 some 1350 metres of diamond drilling in 10 holes was done to explore the region. The most recent exploration was initiated by Odessa Explorations in 1987. The grade of copper found in the area was not economically viable to develop a mine.

Near the top of Mount Ottomite   PHOTOGRAPHER: ALAN TOON, 2015

Mount Ottomite Trail

ACCESS: Drive north on Highway 5 (Coquihalla) to just past the Box Canyon Exit 271 sign. A right-hand exit is easy to miss just opposite the Zopkios rest area on the opposite side of the road. Go through the tunnel under the highway and turn left to the Zopkios rest stop. Park to the side, out of the way of transport trucks and other vehicles.

RATING: easy terrain

SEASON: late December to mid-March

MAP: 92H11 Spuzzum

BEGINNING ALTITUDE: 1200 m

DESTINATION ALTITUDE: 1470 m

DISTANCE: 8.6 km round trip

TIME: 2½–3 hours round trip

CELLPHONE ACCESS: yes

FOOD AND DRINK: Hope

WASHROOMS: Zopkios rest area

DOGS: yes

AVALANCHE CONDITIONS: **avalanche.ca**

This pleasant snowshoe trail is an easy one for beginners, with a gentle upward climb along an unused access road to a forested summit. Although for many years the top of Ottomite was a location for studying snow depth in the area, this is now inactive. During early winter and late spring or if there is a thin snow cover there are many bushes that may poke their way through the snow, although the Hope Mountain Centre for Outdoor Learning tries to keep it brushed out. They also use this trail for several of their snowshoe programs, so it often is well tracked. To avoid disappointment and/or frustration the route is best done in mid-winter. As well, until a new wooden and steel bridge is built here to provide

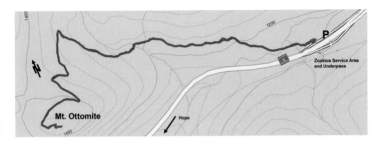

a continuation of the road, deep snow is needed to fill in the river bed and create a snow bridge.

Directions

From the parking lot, pass to the right of the restrooms and walk towards a large pile of dirty snow dumped here from road clearing. To the right of the pile a clear pathway can be seen leading towards the forest. Snowshoe on this trail straight onto and over a snow bridge. As the trail continues, a concrete bunker can be seen. Once this structure is passed, the road continues straight on. At about 2 km a second bridge, made of logs crookedly lodged in the creek, leads to a gently winding path that makes a sharp left turn at about 3 km. The trail then continues on with short and long traverses to the top. Looking upwards from this modest summit there is a panoramic view of the tall surrounding mountains of Thar, Nak and Yak, and to the northeast, Needle Peak can be identified. Return on the same trail used to reach the top.

Another snowshoe trip that uses the first part of this trail is to Iago Peak (12.3 km round trip from the rest area). The trail branches off to the right at the left-hand turn in the Ottomite trail at about the 3 km point. This route is often tracked by backcountry skiers but this is not guaranteed, so carrying a topographic map is necessary.

HOW DEEP DOES SNOW GET?

In the early 1900s American scientist Dr. J.E. Church developed a method to measure the depth of snow and assess its water content to predict runoff and potential for spring flooding. Between 1980 and 1990 data was collected at the snow survey site at Mount Ottomite and later by automated measurement at the Great Bear snowshed. Both of these sites are now inactive. Here is a sample of changes in snow depth and water equivalents during that time:

1980:

January	163 cm snow, 578 mm water
April	299 cm snow, 1140 mm water

1990:

January	207 cm snow, 612 mm water
April	375 cm snow, 1710 mm water

The closest site for measurement at a similar elevation today is Blackwell Peak, in Manning Park, where in March 2015 the snow water equivalent was 600 mm, down from about 850 mm at the same time in 2014. Climate change? El Niño? The scientists are tracking all the information to give us answers. We are the solution.

ACCESS: Drive north on Highway 5 (Coquihalla) to Zopkios Exit 217 and the BC Highways works yard. Turn right towards the yard buildings and park out of the way so that graders, sanding trucks and snowplows can get in and out. An alternative is to park at the Zopkios rest area by exiting at 217, continuing on the side road to go through the vehicle underpass on the left and turning south to park in the pullout. Retrace your car route on foot to the start of the trail. Another possibility is to park on the road by the forest trail start.

RATING: moderate – possible trail finding and track breaking skills needed on the steep initial ascent, followed by an easy ridge walk

SEASON: December to April

MAP: 92H11 Spuzzum

BEGINNING ALTITUDE: 1219 m

DESTINATION ALTITUDE: 1719 m to ridge lookout

DISTANCE: 5 km round trip to the lookout on the ridge; additional 2.4 km round trip to the lookout over the lake and Flatiron Mountain

TIME: 4–5 hours round trip to ridge lookout

CELLPHONE ACCESS: variable

FOOD AND DRINK: Hope

WASHROOMS: rest area at Zopkios pullout; environmentally considerate use of the forest

DOGS: dogs must be on leash in provincial parks

AVALANCHE CONDITIONS: **avalanche.ca**

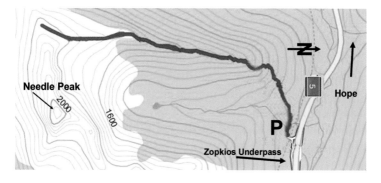

A long-time favourite of backcountry skiers, this trail in Coquihalla Summit Recreation Area has gained popularity with snowshoers in recent years. With any luck, you will find that skiers have created a well-packed trail that traverses through the forest and onto the subalpine ridge. The (steeper) summer trail is well marked with orange flashes, but in winters with high snowfall the markers may be covered. By late spring, although there often is plenty of snow in the surrounding forest, the summer trail becomes a runoff creek and often turns into an icy path with areas of rotten snow. Micro crampons are essential for these kinds of conditions.

Directions

Start the trail either by scaling the snowbanks south of the BC Highways buildings and progressing past the small falls on the left by way of a snow bridge over a log, or by going west along the edge of the access road to a sign on the left indicating the Needle Peak trail. If you take the snow bridge route, head to the left into the forest, where a cutline leads to the summer markers and intersects with the trail from the access road entrance. Follow the flashes (if they are visible) or previous ski and snowshoe trails (if they are present) or head upwards, staying on the central ridge above the Boston Bar Creek valley on the left.

The trail passes first through thin forest, then thicker but scrubbier trees and then, after close to an hour of snowshoeing – only approximately 760 m of distance but 300 m of steep elevation gain – it emerges onto a small plateau. After another 30 minutes and about 500 m total elevation gain, a larger viewpoint is found where there is a sign reminding skiers and hikers that only stove fires are allowed. The first unimpeded view of Needle Peak is to the left from here, as well as a view back to the mountains in the north named after ruminant animals living in alpine areas of the world. From east to west the mountains of Thar, a goat-like animal; Nak, a female yak; and Yak, a cow-like animal with a furry coat, can be seen. As you continue upwards, the trees are now thinning and the highest point of the immediate ridge is in view at about 1.8 km. But don't stop – there is more! When this next ridge is climbed it provides a view of the next higher and larger "summit" that can be your destination for lunch. Follow the narrowing ridge through the trees and then climb upward in a short, open ravine between steep sides, leading to the second ridge. Ascent here can also be done by continuing through the trees along the side of the ridge.

When climbing the third and final ridge (which starts off narrow and then widens), stay well to the middle or go along the left side of the ridge beside scattered trees and then ascend it diagonally from the left. Staying to the left side of the ridge near the top is the favoured path if there is wind, since the ridge provides protection. There are cornices on one side and a steep drop-off on the other. At the end of the ridge, at about 2.5 km, there is a granite rock outcropping that in spring provides a warm, sun-filled place to stop and eat. From this vantage point of about 1719 m elevation can be seen Needle Peak to the northeast and the alpine ski tracks leading from the open areas of Flatiron Mountain to the southwest. The trails of snowshoers and backcountry skiers

Sandra and Doug with the "ruminant" mountains behind them

lead to the far western ridge on the way to the lake below Flatiron Mountain. If a decision is made to go on, it will take about one hour and approximately 2.1 km round trip to descend to the left of the rocky lookout and climb south toward the ridge to where it overlooks the lake. It is approximately 13 km round trip (from the parking area) to continue on to the small lake.

The return trip can be made on the same trail as the ascent, since in deep snow, finding any tree markers on the way down is even harder than on the climb up.

Portia to Iago Station Trail

ACCESS: Drive Highway 5 (Coquihalla) to Portia Exit 202. Cross over a cement bridge, following signs indicating the route to Merritt. Park close to but not impeding access to a yellow metal gate extended across a wide road.

RATING: easy terrain

SEASON: late December to mid-March

MAP: 92H06 Hope; 92H11 Spuzzum

BEGINNING ALTITUDE: 596 m

DESTINATION ALTITUDE: 762 m at Iago Station

DISTANCE: 12.4 km round trip to Iago Station

TIME: 4–4½ hours round trip

CELLPHONE ACCESS: variable

FOOD AND DRINK: Hope

WASHROOMS: environmentally considerate use of the forest

DOGS: yes

AVALANCHE CONDITIONS: **avalanche.ca**

This low-level trail is suitable for beginner snowshoers and provides views along the Coquihalla corridor, numerous waterfalls and a journey along part of the historic Kettle Valley Railway. The trail is also a portion of the 24.4 km Trans Canada Trail (TCT) from Portia to Coquihalla Lakes.

Directions

The trail begins by passing by the yellow metal gate and snowshoeing along a Kinder Morgan maintenance road under which a high-pressure gas pipeline runs. Continue for 20 minutes and about 1.4 km to a Y junction. The road to the right dips downward, while to the left a marker indicating the Trans Canada Trail can be found. Take the left trail and after about another

Frozen falls and icicles along the trail

15 minutes and approximately 800 m of snowshoeing along the tree-lined trail, it will emerge into a flat area with a large boulder in the centre. Continue to the right up a small incline where the trail rejoins the wooded path. In about 20 minutes the moss-covered cement abutments of an old railway bridge can be seen. Continue snowshoeing in a gentle curve to the left and over a small (usually frozen) stream to regain the railbed on the other side. Although there have been several small, icy waterfalls beside the trail up to this point, a grander, taller one – in winter often surrounded by glimmering icicles – now comes into view at about 3 km from the trailhead. The end of this restored

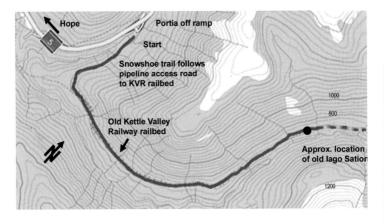

section of the Trans Canada Trail/Kettle Valley Railway is at about 3.4 km, where the TCT meets the continuation of the pipeline road. A small log cabin is in a clearing below the pipeline road to the right.

The wide pipeline road makes for easy snowshoeing for a total of approximately 6.2 km to the destination of Iago – one of the "whistle stops" along the Kettle Valley Railway that today is overgrown with trees and vegetation and identified only by the TCT marker. This place makes a good lunch spot, but for those who wish to go a bit farther the trail continues on the pipeline road. After another approximately 2.5 km there is an old concrete snowshed – but stay far back for viewing this. The snowshed is one of 15 such structures originally built between Romeo station and Coquihalla station. Save exploring this route until a summer hike or bicycle tour – it is not advisable to snowshoe in this high-risk avalanche area.

The upward railway grade on the way to Iago and the Coquihalla Lakes sometimes exceeds the usual rail grade of 2.2 degrees, but this downward slope makes the trip back much faster and should take less than two hours.

KETTLE VALLEY RAILWAY

Andrew McCullough was the chief engineer of the Kettle Valley Railway, a track that was built to link the Kootenay with the West Coast. McCullough enjoyed reading Shakespeare and used characters from the plays to name a number of the whistle stops along the Coquihalla and Hope section of the railway route. Consequently the names Jessica, Romeo, Juliet, Lear, Portia, Iago, Othello and Shylock can be seen along the main highway. The Coquihalla section provided many challenges, not the least of which was more than 14 feet of snow each winter, plus washouts and rockslides that led to this area being the first part of the railway to be abandoned in 1961. The Kettle Valley tracks were officially declared abandoned in 1978 in all areas, and in 2000 the route became part of the recreational Trans Canada Trail.

ACCESS: Drive Highway 5 (Coquihalla) to Exit 221, the Falls
   Lake turnoff. Go through the vehicle underpass and park
   facing south by the side of the road closest to the wide access road that is the beginning of the snowshoe trail.

RATING: easy terrain with elevation gain and long upward
   sections

SEASON: mid-December to late March

MAP: 92H11 Spuzzum

BEGINNING ALTITUDE: 1190 m

DESTINATION ALTITUDE: 1833 m to first summit; 1872 m
   to Zoa Peak

DISTANCE: 8.5 km round trip to first summit; 11 km round
   trip to peak

TIME: 5–5½ hours round trip

CELLPHONE ACCESS: intermittent

FOOD AND DRINK: Hope

WASHROOMS: environmentally considerate use of the wilderness; Zopkios highway rest stop (south of the parking area)

DOGS: yes

AVALANCHE CONDITIONS: **avalanche.ca**

*This snowshoe trail is short, steep and sweet. It is a favourite of
backcountry skiers, which is useful for packing down a trail if there
is a new snowfall. Perhaps that should read "when there is a new
snowfall," since the Coquihalla summit has been known to have
snowstorms in August.*

Directions

The trail begins at the roadside parking area, where often snowmobiles are revving for a trip into the backcountry. They generally

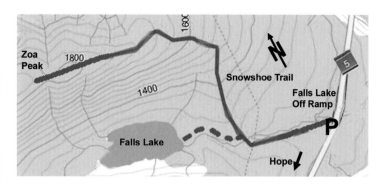

go to the left, up the pipeline cuts, leaving the right-hand trail for snowshoers and skiers to use. Follow the wide road for 20 minutes and about 1 km, passing two pipeline cuts on the left. Turn right at the flat area (used for parking in summer).

Immediately ahead a steep pipeline cut awaits, as does a decision. Following the pipeline for about an hour and 1 km is the best choice, since the trail may already be packed down by other snowshoers or backcountry skiers, saving you the effort of breaking trail. As well, the entrance to the forest trail is readily apparent on the left, close to the top of the last rise.

An alternative route that on the surface appears to be a less strenuous choice is the old Coldwater road, which leads off to the right. This joins the pipeline cut, first with the old Falls Lake 4 × 4 road, and farther along loops back south and then rejoins the pipeline cut close to but above the winter forest trail access. This way is not used often enough by either skiers or snowshoers to have a packed trail, so it will involve some pretty heavy track breaking.

After you've been climbing the pipeline-cut hill for about 50 minutes the slope levels out briefly. Continue on to just before the crest. If anyone goes far enough to begin descending, they have gone too far. However, the ribbon-adorned and marked entrance to the forest on the left used by alpine skiers is easy to spot and it

Heading towards Zoa Peak

is the beginning of a steady climb through the trees. Stay to the more open areas within the forest and follow some intermittent flagging and the general trails of skiers. This helps keep the direction upwards and along the spine of the ridge, heading slightly to the left. After about 1.3 km from the forest entrance a large open area appears on the south side of the ridge. This spot provides a panoramic view including the first summit of Zoa Peak. It is often chosen as a lunch spot, leaving the approximately 600 m distance and 100 m elevation gain to the first summit for a post-picnic push.

The first summit, at about 1833 m, provides a view in every direction. Immediately to the south is Thar Peak; to the southwest are Nak and Yak peaks (part of Zopkios Ridge); and below is snow-covered Falls Lake. The Coldwater River valley can be seen to the north.

To gain the main peak of Zoa the trail loses and then regains about 54 m in elevation before rising to its ultimate height of approximately 1872 m, so many people decide that the first summit is their destination.

The return route is a fast descent on the same trail taken to arrive at the top, with lots of opportunity for shooshing on snowshoes or sliding on backsides in openings in the forest and down the pipeline cut.

COQUIHALLA NAMES

The peaks surrounding Zoa Ridge were named in 1975 by BC mountaineer Philip Kubic after various mountain ruminants (animals that chew their food twice) such as Thar, Yak, Vicuna, Guanaco and Nak. Mountains to the west were given European ruminant names, while the centre peaks were given American ruminant animal names. For instance, a zopkios is a cross between a cow and a yak that is used by porters in the Himalaya for carrying goods. A zoa is the female calf of a bovine bull and a yak. See *Coquihalla Trips & Trails* (2007) by Murphy Shewchuk for a description of all the animals and their relationships to one another that are the names of many of the mountains in the Coquihalla range.

FRASER VALLEY

Burke Ridge Trail via Harper Road

ACCESS: Travel north on Coast Meridian Road in Port Coquitlam until near its end. Turn right on Harper Road and drive to the end of it, just outside the gates to the Port Coquitlam & District Hunting & Fishing Club.

RATING: easy terrain but long distance

SEASON: January to March when snowline is down to at least 500 m

MAP: 92G07 Port Coquitlam

BEGINNING ALTITUDE: 325 m

DESTINATION ALTITUDE: 1032 m

DISTANCE: 12.9 km round trip to old ski lodge site

TIME: 5½–7 hours round trip

CELLPHONE ACCESS: yes

FOOD AND DRINK: Port Coquitlam

WASHROOMS: environmentally considerate use of the wilderness

DOGS: dogs must be on leash in provincial parks

AVALANCHE CONDITIONS: **avalanche.ca**

In choosing this trail, be prepared to carry your snowshoes partway up it to reach the snowline on that particular day. With a beginning altitude of about 325 m, and increasingly unpredictable weather, it is probable that at least the first 15–45 minutes will be on a rocky gravel road. Also be warned that at any time of year and on any day, persistent shooting from the gun club can be heard for about the first hour of climbing. The trail is also used by snowmobilers to get to their cabins below the ridge. Thank them for packing down the track.

**Burke Mt. Lodge
(Bert Ball, Owner/Operator)**

Burke Mountain Ski Lodge ca. 1968
PHOTOGRAPHER UNKNOWN, COURTESY OF DON CUMMINGS

Directions

The trail itself winds upward with a steady elevation gain, then levels out somewhat, returning to a steady climb towards the end. The distant but wide perspective on the city of Vancouver and the Fraser River extending through Delta and Richmond that can be seen from the top is worth the somewhat long slog upward.

Start at the end of Harper Road just before the gun club. There is a locked yellow gate and BC Parks signposts for Pinecone Burke Provincial Park. After 5 minutes of walking there is an upward road branching to the left. Stay right and continue another

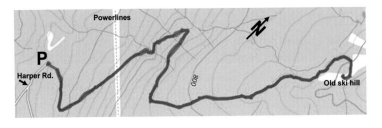

5 minutes until the next left branch. Take this road and continue climbing, reaching the new BC Hydro line-twinning project after about another 25 minutes. A view over the rapidly developing bedroom communities of Vancouver is provided here. Another half hour of climbing leads to an old metal gate; take the right-hand road to pass between the gateposts and continue upward. Hopefully there is now snow on the trail. There are some fairly long sections of gentle climbing in this part, so enjoy the woods, trees and snow scenes without too much effort. At one turn there is a clearing surrounded by coniferous trees that would make a nice sheltered spot for a snack and drink break. After about 1½ hours of snowshoeing and approximately 3.3 km of distance from the trailhead there is a sign on a tree on the right for Gunner's Trail, one of many mountain bike routes on the side of this ridge.

Continue left on the trail until you reach another Y junction at about 4.1 km. On the right trail is an orange square marker that indicates where Village Lake Trail begins. On the left is the trail to the top of the ridge, another 45 to 60 minutes of snowshoeing.

For the way to the top, continue on the left trail for another half hour through an open area with new tree growth rapidly crowding in. Stay to the right on the narrowing and curving road for another 15 to 20 minutes that will take you to the top of the ridge after about 6.4 km. Below the ridge knob are small tarns, so beware that throughout the winter they may be covered with snow but not stable to walk on. Also beneath the snow is a bit of history: remains of the short-lived Burke Mountain Ski Lodge, parts of its tow machinery, an old oil tank and large sled runners.

Enjoy lunch and the view and return the same way you ascended.

BURKE MOUNTAIN: SOME HISTORY

In 1959, Coquitlam councillor René Gamache and area Boy Scouts built the first cabin on Burke Mountain. Initially the additional cabins that were constructed were used for summer recreational escapes. But the idea of having a ski lodge in the area gradually developed, and on New Years Eve 1967/68, Burke Mountain Lodge was officially opened. Numerous difficulties such as financing road maintenance (still mainly paid for by the cabin owners) and unpredictable snowfall eventually resulted in closure of the lodge by the 1970/71 season. It accidently burned down in the 1980s. Thanks to Lyle Litzenberger, author of *Burke and Widgeon: A Hiker's Guide*, for this historical information.

Burke Mountain and Burke Ridge were named after Edmund Burke, a prominent 18th-century British statesman and political thinker. Captain George Henry Richards of the Royal Navy named Burke and other local mountains ca. 1859 when he was surveying Burrard Inlet.

The 38,000 hectare Pinecone Burke Provincial Park was established in 1995. It includes part of the traditional territory of the Katzie First Nation and adjoins one of their reserves. The Katzie are working in conjunction with BC Parks to develop a new management plan for the park.

MANNING PARK

Cambie Creek Loop Trail

ACCESS: Drive on Highway 3 (Crowsnest) towards Manning Park. Heading east, shortly after reaching Allison Pass, pass some highway maintenance buildings on the right and turn left into the signed Cambie Creek plowed parking area (usually hidden behind a high bank of snow).

RATING: easy terrain and short distance

SEASON: December to April

MAP: 92H02 Manning Park

BEGINNING ALTITUDE: 1320 m

DESTINATION ALTITUDE: 1380 m high point on the loop trail

DISTANCE: 5.3 km loop trip

TIME: 1½–2 hours

CELLPHONE ACCESS: no

FOOD AND DRINK: Manning Park Resort

WASHROOMS: outhouse at the parking lot

DOGS: dogs must be on leash in all provincial parks

AVALANCHE CONDITIONS: **avalanche.ca**

This pleasant short-loop trail provides an easy outing for families or for those who want a short snowshoe adventure or a trail to provide a break in a road trip to the Okanagan. Parts of the trail are frequently used by backcountry skiers on their way to Fat Dog Ridge as well as by snowshoers, which often decreases the need to break a new trail.

Directions

The trail begins at a sign on the north side of the parking lot. The initial part is a wide forest track that parallels Cambie Creek.

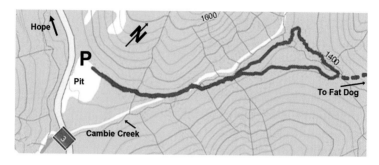

After about 410 m and 10 minutes of snowshoeing, there is a sign and map indicating the way to both the 2.5 km loop trail and the 5 km one. Continue on the trail to the right and, at approximately 980 m, cross a wide bridge over Cambie Creek. Another half hour of snowshoeing, and about 1.4 km from the start, there is a Y junction and a sign again indicating the 2.5 km Cambie Creek Loop and the 5 km loop trail. Continue to snowshoe along this trail on the left, parallel to the creek. At some times during the winter, at about the 1.7 km mark, there may be strange snow mounds that are large snow caves. These will have been built by students in the outdoor education program of a Vancouver secondary school (and may be inhabited if the students are on their winter outing that week).

Another sign showing the same information as earlier (2.5 km and 5 km loops) may be leaning against a tree. Continue along the trail and up a gradual grade. This logging road climbs to the high point of the trip, and after a gradual right turn there is a choice to go straight ahead (narrow road and bent bushes – the wrong way) or to turn right and begin descending, which is the correct trail. The bridge on this trail was replaced in 2016 and makes for an easy crossing of the creek. About 3.1 km from the trailhead, the intersection for the trail to Fat Dog Ridge occurs. As the road descends there are two short

Snow cave along the Cambie Creek Loop

possible avalanche zones on the left where steep open terrain below trees makes room for heavy snow to slough off. Descend the long hill to the next intersection, at about 3.9 km, where the trail (on the right at the intersection) originally branched off to begin the loop. The rest of the trail uses the same track it began with before the loop, and leads back to the parking lot after approximately 5.3 km of snowshoeing.

HOW TO BUILD A SNOWCAVE

You will need several shovels and lots of consolidated (firm, not crystalline) snow. Avalanche shovels will work well.

Select a level patch of ground, with a solid base of snow on it, that is safely away from avalanche danger. Pile up a large heap of snow with a circumference as big as you want the snow cave to be to fit two or more people. Pack the snow as firmly as possible to a height that will allow people to move around inside the cave (though probably not stand upright). Allow the cold air to harden the snow. Dig a tunnel into the mound, sloping slightly upwards for several feet. Hollow out a cave that is big enough to sleep and sit in. Make a sleeping bench by leaving a ledge slightly higher than the entrance tunnel. Smooth the ceiling to minimize drips and direct the meltwater along the walls. Cover the sleeping benches and floor with a firm, closed-cell-foam type of padding. (Inflatable pads will bounce and not be as warm as a firm bottom layer. Clothing as a mattress will not keep the cold away.) Make two ventilation holes at an angle in the ceiling where snow is about 12 inches thick so you do not suffocate. When inside, block the door with a backpack to keep the cold air out. Keep several shovels inside with you in case there is a massive snowfall in the night that might block the door. On the outside, mark the entrance and roof with poles and sticks so others can see the structure and do not inadvertently walk on the roof if new snowfall occurs.

Thanks to Canada West Mountain School for reviewing this description of how to build a snow cave. They offer courses in how to build snow caves and igloos.

Disclaimer: The authors and Canada West Mountain School assume no liability for the safety of individuals using these directions to build or stay in a snow cave.

MANNING PARK

This now 83,671 hectare provincial park was created in 1941 and named for E.C. Manning, who was the Chief Provincial Forester from 1936 until his death in an airplane accident in 1941. During his tenure in office he was a champion for setting forested land aside for the enjoyment of all. Thank you, Mr. Manning.

Fat Dog Ridge Trail

ACCESS: Drive east on Highway 3 (Crowsnest) towards Manning Park. Shortly after reaching Allison Pass, go by some highway maintenance buildings on the right, then turn left at the Cambie Creek sign into the plowed parking area (usually hidden behind a high bank of snow).

RATING: easy terrain but long distance

SEASON: December to early April

MAP: 92H/02 Manning Park

BEGINNING ALTITUDE: 1320 m

DESTINATION ALTITUDE: 1965 m

DISTANCE: 15.4 km round trip

TIME: 5–5½ hours round trip

CELLPHONE ACCESS: no

FOOD AND DRINK: Manning Park Resort

WASHROOMS: outhouse at Cambie Creek parking lot

DOGS: all dogs must be on leash in provincial parks

AVALANCHE CONDITIONS: **avalanche.ca**

This lengthy hike with its steady upward climb is best done in springtime when the days are longer. As well, the final elevation is over a mile high (1.22 miles), so some individuals may feel the effect of this higher altitude and walk slower.

Directions

The trail begins at a sign on the north side of the parking lot. The initial part is a wide forest track that parallels Cambie Creek. After about 410 m and 10 minutes of snowshoeing there is a sign and map showing the trail. Continue on the trail to the right and at approximately 980 m cross a wide bridge over Cambie Creek. After about another half hour of snowshoeing, and about 1.4 km from

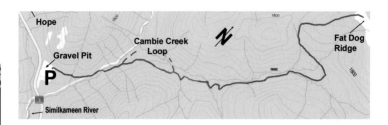

the start, there is a Y junction and a sign indicating the 2.5 km Cambie Creek Loop Trail and the 5 km loop trail. Stay to the right, where at about 2.4 km the final sign marks Fat Dog Trail. The trail winds steadily upward on a forest road to the right, first heading northeast, then westward after a long curve. At approximately 4.25 km there is a wide, open area with a left-hand trail heading into trees that leads once more onto a wide forest road. Another approximately 400 m of snowshoeing brings you to a small clearing and then back into the forest for a short time. The road now skirts a ridge with emerging views of Hozomeen Mountain in the distance and alpine ski trails on a smaller hill in the immediate view. On a sunny day this ridge makes an excellent spot to stop for early lunch if group members choose to forgo their lunch at the final ridge.

The right-hand turn from the road at approximately 6.3 km and elevation 1826 m to gain Fat Dog Ridge is seldom marked by anything other than tracks of backcountry skiers. Sometimes these tracks create a packed upward path through sparse trees to a large grove of trees. This area often is selected by skier/backpackers who choose to stay overnight on the ridge. On a windy day the trees make a sheltered lunch site.

Continue on from the grove of trees, aiming for the summit ridge while walking through scattered snags and some coniferous trees. If previous skiers or snowshoers went to the summit in windy conditions, the trail may zigzag through the more protected areas offered by the small clusters of alpine trees.

Heading home from Fat Dog Ridge

The top of Fat Dog Ridge, reached after about 3–3½ hours, is at approximately 1965 m and a distance of about 7.7 km from the parking lot. Be alert to the steep drop-off and large cornices that develop on this ridge.

From this lofty vantage point there is an unimpeded view to the southwest towards Hozomeen Mountain in the Northwest Cascades and Frosty Mountain in Manning Park as well as of the Big Buck and Three Brothers summits to the east.

Return is by the same trail, with descent taking a shorter time of approximately 2 to 2½ hours.

Lightning Lake Loop Trail

ACCESS: Drive east on Highway 3 (Crowsnest) to just past Manning Park Resort. Turn onto Gibson Pass Road and at a Y junction take the left fork, which leads to the Lightning Lake day use parking lot. Park at the far end of the lot.

RATING: easy terrain on Rainbow Bridge loop; moderate difficulty with some narrow tracks on the east side of Lightning Lake back to Rainbow Bridge; narrow tracks on a slope on parts of the Flash Lake sections (if open)

SEASON: mid-December to March

MAP: 92H02 Manning Park

BEGINNING ALTITUDE: 1245 m

DESTINATION ALTITUDE: Basically a flat trail around the edge of the lakes

DISTANCE: 7 km loop around Lightning Lake via Rainbow Bridge; 9 km loop around entire Lightning Lake; 3.5 km Flash Lake loop; (none of these require a lake crossing)

TIME: 1½–2 hours around Lightning Lake via Rainbow Bridge; 2–2½ hours around entire Lightning Lake; 3½–4 hours around both Lightning and Flash lakes

CELLPHONE ACCESS: no

FOOD AND DRINK: Manning Park Resort

WASHROOMS: Lightning Lake day use parking lot; Lone Duck campground; Manning Park Resort Nordic Centre

DOGS: dogs must be on leash in all provincial parks

AVALANCHE CONDITIONS: **avalanche.ca**

This trail can be done in a variety of loops, allowing for families to easily complete the first part, while more experienced, energetic snowshoers may want to extend their trip and also the type of terrain through which they are snowshoeing. For obvious reasons it is

Cross over the bridge – Rainbow Bridge

not advisable to walk on the lakes as a means of completing this loop trail. Ask Nordic Centre staff about current avalanche dangers and snow stability on the trails before you begin the trip.

The winter trail generally follows the summer trail through the forests around Lightning and Flash lakes. The Lightning Lake section crossing at Rainbow Bridge is frequently used, so hopefully a new path will not need to be tracked. The initial part of the trail to Rainbow Bridge and around the eastern shore of the lake back to the parking lot could be easily completed by a beginner snowshoer. However, in the winter, on some sections of the trail between the Skyline turnoff and the bridge between Lightning and Flash lakes and then back along the east side of Lightning Lake to Rainbow Bridge, parts of the route take the form of a snowshoe-width narrow ledge high above the lake. Steep, treed terrain looms above

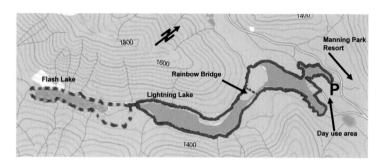

and the trail passes by several small open slopes that present some avalanche danger. It is for these reasons that this loop is deemed moderately difficult in places and is not suitable in those areas for children or novice snowshoers.

Directions

Start this trail at the Lightning Lake day use parking lot and progress in a counterclockwise direction. It is not advisable to cross the short distance across the mouth of Spruce Bay from the Lightning Lake parking area to get on the trail. During mid-winter this is the shortest way but during early and late season the ice may be rotten and/or have flowing water under thin ice. The safest trail is the one on the right, close to the end of the parking lot, which heads gradually up a small slope and through the trees along the edge of Sandy Bay. Pass by the Lone Duck campground and shelter and snowshoe alongside the cross-country ski tracks without disturbing them. Continue on the track and head up a modest hill to the left to reach an intersection. One trail continues along the shoreline to Rainbow Bridge, but the one to take stays on the main route, which is a wide track through the forest. At about 2.4 km there is a sign indicating this is the path to Strike and Thunder lakes and the Skyline trail. Continue until you reach a Y junction at about 2.8 km. The left-hand path leads to Rainbow Bridge in about 60 m and is a good trail to take for families with children.

The main, right-hand path continues somewhat inland but still parallel to the shores of the deceptively long, narrow southern section of Lightning Lake. A second Y junction on the left leads to a summer favourite fishing spot and Fisherman's Trail. Stay to the right and soon a right-hand turn and sign at about 3.2 km indicates Skyline Trail. Follow the trail on the left, which now begins to be more challenging, with the path narrowing, steep sides above and below, and at times dead trees blown down onto the trail. After about 4.18 km and 1½ hours of snowshoeing since the parking lot, the small bridge crossing the end of Lightning Lake can be seen to the left. As noted, after crossing this bridge the return trail on the east side of the lake is along a narrow 2 km path with some sections that have steep sides (similar to the area just passed) until Rainbow Bridge is reached after about 40 minutes more of snowshoeing. The lakeside trail curves along the lake and past the start of the Frosty Mountain trail and then left onto the dam at the end of Lightning Lake. From here it is an easy return by snowshoeing straight ahead to cross a bridge with green metal railings and head for the parking lot.

Flash Lake Loop Trail

A possible addition to the Lightning Lake loop is to continue around Flash Lake, the next lake in the series. The Flash Lake loop is not as frequently used and may need tracking, although the trail itself is closer to the shore and thus does not have the steep sides found along the eastern part of Lightning Lake. At present this route does not have signage for winter travel, and if snow is thin, trailbreaking will be necessary to avoid boggy areas. As well, it is prone to a lot of blown-down trees, so check about conditions before venturing onto this part of the trail.

Directions

Continue straight ahead at the southeast end of Lightning Lake. Upon reaching the end of Flash Lake, at about 6.5 km and 2 hours since the parking lot, pass over the bridge and continue through scattered trees, then turn left to regain the lake trail. The track first heads away from the lake through the forest. Early and late in the season there may be considerable water flow from the many diversions of the streams in this area. Continue by generally following the edge of the lake, passing by a wide, open rock avalanche area. The trail then regains a bench along the edge of the lake until near the Lightning Lake bridge, where on the left there is a log bridge. While this span is safe in the summer and is used to access the Lightning Lake bridge to cross back over to the north side, it is too narrow for snowshoes, and if snow covered or slippery it is not a safe crossing. Continue straight on through low brush (though in early winter and spring this may also have stream water and be marshy) to the Lightning Lake bridge. Remain on the east side of the lake, pass by the narrowest neck of Lightning Lake on the left and arrive at Rainbow Bridge at about 8.7 km. Follow the rest of the Lightning Lake loop trail to the dirt dam at the end of the lake, arriving after approximately 12.5 km and about 4 hours. Snowshoe straight ahead to cross on a bridge with green metal railings and then head to the parking lot.

ACCESS: Drive east on Highway 3 (Crowsnest) past Manning Park Resort and continue for several kilometres. Turn right at the sign for the parking lot at Monument 83 and Monument 78 trailhead.

RATING: easy terrain but may need trail-breaking

SEASON: late December to mid-March

MAP: 92H02 Manning Park

BEGINNING ALTITUDE: 1127 m

DESTINATION ALTITUDE: 1200 m at Castle Creek Meadows

DISTANCE: 7 km round trip (length varies depending on creek flow and snow bridges)

TIME: 3–4 hours round trip

CELLPHONE ACCESS: no

FOOD AND DRINK: Manning Park Resort

WASHROOMS: outhouse at trailhead parking lot; indoors at Manning Park Nordic Centre and Manning Park Resort

DOGS: dogs must be on leash in provincial parks

AVALANCHE CONDITIONS: **avalanche.ca**

For a taste of easy access backcountry snowshoeing where you will seldom meet other adventurers, this trail will fit the bill. It is used by cross-country skiers but few snowshoers. The destination in the meadows of Castle Creek provides open views of the surrounding mountains. The end of this trail – the actual Monument 78 at the international border – is 12 km one way, which for most snowshoers is too far for a day trip. As well, there may be (usually are) obstructions caused by beavers in the creek and deadfall from pine-beetle-infested trees on the trail, so check with the Nordic Centre about trail conditions.

Miss the signpost and you may find yourself on the Monument 83 trail

Directions

Climb over the piled-up snow left from parking lot clearance and head east along a forest service road that follows the Similkameen River for about 800 m before the trail crosses a bridge. Ahead is a junction, with the left trail going to Boyd's Meadow. Stay to the right and continue for about another 150 m to cross a second bridge. The trail begins a modest climb for the next 20 minutes or so, and at about 1.9 km there is a marker post indicating the right-hand trail to Monument 78. The left-hand

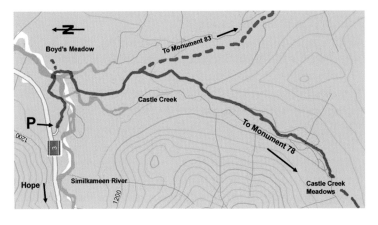

one (straight ahead) goes to Monument 83. Turn right and continue to gently climb along the trail – bordered sadly by many dead lodgepole pines devastated by the pine-beetle infestation. After a brief downhill section at about 3.4 km there is a T junction and trail marker post, with the right-hand branch leading to Similkameen Trail. This trail has not been cleared for years and is impassable from this intersection. Turn left and continue on until you come to a large meadow with numerous deciduous bushes and small trees as well as coniferous trees. Depending on snow cover and whether the beavers have been at work causing stream diversions of Castle Creek, the unmarked trail initially winds through the meadow and keeps the river on the right. As it continues through the valley, views emerge of Frosty Mountain and Windy Joe to the right and Mount Winthrop in the US on the left. Castle Peak at 8,360 feet, one of the highest mountains in the Cascade Range, can be seen straight ahead. Select a sunny spot for lunch, assess how much daylight is left and decide whether time and snow conditions will allow you to continue. The rest of the trail may require crossing snow bridges over side creeks. Return the way you came.

THE PACIFIC CREST TRAIL

Monument 78 is one exit (or entrance) leading to the border crossing and the beginning or end of the 4000 km Pacific Crest Trail through the United States to the Mexican border. This border crossing was the 78th boundary monument from the Pacific along the line of the 49th parallel. The PCT became even more famous after the 2014 movie *Wild*, but it has long held an allure for hikers who seek long-distance challenges. The Pacific Crest Trail Association has tracked 3,844 people who have completed the trail, and 77 did it more than once. Read some of their comments about their experiences in the logbook at the reception desk of the Manning Park Resort.

ACCESS: Drive Highway 3 (Crowsnest) past the Manning Park Resort and turn immediately onto the road leading to the downhill ski area. Continue on the road to Gibson Pass and park in front of the Orange chairlift if possible.

RATING: easy terrain but a fairly long distance

SEASON: late December to late March

MAP: 92H02 Manning Park

BEGINNING ALTITUDE: 1455 m at bottom of Orange chairlift

DESTINATION ALTITUDE: 1755 m at lake; 1843 m at high point

DISTANCE: 11.4 km round trip to lake (from bottom of Orange chairlift)

TIME: 5–5½ hours round trip

CELLPHONE ACCESS: no

FOOD AND DRINK: at downhill ski lodge café and Manning Park Resort

WASHROOMS: at downhill ski lodge; outhouse at far side of Poland Lake

DOGS: dogs must be on leash in all provincial parks

AVALANCHE CONDITIONS: **avalanche.ca**

The trail to Poland Lake offers a good workout and spectacular views. It is in an avalanche area, so definitely check reports for avalanche conditions before attempting this trail. On weekends during the ski season the trip can be shortened by taking the chairlift (a snowshoe ticket is needed) to the top of the Orange Chair ski run.

Directions

Ski-run approach: On weekdays or after the ski season is finished but there is still lots of snow on the upper levels and the

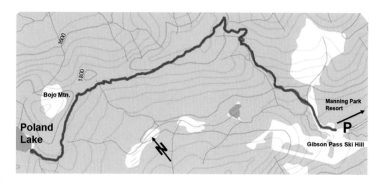

days are getting longer, it is often the nicest time to do this snowshoe trail. Start to the left of the Orange Chair and snowshoe along the side of the run. Ascend on Junction Run. Then, once past Loop Run, go to the left onto Horseshoe Run, reaching the top after about 45 minutes and an elevation gain of about 280 m. On a tree there is an old sign indicating the direction to Poland Lake. Go along this narrower corridor and choose to go left and follow pink tapes to the beginning of the main trail. To the right you'll find a short connecting trail used by those who take the Orange Chair to get to the main trail. Either choice arrives at the main trail, which then begins to rise gently as it winds around to the west. The trail has a number of orange flashes to follow but it is well used and often has a good path. Soon, at a corner, a wide view opens and the Three Brothers can be seen in the distance to the right. The trail turns west and continues with steady but small increases in elevation until, at about 2.7 km, the terrain opens up in all directions. With steep above, steep below and open terrain, this is prime avalanche country. This area is sometimes used for teaching how to read snow layers for assessing stability, which would explain the square holes you may see in the side of the hill along the path. This is also the high point on the trail, at about 1843 m.

Hozomeen Mountain in the USA, seen from the Poland Lake trail

Views of Red Mountain and Lone Goat Mountain, with the sharp-edged Hozomeen in between and the Cascade Range behind, remain in view as the trail descends slightly and curves around, eventually heading into the forest. After about 2¾ hours of snowshoeing, you'll see a sign directing that horses are to be left at the bottom of the ravine. Climb the path along the side of the small ravine while remaining aware that there is probably running water down the middle since this is the outlet from the lake. Within minutes the lake is in view at an elevation of about 1755 m and approximately 5.7 km from the start at the ski hill. Across the lake are a small log shelter and an outhouse. There is a trail around either shore, so there is no need to walk over the ice to reach these structures. Close to the cabin is the beginning of the Memaloose trail – an alternative route intermittently marked with flagging and following Memaloose Creek for much of its approximately 9 km, to return to the Allison Pass highway maintenance yard. If cars were left at either end

(Gibson Pass or Allison Pass), this could be a long trip back to the highway. This trail is seldom tracked, so some effort will be needed to break trail. Completing this route not only requires coordination of cars but makes for a very long day. Historically the Memaloose trail was used for access to traps in the valley drained by the creek.

Orange Chair ski-lift approach: On weekends and holidays until the end of the ski season, riding the Orange Chair at a cost of $10 turns the trail from fairly strenuous into an easy snowshoe. After getting off the chairlift, turn left and proceed along a narrow track for about 500 m to a sign indicating an avalanche area and the way to Poland Lake. Turn right at this cross trail, which shortly meets the beginning of the main trail that goes around the shoulder of Bojo Mountain to Poland Lake. Continue on the trail as described above.

Strawberry Flats approach: This 16 km round-trip trail offers a slower and much longer approach without the rather steep elevation gain the side of the ski run provides. The trail starts at the Strawberry Flats parking area. On the right is the North Gibson cross-country ski trail, but the old forestry road on the left is the one to take. The trail is level at first and then begins to switchback upward until, after going north and west, it emerges close to the top of the ski hill near the Orange Chair lift. Now follow the directions for the Orange Chair approach to get to the beginning of the upper trail.

The return route for any of these approaches follows either the snowshoe ascent route or a return to the top of the ski runs and a rapid descent along the side of the runs.

Skagit River Trail

ACCESS: Drive east on Highway 3 (Crowsnest) to 12 km past the Hoary Marmot sign that marks the western entrance of Manning Park. The trail begins from the parking lot of the Sumallo Grove turnoff, where a signpost (without a sign in winter) and a snowplow pullout indicate the park entrance. (See below for additional access instructions.)

RATING: easy terrain

SEASON: late December to mid-March

MAP: 92H03 Skagit River

BEGINNING ALTITUDE: 605 m

DESTINATION ALTITUDE: 596 m

DISTANCE: 7.8 km round trip to Delacey Wilderness bear cache

TIME: 2½–3½ hours round trip

CELLPHONE ACCESS: no

FOOD AND DRINK: Manning Park Resort

WASHROOMS: outhouse in parking lot at the beginning of trail; Manning Park Resort

DOGS: dogs must be on leash in all provincial parks

AVALANCHE CONDITIONS: **avalanche.ca**

This easy, family-friendly trail begins at the south end of the Sumallo Grove parking lot. In winter the BC Parks sign is not hanging on the post at roadside and the parking lot is no longer plowed, leaving only the snowplow turnaround at the entrance. This means the trip requires a drop-off of snowshoers and an arranged pickup time, or good spring weather when the snowplow will not need to be on the roads.

Directions

The walk in to the parking lot will add another 500 m each way. The large cedars and firs in this grove will give a taste of the trees in the magnificent forest on either side of the trail along the Skagit River. Unfortunately, timber thieves cut down a number of these trees and this is why the parking lot is closed with a locked gate over the winter.

After leaving the parking lot proceed southward for several minutes along a wide trail to reach the river. Turn left, remove your snowshoes and cross a high metal bridge over the Skagit. The trail has left the Manning Park boundary and is now in Skagit Valley Provincial Park. Looking to the west you can see the Sumallo River where it joins the Skagit. The historic Whatcom Trail, used as an overland route from the Puget Sound area during the Fraser Canyon gold rush of 1858, was part of this trail. The route follows the river at first, then heads off into the woods. At approximately 1.3 km and after about 30 minutes of snowshoeing, there is a sign on the left indicating the beginning of an access trail to the Silverdaisy Mountain trail, where the Invermay lead and zinc mine operated between 1933 and 1938. Close to this area, also on the left, slightly uphill and through the trees by a falls, is a small collapsed shed, an abandoned mine entrance and an old vehicle that provides a glance into mining history and broken dreams.

At approximately 1.8 km there is an open area on the left that will provide some light and views of sky in comparison to the dense cover created by the gigantic trees that tower over most of the route. For another 30 minutes the trail continues with a gradual increase in elevation. At about 2.7 km some orange flashes can be seen on the trees. These indicate the direction of the trail is to the left, down a small gully and rising again to an elevation of about 635 m. Continue on the trail as

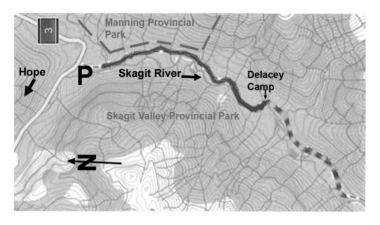

it makes small elevation gains and losses and then descends towards the river and Delacey Wilderness camp at approximately 3.6 km.

The first part of the camp is beautifully located close to the river, although during spring runoff this area becomes flooded. Continue on for another 300 m to the second part of the camp, at about 3.9 km, where a bear cache and a picnic table (possibly covered in snow) are located. Unfortunately there are no washrooms in either part of the camp. Still, this may make an excellent turnaround and/or lunch spot for families with small children.

There are approximately 1½ additional kilometres that can be travelled safely here in winter. However, the next part of the trail is not marked clearly with flashes, and the snow-covered forest may not readily show the way. If you decide to continue, go up the hill on a diagonal traverse to the left at the south end of the campsite. At 4.1 km there is a bridge crossing Twentysix Mile Creek. The trail continues through the woods for about another 20 minutes, heading towards the river, but then becomes narrow and too dangerous to negotiate on snowshoes. It returns to high above the river, and even in the summer it requires walking a narrow pathway on a ledge of steep cliffs with large rocks intruding on one side.

Return to Delacey campsite and enjoy the opportunity to admire once again the tall, ancient giants and the stumps of even larger trees that were logged in the early years of the last century. As well, for the fly fishers in your group, this would be a great spot (from July 1 to October 31) to catch and release rainbow trout and Dolly Varden char. As outdoors writer and fly-fisher Ian Forbes put it, "For sheer physical beauty, none can top the Skagit River." His words ring true during the winter as well.

THE SKAGIT RIVER: DAMMED OR DAMNED?

Rising in Manning Park at Allison Pass, the Skagit is named for the indigenous people who have lived in the region of the present-day [US] Ross Lake National Recreation Area for over 8,000 years. The river and its tributaries drain some 6900 km² (1.7 million acres) of the Cascade Range.

The Skagit is also a river that nearly disappeared under political pressure for hydroelectric development. For decades, controversy had plagued attempts by Seattle City Light Co. to obtain a stable power source. Seattle felt entitled to hydroelectric dams on the river, while British Columbia wanted economic benefits as well as environmental preservation where its territory was affected. Interim agreements resulted in financial compensation for such events as in 1953, when Seattle raised the Ross reservoir by five feet, flooding 500 acres of Canadian land. Finally the parties made an agreement in 1967 for SCL to pay US$34,566.21 in annual rent to BC, either in cash or in kind in the form of electricity at the discretion of BC. The figure amounted to only about $100 per mile for the 35.3 miles of the Skagit River that lies in Canada. As well, the BC resources minister at the time made a 99-year deal to permit raising of the Ross reservoir in the US that would result in flooding of Canadian land well beyond the 500 acres that occurred in 1953. When these facts became publicly known, years of protests ensued (on both sides of the border) against the possible destruction of the river valley. It was only in 1984, after 20 years of unrest and a number of years of negotiations, that a treaty was signed exchanging Canadian hydro power for the protection of the Skagit valley and an equitable settlement related to the power provided to Seattle.

Windy Joe Trail

ACCESS: Drive Highway 3 (Crowsnest) to east of the Manning Park Resort. Turn on to Gibson Pass Road heading to the downhill ski area. Drive about 1.2 km to a cement bridge and park in the pullout on the southeast side of the road.

RATING: easy, but a long distance with steady elevation gain

SEASON: late December to late March

MAP: 92H02 Manning Park

BEGINNING ALTITUDE: 1185 m

DESTINATION ALTITUDE: 1838 m at fire lookout

DISTANCE: 15.8 km round trip

TIME: 5–5½ hours

CELLPHONE ACCESS: no

FOOD AND DRINK: Manning Park Resort

WASHROOMS: Manning Park Resort; Manning Park Nordic Centre; outhouse at lookout

DOGS: all dogs must be on leash in provincial parks

AVALANCHE CONDITIONS: **avalanche.ca**

This trail is an enjoyable snowshoe, with 360 degree views from the historic forest fire lookout at the top. For most of its length the trail uses an old forest access road to the lookout. The grade is mild but the distance requires starting early, especially during short winter days.

Directions

Start the trail to the southeast of the bridge by the parking area, where there is a BC Parks sign giving trail choices. Head towards the forest and follow the generally flat Similkameen Trail signposted to Frosty Mountain. The trail is nearly always tracked

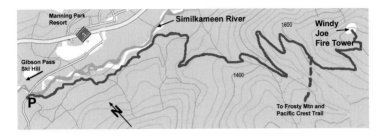

by walkers, snowshoers and backcountry skiers. It is to the right of the Similkameen River and crosses the drainage from Windy Joe three times. There are orange BC Parks markers giving distances, although the km 5 and km 6 signs are strangely very close together. Most marker distances varied somewhat from our current GPS readings.

After about three-quarters of an hour of snowshoeing, and approximately 2.3 km, there is a signpost showing the direction to the Pacific Crest Trail and Windy Joe, both of which require beginning a gradual ascent on long switchbacks. When an intersection signpost occurs at about 5 km it indicates the trail to Windy Joe to the left and the trail to Frosty Mountain and Pacific Crest Trail to the right. Continue on the left through gradually thinning forest with some views to the southwest. Just before the curve in the trail that leads to the top of Windy Joe there is an open area to the left with views of the southwesterly mountains. Follow the curving path around past the outhouse and continue to circle to the left up to the top to reach the lookout. An orange BC Parks sign on the outside wall says 8 km. A recent GPS reading of ours showed approximately 7.9 km one way, but if boasting rights are at risk, go for the 8 km.

The lookout building has a pleasing architecture with two levels of glass-walled observation rooms, originally built to enable detection of possible fires in all directions. Inside on the upper

Windy Joe Fire Lookout   PHOTOGRAPHER: DOUG FARENHOLTZ, 2014

level is a sighting mechanism for identifying locations of fires, and paintings that help orient the viewer to the surrounding mountains and landmarks. To the southwest are Castle Peak and Frosty Mountain. To the east are Monument 83, Ptarmigan Peak and Mount Winthrop. To the west are Mount Outram, Mount Ford and Mount Dewdney. And finally to complete the picture, to the north, Blackwall Peak and Three Brothers Mountain, and Highway 3 and the Similkameen River that wind their way through a valley. Although the fire lookout has not been used since 1965 it has been well maintained. The structure is registered as one of Canada's heritage buildings. Contribute to its care by shutting the door upon leaving and taking all refuse to your car.

Return by the same route – a fast jaunt with only one short uphill – which will take about 2 hours.

Windy Joe Mountain was named after a local pioneer trapper, Joe Hilton, who is reported to have said the wind was so strong at the summit that no snow could stay there. During any winter, this perception is challenged by the snowshoers who track through the deep snow around the fire lookout.

Additional trails close to Manning Park Resort

Manning Park has numerous short snowshoe trails that are readily accessible from the resort. A map to help you find Meadow Loop, Lynx Hollow and Snowshoe Hare Challenge is available at the Nordic Centre.

Monument 83 Trail

The parking area and beginnings for both Monument 83 and Monument 78 are the same. Monument 83 begins to the left at the Y junction of 78 and 83, which occurs after about 1.9 km of snowshoeing from the trailhead. If the snow is deep and covers the marker post, or if others have already created tracks on both 78 and 83, it is easy to find yourself on the 83 trail (on purpose or inadvertently) since it leads straight on from the main route, while Monument 78 is a right turn.

Monument 83 begins with a deceptively gentle uphill slope, but after about 2.3 km and a wide bridge crossing it starts in on the real climb (859 m elevation change in total), which continues to the border crossing at 16 km from trailhead. From the bridge onward the trail also increasingly has deadfall obstructions from the numerous lodgepole pine trees killed by the pine beetle. If these challenges do not seem like much fun and decrease the wish to go further, then snowshoeing just to the bridge and back can be used as an add-on to the Monument 78 route.

Boyd's Meadow

After crossing the first bridge on the Monument 78 trail there is a sign on the left indicating Boyd's Meadow. The trail is about 3 km return from the trailhead and is an easy, rolling logging road. As on most trails in Manning it will have yearly deadfall that may not be cleared for winter travel. This open area is a great place to play some of those snow games found in the "Snowshoeing with Children" section of the book, but remember to stay away from tree wells and possible bog holes.

Memaloose Trail

Turn off Highway 3 into the Allison Pass highway maintenance yard. Park somewhere that does not interfere with operations and won't trap your car inside a locked area after hours. The trail is not well marked even in summer but gradually gains elevation along the side of the ridge. It also makes for a very long day trip if your destination is Poland Lake (18 km round trip), so it is advisable to do this route in late spring for maximum daylight. It can be done as a crossover from Strawberry Flats to Poland Lake and exiting via Memaloose Trail, but that is an even longer total distance. The trail follows along the side of the drainage of Memaloose Creek for most of its path, and from the 1890s it was used as a route for trappers in the valley. When it reaches the top of the ridge it turns north towards Poland Lake, where there is a small shelter and an outhouse at the south end the lake.

Cascade Lookout

Exit from the Manning Park Resort area, cross Highway 3 and enter the road directly across from Gibsons Road. There may not be parking spaces and room has to be left for a snowplow, so walking from the resort parking is the best idea. Turn left going past a number of small cabins. Turn right and begin a long and winding road that will be double-tracked for cross-country ski-ers for most of the season. Stay to the side of the tracks; do not cross back and forth or walk on the tracks. It is 8 km from the start of the switchbacks to Cascade Lookout, but once there it is a wonderful view of the surrounding mountains to the south and west. A sign at the lookout parking area indicates that, starting on the left, the mountains are Monument 83, Sheep Mountain, Windy Joe, The Parks USA, Mount Winthrop, Frosty Mountain, Hozomeen Mountain, Mox Peaks (the highest, at 2496 m), Sky-line Ridge and Red Mountain.

An additional 8 km leads to subalpine meadows (covered in wildflowers in the summer) and Blackwall Peak. Because of the length of this total round trip to get to Blackwall Peak, it is defi-nitely not a day trip for snowshoers but best left to the alpine backcountry skiers.

Black Mountain Loop Trail

ACCESS: Drive Highway 1/99 towards Whistler and turn off at Exit 8 signed for Cypress Bowl Road. Drive 18 km to the downhill ski area parking lot. Park by Black Mountain Lodge (the old day lodge) in the lower parking lot. Cypress Coachlines provides a shuttle bus service to the downhill ski area, with pickup stops in Richmond, Vancouver and North and West Vancouver. For schedules and fares see **cypresscoachlines.com**.

RATING: Black Mountain Loop Trail – easy terrain with a few steep sections; Eagle Bluffs Trail – moderate with some short, steep, challenging terrain and possible route finding and trail tracking

SEASON: mid-December to late March

MAP: 92G06 North Vancouver

BEGINNING ALTITUDE: 920 m

DESTINATION ALTITUDE: 1217 m at Black Mountain south summit; 1071 m at Eagle Bluffs

DISTANCE: 4.2 km round trip from backcountry entry gate to Black Mountain south peak via Cabin Lake; 500 m round trip side trip to Yew Lake Lookout (Black Mountain north peak); 5.6 km round trip Black Mountain via Cabin Lake with return via Sam Lake and Theagill Lake

TIME: 3½–4 hours round trip Black Mountain loop via Cabin Lake and return via Sam and Theagill lakes; 2½–3 hours to Black Mountain via Cabin Lake and return the same way

CELLPHONE ACCESS: yes

View to the north from Black Mountain south summit

FOOD AND DRINK: Crazy Raven Bar & Grill and Cypress Creek
    Grill, both in Cypress Creek Lodge
WASHROOMS: Black Mountain Lodge and Cypress Creek Lodge
DOGS: All dogs must be on leash in backcountry areas of pro-
    vincial parks
AVALANCHE CONDITIONS: **avalanche.ca**

*This trail offers a number of choices for both long and short excur-
sions. There is the trail to Cabin Lake and Black Mountain as a solo
short trip with great views, and an easy addition is a side trail to
Yew Lake Lookout (Black Mountain's north peak). The Black Mountain Loop is a good half-day excursion, while the trail to Eagle Bluff
is more challenging and makes a full-day adventure.*

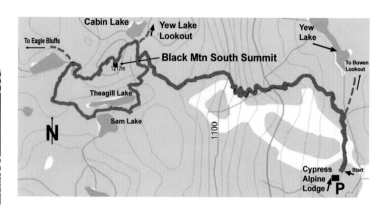

Directions

The starting point is the backcountry entry just west of the new Cypress Creek Lodge built preceding the 2010 Olympics. A free backcountry pass must be obtained from Black Mountain Lodge (the old day lodge) in the lower parking lot and displayed on jackets before passing through the entry. Go past the Eagle Express chairlift. The entrance to the trail is in the forest directly ahead, to the left of the large map showing the ski runs on the surrounding mountains.

Shortly after entering the forest, you will see a Y junction, with the trail to Black Mountain to the left marked by orange poles and on the right the trail to Yew Lake and Bowen Island Lookout. For approximately 50 minutes the trail leads upward in a series of switchbacks and parallels the "Maëlle Ricker's Gold" downhill ski run. Ricker won the top medal in snowboard cross in the Vancouver 2010 Winter Olympics. After the first 25 minutes of climbing, there is an area at the turn of a switchback that provides an open view to the north, with the Mount Strachan ski trails to the right and Yew Lake and meadows below. To the west, hiding in the trees on the hill north of the meadow, is the switchback trail leading to Bowen Island Lookout. The West Lion can be seen peeking from behind Mount Strachan, while the Tantalus Range rises to the northwest.

Continue on the steep trail and after a total of about 35 minutes and approximately 1.3 km of climbing, emerge at a level area slightly below the top of the Eagle Express chairlift and the ski run. Keep following the marker poles leading slightly to the left and upwards for another 15 minutes, arriving after a total of approximately 1.8 km and 270 m elevation gain at the BC Parks directional post at the top of this switchback climb. A sign indicates the Black Mountain Loop trail and Eagle Bluffs to the left. The shortest hike straight to the top of Black Mountain via Cabin Lake is by going to the right.

To the right of Cabin Lake there is a short trail – about 500 m round trip and not often tracked – that leads to Yew Lake Lookout (the north summit of Black Mountain) and can be completed before going to Black Mountain.

Turn right at the BC Parks board sign and snowshoe about 80 m towards Cabin Lake. Turn left at Cabin Lake and proceed in a southerly, then southeasterly direction, climbing gently to reach Black Mountain's south peak at about 2.1 km from the beginning. On a clear day the south summit of Black Mountain offers a 360 degree view to Mount Baker in the southeast, the Gulf Islands and mountains on Vancouver Island to the southwest, and northwest to the north summit of Black Mountain, the Sunshine Coast, the Tantalus Range and Howe Sound. North and east vistas present Mount Strachan (pronounced "strawn" even if you aren't Scottish) with its web of downhill ski trails and the East and West Lions. If the summit of Black Mountain was the goal, return on the same ascent path.

To complete a counterclockwise loop, return to the trail where the final rise occurred that led to the summit. Snowshoe towards the forest and begin a rapid descent through the trees on a series of switchback traverses following orange tree flashes. The path leads to a small frozen lake and a trail that circles around the lake to the right to gain the southern shore. Follow the path (do not cross the lake) that then passes through trees to a Y intersection where a signpost indicates the way to Eagle Bluffs (another 1.7 km to the right; see the next route description) and back to Black Mountain and Cabin Lake. There is also a sign on an old snag that has the Baden-Powell insignia, since the Eagle Bluffs trail is part of the B-P trail.

For the Black Mountain loop, take the trail heading southeast as it continues around the lake and begins a long, steady descent along the slope of a hill on the right side. From this path both Sam Lake on the right and long, narrow Theagill Lake on the left can be seen as the trail passes between them and turns uphill to the left. A direction post appears at a T junction: the trail to the right goes to the top of the Eagle chairlift; the one to the left goes to the top of Black Mountain and to Cabin Lake. Take the trail to the left and continue for about 260 m to return to the signpost that was at the top of the hill on the original switchback ascent from the lodge. Turn right and begin the downward snowshoe.

If by chance or choice a decision was made at the previous directional sign to go to the top of the Eagle Express chairlift, it is necessary to avoid all skiers when emerging onto the hill, and snowshoe on the far left of the ski run to the first crest of the ski hill. Continue for about 20 m past a snowmaking machine on the left side, where a cross trail leading southwest intersects with the downhill snowshoe trail.

Eagle Bluffs

RATING: moderate with some challenging steep sections and possible trail tracking

DISTANCE: 8.6 km round trip

The Eagle Bluffs trail can be added to the Black Mountain one to create a longer and more challenging trek for those snowshoers who are able to manage steeper terrain, ice, exposed rocks and uneven ground. On this trail there are several short vertical sections and during early and late season there are a number of narrow streams to be crossed. Markings on the trees are far apart at first, so if the trail has not been tramped down, good route-finding methods are needed. Ensure the lead person can see the next marker each time before the rest of the group continues.

Directions

Turn left at the BC Parks directional post at the top of the initial steep switchback ascent (instead of going to the right toward Cabin Lake and Black Mountain). This trail goes in a clockwise direction rather than the one described above that follows a counterclockwise loop. Follow the orange markers eastward. The marker poles and orange flashes lead on for about another kilometre and 25 minutes of snowshoeing, passing between Theagill and Sam lakes and turning right and up a gradual climb along the side of a hill. Turn right, proceeding to a Y junction where a BC Parks directional post indicates the trail to Eagle Bluffs. Head left in a southwesterly direction and then easterly, following the orange diamond markers on the trees. The trail passes around several small tarns and through small snow-covered alpine meadows that in the sunshine look like fields of crystals. Beware: the boggy ground or the lakes may not be completely frozen, so stay on the trail and do not do shortcuts across the tarns. After a steep downward section (at the bottom of which there is a marker on the right indicating a summer trail to Doughnut Rock and one on the left giving assurance that this is indeed the Eagle Bluff trail), the markers become much more frequent. After about 1.7 km and 45 minutes from the Y junction, the final destination is reached. The large granite rocks provide a platform for viewing the Lower Mainland, Mount Baker, the Sunshine Coast and the Gulf Islands and also a spot for lunch. Gigantic and very canny ravens may invite themselves to the picnic. They have long ago lost their fear of people, so keep backpacks zipped and guard food carefully or it will disappear in their beaks. Return to the Y junction by the same route and go left and on steep traverses upward for about 350 m and 15 minutes to the summit of Black Mountain. After enjoying the view, proceed along the trail on the side of Black Mountain summit to Cabin Lake. Turn right at the Cabin Lake junction and head back to the sign for Black Mountain Loop Trail. Turn left and descend in about half the time it took to climb up the switchback trail.

TRAILS ON THE NORTH SHORE

The majority of the Black Mountain Loop trail follows the Baden-Powell Centennial trail, named after Lord Baden-Powell, an Englishman who was the founder of the Boy Scout movement. The fleur-de-lys symbol on a triangular metal sign with the initials B-P indicates the trail that extends from Horseshoe Bay to Deep Cove. Over 200 summer trail runners use the BPT for the Knee Knackering North Shore Trail Run each July between these two communities. Think a run (started in 1989) that goes for some 48 km of roots, rocks and steep trails. *Running Wild* magazine has recognized this run as one of the 25 toughest in North America. Thankfully, the snow usually covers all the roots and most of the rocks and allows claims to be made by snowshoers of completing part of the course.

The official opening of the Lions Gate Bridge in 1939 resulted in an increase in North Shore population and use of Cypress and Hollyburn areas for skiing and other recreation. Cypress Provincial Park, in which this trail is located, was created in 1975 in response to protests about logging in the Cypress Creek Valley and on Hollyburn Ridge. There is no Cypress Mountain as such. The area gets its name from the yellow cypress trees that grow in the alpine above 1000 metres.

CABIN LAKE

Cabin Lake did once have a cabin located near its shores. Mary and David Macaree noted in the 1976 edition of their *109 Walks in British Columbia's Lower Mainland* that there was "an old wooden building in the dip between them" (the north and south summits of Black Mountain).

ACCESS: Drive Highway 1/99 and take Cypress Bowl Road Exit 8. Travel 18 km to the downhill ski area parking lot. Cypress Coachlines provides a shuttle service to the downhill ski area, with pickup at various city and regional locations: **cypressmountain.com** or 604-637-SNOW (7669)

RATING: easy

SEASON: December to March

MAP: 92G06 North Vancouver

BEGINNING ALTITUDE: 920 m

DESTINATION ALTITUDE: 1017 m at the Lookout

DISTANCE: 4 km round trip to Bowen Lookout; 2 km entire Yew Lake loop; 300 m Old Growth Loop

TIME: 2–2½ hours round trip to Bowen Island Lookout, including part of Yew Lake Loop

CELLPHONE ACCESS: yes

FOOD AND DRINK: Cypress Alpine Lodge

WASHROOMS: Cypress Alpine Lodge; Black Mountain Lodge

DOGS: all dogs must be on leash in provincial parks but are not allowed on the Yew Lake section of this trail

AVALANCHE CONDITIONS: **avalanche.ca**

This pleasant short trail is located in 3012 hectare Cypress Provincial Park. It starts to the west of Cypress Alpine Lodge close to the downhill ski area of Cypress Bowl. A free backcountry pass is required from December 1 to the end of the winter season. This can be obtained from Black Mountain Lodge (in the Brown Bag Room opposite the washroom entrance) in the lower parking lot.

Directions
After passing Cypress Alpine Lodge (built in 2008 in anticipation

View from Bowen Island Lookout

of the 2010 Olympics), saunter past all the people on the left who are lined up waiting for the Eagle Ridge chairlift that accesses Black Mountain. At the forest edge on the right is a large map showing the ski hill runs and surrounding areas. Straight ahead the trail starts in the woods and is marked with a sign indicating the Back-country Access Trail. An avalanche danger level sign is a few metres beyond. Part of this trail is a section of the longer Howe Sound Crest Trail that leads to the meadows of Mount Strachan and eventually to the coast, exiting close to Porteau Cove Provincial Park.

During the winter the trail is well marked by orange-topped poles to the lookout. About 30 m from the start, and 5 minutes from the forest entry, there is a signposted junction with the Black Mountain trail leading upward to the left and Yew Lake Loop Trail and Bowen Lookout Winter Trail heading to the right. Cross over the snow-covered bridge on the right, turn up the small hill and continue through the woods in a westerly direction. This trail will proceed along part of the Yew Lake loop and provides an opportunity to view open areas of what may look like meadow. In fact,

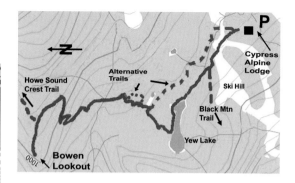

though, these are boggy parts around Yew Lake and often have streams and saturated snow, so do not use them as a shortcut to the service road. Continue in a westerly direction around the Yew Lake loop for about 1.1 km and eventually arrive at a Y junction. Turn left and continue on to the next post, which indicates the lower part of Old Growth Forest Loop to the right and Howe Sound Crest Trail to the left. Turn left and in a short distance another post marks the end of the upper part of Old Growth Forest Loop (the path to take on the return trip if marvelling at more giant trees is on your list). Take the Howe Sound Crest trail leading uphill.

Upon your exit from the forest, a service road (Pumphouse Road) is immediately in front. There is a cement block building on the right; take the road to the left. Although this road appears to head straight northwest and perhaps result in a viewpoint, it in fact ends after a brief time and changes into steep, bush-covered terrain. Snowshoe only as far as a bridge that crosses a shallow creek to the right – about 200 m. Assess the safety of the bridge – it does not have sides and at times get piled dangerously high with snow, requiring balancing skills to cross it.

Begin a steady upward ascent on gradually inclined switch-backs – a short one, a long one, another short one and three longer ones. As you gain elevation, look southeast to see the downhill ski area on Black Mountain's Raven Ridge. This was the site of the 2010 Olympics freestyle ski, ski cross and snowboard competitions.

A Y junction occurs – the right-hand trail heads into the forest as the continuation of the Howe Sound Crest Trail, while the left-hand one leads 240 m to Bowen Island Lookout. The lookout is the final destination after a total of about 50 minutes of snowshoeing. It is a flattened promontory with panoramic views. At times, enterprising individuals build a snow seat which provides a comfy resting spot to view Snug Cove on Bowen Island, and to the southwest, Point Grey and beyond to Vancouver Island. Gambier Island sits in Howe Sound with the Tantalus Range as a backdrop. BC Ferries vessels can often be observed on their way to Langdale on the Sunshine Coast and to Nanaimo.

To return, an easy trek of about 50 minutes, retrace the path down the switchbacks and over the bridge. When you reach the road, resist the urge to walk east and then down the side of the ski hill. Return by entering the forest at the right, before the cement building. After a brief time on this trail, you'll see the upper part of Old Growth Forest Loop. Follow this loop if you want to see more big trees. (Old Growth Forest Loop circles back to intersect with the Howe Sound Crest segment that is part of the return trail.) If another visit to the ancient trees is not planned, continue to walk south on Howe Sound Crest Trail. Pass by an open area on the left and the path on the right that was the exit from the path around Yew Lake to start the trip. Turn left on the Yew Lake upper trail that runs parallel to the Yew Lake trail taken in the morning. Exit the forest and head towards the lodge and the parking lot.

CYPRESS BOWL

Cypress Bowl receives its name from the trees that are found in the park. The trees are also known as Alaska yellow cedar and Nootka cypress. These coniferous trees have a flattened, scale-like, yellow-green foliage and a small, round, green cone that darkens as it ages. They grow in wet, mountainous places, often close to other conifers. The tree produces an oil called cypressine which acts as a natural preservative and creates a wood that is durable and resistant to harsh weather, fungus and insects. The cypress is the provincial tree of British Columbia and the wood has often been used in First Nations carving of masks, paddles, bows, dishes and other small objects. It is also used for siding, shutters and shingles and as structural timber in houses and bridges.

Along with the cypress, the towering amabilis fir and hemlock trees that can be seen on Old Growth Forest Loop, many of which are over 1,000 years old, were spared from the logging that occurred on Cypress Mountain during the early 1900s.

Dog Mountain and First Lake Loop Trail

ACCESS: Take Mount Seymour Parkway after exiting from Highway 1 or, after crossing north on Ironworkers Memorial/Second Narrows Bridge, take Exit 22A. Proceed about 4 km to lights and the Parkgate Village shopping centre. Turn left on Mount Seymour Road and continue about 13 km to the Mount Seymour snowshoe parking along the side of the road just before the resort ski parking. There is a shuttle bus that leaves from Parkgate Community Centre and/or Lonsdale Quay. Check the Mount Seymour website for the schedule: **mountseymour.com**.

RATING: easy terrain when there is deep snow cover; a few short steep sections

SEASON: December to March

MAP: 92G07 Port Coquitlam

BEGINNING ALTITUDE: 1020 m

DESTINATION ALTITUDE: 1050 m at Dog Mountain

DISTANCE: 6 km round trip to Dog Mountain with return by lower loop; 3 km First Lake Loop trail

TIME: 2 hours round trip to Dog Mountain; 3 hours if snow cover is thin

CELLPHONE ACCESS: yes

FOOD AND DRINK: Three Peaks Lodge – Elevations 1020 Restaurant, Grill Works Cafeteria, Whiskey Jack Brown Bag lunch room

WASHROOMS: Three Peaks Lodge; also washrooms by the first aid station

DOGS: Dog Mountain Trail is not in the provincial park. However, all dogs must be on leash in high population areas of Metro Vancouver and in backcountry areas of provincial parks (the ascent and descent routes beside the ski run).

On a weekend, get in line to go to Dog Mountain

AVALANCHE CONDITIONS: **avalanche.ca**

NOTE: This ascent/descent trail is in Mount Seymour Provincial Park, so a trail fee does NOT have to be paid. If snowshoes are rented from the Adventure Centre, a snowshoe trail ticket has to be purchased that also allows use of the trails in the 81 hectare CRA (controlled recreation area) to the east of the ski runs.

Easy access from Vancouver and a rewarding view with minimal elevation gain have made this an extremely popular trail. As a result the well-marked trail is usually hard packed and many other snowshoers (and dogs) may be encountered, even during midweek. It is best travelled early in the morning or on weekdays. Otherwise, there may be a long walk along the side of the road from the lower parking areas designated for snowshoers and backcountry skiers. Families with young children will welcome the fairly easy terrain and an option for a shorter, 3 km loop via First Lake. Those looking for an after-work outing during short winter days will appreciate the reflective route-marker poles allowing for a potential after-dark adventure.

Directions

The trail begins to the north of the BC Parks information kiosk and ascends on the left of the roped edge of the groomed ski run. Pass by the first signed entrance for First Lake Winter Trail – this will be the exit on the return trip – and proceed uphill, passing a second sign showing one route to Dinkey Peak. Continue a rapid ascent (about 15–20 minutes) for the first 700 m.

At the marker post for the intersection of First Lake Trail/Dog Mountain and Mount Seymour the trail turns left. Shortly after, by snowshoeing to the left off this trail, on an unmarked but often tracked path, there is a short trail of about 460 m round trip to Dinkey Peak (elevation 1122 m) with southerly views. If the First Lake loop (which does not have any wide vista views) is the trail of choice for the day, then the short Dinkey Peak trail can provide a view. The path leads gently upwards until it begins to curve to the left. Soon there are several tree flashes and BC Parks tree signs in this area. The path to Dinkey Peak rock is on the right. Snowshoe around the right side of the rock and climb it on a diagonal to the left. There are sharp drop-offs on all sides except in the ascent area, so stay to the middle of the viewpoint.

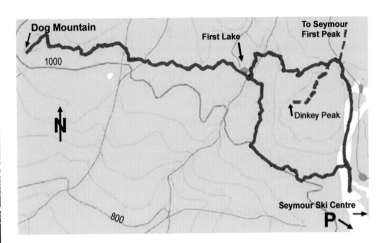

THE TRAILS

By staying on the main track to the left for about 550 m, you will reach First Lake after approximately 15–20 minutes. There is a winter trail to the right that hugs the edge of the lake in a counterclockwise direction. Although crossing the lake is a temptation, fate is also being tempted and the ice may be soft and/or thin during mild winters. Use the lakeside trail on the left as the safest method to reach the bridge at the southwest side of the lake. Go right at the intersection and cross the bridge. (By going left at the intersection, the trail becomes the rest of the First Lake Loop trail that returns to the parking lot.) Skirt the lake to the west, following the poles that mark the way to Dog Mountain. There are also tree markers (and usually a well-worn snow track) leading to the top. One sign indicates 1.5 km to Dog Mountain. As well, there are yellow markers with a black stripe (BC Parks markers) and orange markers on trees, so it is very difficult to get lost on this trip. The trail upward is gradual with several short steeper sections to gain the top of the mountain. Once you've arrived there, the "mountain" description may seem overrated. The area is really a flattened space with a view at the end of a ridge. Snowshoers are rewarded with 360 degree views that include the Lower Mainland, Sunshine Coast and coastal peaks north of Grouse Mountain. The closest summits are Grouse Mountain, with its wind turbine, and Lynn Peak, with Coliseum Mountain farther north. The Seymour River is immediately below in the valley.

On the way back down the trail, look for an aluminum heritage marker high on a tall tree on the left of the trail just before the last slope to the lake. It says SKI LODGE and has been there long enough to have the bark of the tree grow in around it. From the lake area, by looking up in a northerly direction, a log cabin can be seen. This structure belongs to North Shore Search and Rescue, one of Canada's oldest and busiest SAR organizations.

After crossing the bridge, return by taking the loop trail option straight ahead. Follow the orange-topped poles and orange flashes on the trees for approximately 900 m and about 25 minutes through stands of old growth amabilis fir, yellow cedar and mountain hemlock to the exit close to the parking lot. A large map and sign provided by Metro Vancouver is close to the exit.

"DOG MOUNTAIN"?

Dog Mountain often seems to have been given its name because of the numerous dogs leading humans that one meets on the trail. Records of the first time it was named Dog Mountain were found in a *North Shore Hikes* book published by the BC Electric Railway Company in March 1927. On a 1927 topographic map it was named Dogshead Mountain, referring to the shape of the viewpoint after a light snowfall, which was thought to look like the head of a St. Bernard.

ACCESS: Drive Highway 99 towards Whistler and turn off at Exit 08 signed for Cypress Bowl Road. Proceed to the well-marked right-hand turn for the Nordic skiing and snowshoe area.

RATING: easy terrain with several steep sections

SEASON: mid-December to early April

MAP: 92G06 North Vancouver

BEGINNING ALTITUDE: 900 m

DESTINATION ALTITUDE: 1326 m

DISTANCE: 6.6 km round trip; up to 8 km using parts of the summer trail during low-snow years

TIME: 3½–4 hours round trip

CELLPHONE ACCESS: intermittent

FOOD AND DRINK: Café at Nordic area; Hollyburn Lodge; Cypress Creek day lodge at downhill area

WASHROOMS: Opposite the cross-country ticket booth

DOGS: dogs must be on leash in all provincial parks – this trail is patrolled by rangers on a regular basis

AVALANCHE CONDITIONS: **avalanche.ca**

A snowshoe trip to the top of Hollyburn Mountain provides exercise and views of ocean, city and mountains without having to drive very far. The trail is easily accessible but parking for the backcountry trail, at the base of the Nordic ski area, becomes very crowded on sunny days, holidays and weekends. Arriving at the hill before 9:00 a.m. is essential to avoid a lengthy walk along the road before reaching the trail.

If you are renting snowshoes at the Nordic snowshoe rentals facility, DO NOT buy a snowshoe trail ticket. The backcountry trail described here is in the provincial park and does not require a

ticket. It is located in the 3012 hectare Cypress Provincial Park and is maintained by both BC Parks and the ski facility operator to provide access to the backcountry.

The trail is very popular and therefore the snow is often packed-down all the way to where the Upper Romstad cross-country ski run intersects with the snowshoe trail. Often it is possible to complete this first part wearing only hiking boots and micro-crampons. However, snowshoes are needed for the steep ascent on the backcountry trail leading to the summit from the intersection. As well, descent on the entire trail is faster and more fun on snowshoes.

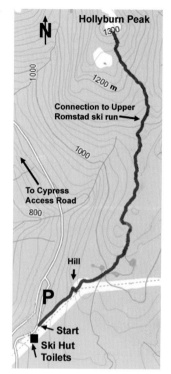

Directions

The beginning of the trail is to the left of the BC Parks signboard, and from December snowfall until the end of March it is clearly marked with orange marker poles to the top of the highest cross-country ski run called Upper Romstad. Initially the trail parallels the wide cross-country ski trail that runs under the power lines, gaining about 100 m of elevation and slightly more than 300 m distance in 15 minutes of climbing. This is followed by a short, steep descent. The powerlines are left behind as the trail winds left into the forest. After a steady ascent and a left turn, a small flat area is reached after another 20 minutes. A trail is often seen leading downwards to

Looking towards the Lions from the top of Hollyburn

the left – this is a shortcut back to the trail just ascended, and the flat depressed area is a small tarn. If entering the forest on this trail, be aware that early and late in the season it has runoff creating hazardous conditions when the saturated snow collapses into the tarn or gully when walked upon. Continue upwards until the trail meets the top of the groomed Upper Romstad Nordic ski trail at an elevation of 1119 m and a distance of approximately 2.3 km and one hour from the beginning. Here signs will indicate the Nordic ski area boundary and the entrance into the backcountry.

A steep ascent now awaits. The perspective upwards presents only the first crest of the hill, which levels briefly, then climbs again, levels slightly and ends with a final steep pitch to the summit that requires good ascent (and descent) snowshoeing skills.

Completing the final approximately 1 km of distance and about 215 m of elevation from the intersection of Upper Romstad and the backcountry boundary to the summit is worth the effort. On a clear day a 360 degree view is provided of the surrounding "North Shore" and Coastal Mountain Ranges and Burrard Inlet, as well as a wide perspective of the city and the bustling Lower Mainland. Looking downwards, the Cypress Creek Day Lodge can be seen as well as the road to the downhill ski facilities. Some of the downhill ski runs on both Black Mountain and Strachan are visible. Whiskey Jacks, ravens and frequently fellow athletes will be found enjoying their lunch and the view from the summit.

The trail back down the hill is often flattened by those who use their snow pants, garbage bags or other adapted equipment to make a luge course on which to hurtle down sections of the trail. Although the fresh powder and occasional ski tracks that head off the main trail may be enticing, the surrounding terrain is extremely steep and unforgiving. Make a choice of safe descent technique and return using your ascent path without straying too far from the trail.

NOTE: with snowfall happening later in the season in recent years, during December and even early January, the snowshoe trail may use parts of the summer trail traced by orange tree markers. Usually, once there is enough snow for cross-country skiing on the upper slopes, there will also be enough to create the winter access trail marked by orange-topped poles to the intersection with the highest cross-country trail of Upper Romstad.

If snow levels are low, it is at the flat meadow and small tarn that the summer trail may be used to attain the top of the cross-country ski area. In that case follow the orange tree markers, criss-crossing the wide ski path several times and passing a signpost indicating 1.8 km to the top of Hollyburn Mountain (summer trail distance), 2.2 km to the parking lot and 2.2 km going west to the alpine ski area. (This western trail is closed during the winter.) Continue following the summer orange tree markers and eventually reach a flat area with a rope strung between trees on the left-hand side. A winding and sometimes narrow ascent awaits before you gain the top. This may be difficult for novice snowshoers or children due to narrow sections and short steep pitches to climb up and down.

Food, drink and hot chocolate are available at the historic Hollyburn Lodge. At the end of your trip, a snowshoe in to this legendary lodge is well worth the 20 minutes and 1 km it takes to get there. The lodge is accessible to snowshoers via the trail at the far end of the parking lot (past the ticket booths and snow tube park) that goes through the woods. Trail tickets are not needed to go along this trail but are needed if you plan to use any of the snowshoe trails in the commercial areas.

Hollyburn ski camp from the top of the First Lake ski jump ca. 1929
BUDDY BARKER/WIN OLIVER COLLECTION, HOLLYBURN HERITAGE SOCIETY ARCHIVES

SOME HOLLYBURN HISTORY

Hollyburn Lodge was built in 1926-27 and still retains much of its original charm. A group of enterprising Swedish community members had the vision of creating a ski lodge and for years successfully operated rope tows and created ski jumps in the First Lake area in front of the lodge. This was followed by the construction of private cottages on land leased from the municipality, and by the mid-1930s there were over 200 homes in the area. Although no new houses can be constructed in the provincial park, some of these original private structures still exist and can be seen by snowshoeing to the south of the ski trails in the area of the lodge. Restoration of the lodge began in 2015 with the intent of keeping the historic building safe and authentic for many more generations of skiers and snowshoers.

ACCESS: Drive Highway 1/99 and take Cypress Bowl Exit 08. Travel 18 km to the downhill ski area parking lot. Cypress Coachlines provides a shuttle bus service to the ski hill, with pickup at various city and local locations: **cypressmountain.com** or 604-637-SNOW (7669)

RATING: easy terrain with a few short steep sections

SEASON: mid-December to March

MAP: 92G06 North Vancouver

BEGINNING ALTITUDE: 920 m

DESTINATION ALTITUDE: 1017 m at Bowen Island Lookout; 1069 m at T junction of Howe Sound Crest East and West Trails

DISTANCE: 5.3 km loop (including trail to Bowen Island Lookout)

TIME: 2½–3 hours

CELLPHONE ACCESS: yes

FOOD AND DRINK: Cypress Alpine Lodge

WASHROOMS: Cypress Alpine Lodge; Black Mountain Lodge

DOGS: all dogs must be on leash in provincial parks; dogs are not allowed in the Yew Lake area

AVALANCHE CONDITIONS: **avalanche.ca**

This trail can be done as its own snowshoe trail or as an addition to Bowen Lookout Trail. A free backcountry pass is required from the beginning to the end of the winter season. The pass can be obtained at Black Mountain Lodge (the Brown Bag Room opposite the washroom entrance) in the lower parking lot.

Directions

Snowshoe past Cypress Alpine Lodge and the Eagle Ridge chair lift that accesses Black Mountain. Straight ahead the trail starts in the woods and is marked with a sign reading BACKCOUNTRY ACCESS TRAIL, while on the right is a map of the ski areas. A few steps on, an avalanche sign shows the risk level for the day.

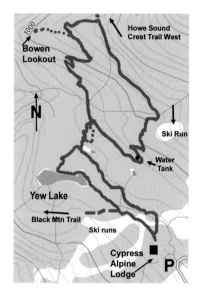

During the winter season the trail is well marked by orange poles to the lookout. After about 28 m from the start, and 5 minutes from the forest entry, there is a junction with the Black Mountain trail leading upward to the left and Yew Lake Trail and Bowen Lookout Winter Trail signposted and leading to the right. Cross over a snow-covered bridge, turn up the small hill and continue through the woods in a westerly direction. This trail runs along part of the Yew Lake loop and provides an opportunity to view open areas of apparent meadow. These actually are boggy parts of the Yew Lake area and often have streams and saturated snow, so do not use them as a shortcut to the service road. Continue around the Yew Lake loop trail for about 1.1 km and eventually arrive at a Y junction. Turn left and soon another post indicates the lower part of Old Growth Forest Loop to the right and Howe Sound Crest Trail straight ahead. Continue on the trail and eventually come to a sign marking the end of the upper part of Old Growth Forest Loop (the path to be taken upon the return trip to see the gigantic trees). Continue uphill on Howe Sound Crest Trail.

Upon exiting from the forest you will see a service road (Pumphouse Road) immediately in front. There is a cement-block building on the right; snowshoe on the road to the left. Although this road appears to head northwest and perhaps result in a viewpoint, it in fact ends after a brief time and changes into steep, bush-covered terrain. Snowshoe only as far as a bridge that crosses a shallow creek to the right – about 200 m. Assess the safety of the bridge – it does not have sides and at times gets piled dangerously high with snow, requiring balancing skills to cross it.

Begin a steady upward ascent on gradually inclined switchbacks – a short one, a long one, another short one and three longer ones. Look southeast as elevation is gained to see the downhill ski area on Black Mountain's Raven Ridge. This was the venue for the 2010 Olympics freestyle, ski cross and snowboard competitions.

When you reach a Y junction and left turnoff for the lookout, visiting Bowen Island Lookout (240 m each way) is an option. Then resume the trail leading up the hill to enter the forest. Snowshoe for about 8 minutes and approximately 290 m to reach another T junction and a BC Parks directional post and sign. The left-hand (west) trail leads to Strachan Meadows, Unnecessary Mountain and the Lions, which is a very high-risk avalanche area in the winter. The right-hand (east) fork leads via Howe Sound Crest East Trail to complete the loop back to parking and the lodges and is the one to take.

Snowshoe in a southeasterly direction along a wide forest trail that was upgraded with funding from the Vancouver Olympic Committee (VANOC) and with support and work by the BC Federation of Mountaineers preceding the Olympics in 2010. The route continues downward and passes over a dirt bridge covering a large culvert. A BC Parks trail post may be seen on the left. There are ski runs just beyond the knoll to the east, but resist that easy exit and follow the trail that enters the forest ahead and slightly to the right, and again begin to descend through the trees. **NOTE:** If there is not a tracked trail through the woods, do not try to make one. Follow the downward trail used by skiers and go for a short while along the edge of the ski run. Turn right and walk west in front of a large green water tank.

If you do take a tracked trail through the forest, you will encounter terrain that includes several brief steep descents and long switchbacks until it evens out and passes along a narrow ledge behind the water tank.

After a brief descent the trail comes out on the level service road. On the left, to the east, are the downhill ski runs and the lodge. Once again resist the urge to use the ski runs as a quick means to reach the trailhead. Instead, turn right and walk past the green water tank and along the Pumphouse service road to the cement building (seen earlier upon exiting the forest on the way to the switchbacks to Bowen Island Lookout). Shortly after this building, the entrance into the forest is on the left. After a brief time on this trail, you'll see the upper part of Old Growth Forest Loop. Follow this loop if you want to see more big trees. (Old Growth Forest Loop curves back to intersect with Howe Sound Crest Trail.) If another visit to the ancient trees is not planned, continue to walk south on Howe Sound Crest Trail. Pass by an open area on the left and the path on the right that was the exit from the trail around Yew Lake that started the trip. Turn left on the Yew Lake upper trail that runs parallel to the Yew Lake trail taken in the morning. Exit the forest and head towards the lodge and the parking lot.

JAYWALKING

If you bring out snack food or a lunch anywhere around Bowen Island Lookout, two favourite winter birds will rapidly appear. The Gray Jay (commonly called a Whiskey Jack) and the beautiful Steller's Jay with its sapphire-coloured wings and body will argue over any bird seeds that are thrown to them.

The Gray is a member of the jay and crow family and lives year round in the coniferous forests of BC. It is unusual in that it stores food wedged in cracks in the bark of trees for future use to feed young or for itself during the winter. Braver than the Steller's Jay that keeps its distance, the Gray will snatch any food from hands with a flyby or even sit as close as on a boot or glove if food is offered. The Gray Jay mates for life and lays two to five eggs each season. The name Whiskey Jack is said to be a variation of the Algonquin name *wiskedjak* or *whiskachon* or *wisakadjak*, given to a mischievous prankster in one of their myths.

Steller's Jay is the provincial bird of British Columbia. It is related to the blue jay found in other parts of Canada but has longer legs and a more pronounced crest. It lives in coniferous forests but also seeks open areas and deciduous trees such as oaks that provide food. Similar to the Gray Jay, Steller's will store some of their food for future use. They can mimic other species' calls and use this skill to imitate predator birds and scare competitors away from food supplies. Steller's Jay will try to steal food from its cousin the Gray if humans are around.

Mount Seymour First Peak Trail

ACCESS: After exiting from Highway 1 (Upper Levels) or after crossing north on Ironworkers Memorial/Second Narrows Bridge, take Exit 22A. Proceed about 4 km to lights and the Parkgate Village shopping centre. Turn left on Mount Seymour Road and continue about 13 km to the Mount Seymour snowshoe parking along the side of the road just before the downhill ski resort parking lot. There is a shuttle bus that leaves from Parkgate Community Centre and/or Lonsdale Quay. Check **mountseymour.com** for schedules and fares. If taking the shuttle, park in the surrounding neighbourhood, not in the community centre's lot.

RATING: moderate terrain with numerous steep sections

SEASON: mid-December to late March

MAP: 92G07 Port Coquitlam

BEGINNING ALTITUDE: 1020 m

DESTINATION ALTITUDE: 1407 m First Peak; 1426 m Second Peak

DISTANCE: 7 km round trip to First Peak; add 1 km round trip to Second Peak

TIME: 3½–4½ hours round trip to First Peak; add 1 hour round trip to Second Peak

CELLPHONE ACCESS: yes

FOOD AND DRINK: Three Peaks Lodge – Elevations 1020 Restaurant, Grillworks Cafeteria, Whiskey Jack brown bag lunchroom

WASHROOMS: Mount Seymour Three Peaks Lodge; also washrooms by first aid station

DOGS: all dogs must be on leash in provincial parks

Elliot makes his first ascent of Mount Seymour First Peak

AVALANCHE CONDITIONS REPORTS: **avalanche.ca**

NOTE: This trail is in Mount Seymour Provincial Park, so you do NOT have to pay a trail fee. If you rent snowshoes from the Mount Seymour Adventure Centre you must buy a trail ticket. This increases the cost but also allows you to use the snowshoe trails in the 81 hectare CRA (controlled recreation area) to the east of the ski runs.

This local trail is easily accessible from the Mount Seymour downhill ski area. Although there are steep portions, the first part to Brockton Point is good for beginning snowshoers, since choices can be made along the way at various viewpoints to end or continue the adventure. Steep ascents are interspersed with flatter terrain, allowing for leg and lung recovery for those not used to rapid elevation gain. However – an encouraging hint – the 360 degree view from First Peak makes the effort worth it all. The trail is in a well-known avalanche zone, so check the avalanche rating and believe the signs just after Brockton Point.

Directions

At the northwest end of the parking lot, by the BC Parks kiosk, the trail begins. Stay to the left of the ropes that indicate the demarcation between the downhill ski area (ticketed) and BC Parks terrain. Orange-tipped trail markers (placed in late December and removed by the end of March) clearly trace the trail, which is maintained by BC Parks rangers in co-operation with Mount Seymour Ski Resort. Because it is used by so many winter activity enthusiasts, the trail often is so packed down that snowshoes may appear unnecessary for the first portion of the trail, but either snowshoes or micro-crampons are helpful for a safe grip. After the first 15 minutes, though, snowshoes are definitely needed, and on the way down the gripping potential of the snowshoes will be appreciated.

Very soon after the start, the first trail going to the left marks the beginning (or end, depending on which of two entrances you've chosen) of First Lake Loop Trail and the trail to Dog Mountain. Continue straight up the hill, to the entertainment of downhill skiers and boarders on your right. Climb for approximately 700 m and 15 minutes to the trail marker for the turnoff to the left to First Lake Loop Trail and Dog Mountain and straight ahead to Mount Seymour First Peak. Continue climbing straight ahead on the steep trail, which at about 1.1 km passes beside the ski run again and then heads downwards and northwest, followed by more climbing. The first good viewpoint of First Peak is at about 1.4 km, followed by an even better one at Brockton Point at approximately 2.3 km. To the left the object of the trip becomes apparent. Initially the large ridge appears to be First Peak, and climbers, backcountry skiers and snowshoers can often be seen on its top. This ridge is named The Face, and during winter it may have steep (VERY steep) paths up its face where the fearless or those practising roped ascents and ice climbing take a shortcut to First Peak. This is not a trail for those who fear heights and is suitable only for experienced snowshoers. Looking south, you can see Mystery Peak and the chairlift exit as well as the first view of surrounding mountains. To the southeast is Mount Baker, with the Canadian and US Gulf Islands to the south and southwest. Shortly after Brockton Point a descent begins and an avalanche information sign comes into view, a reminder that you are entering the backcountry, which is not patrolled and where even steeper terrain exists and avalanches can happen. Another climb upward in a northeasterly direction follows, then a diagonal descent at the left side of a steep hill and into a narrow, flatter area.

The trail now continues in a steep ascent with increased views including the mountains of Golden Ears to the east, the lower hills around the village of Anmore and portions of Indian Arm inlet. The upward climb leads to a small plateau where a danger sign warns of steep drop-offs to the east. A 10-minute further climb brings you to another viewing spot, surrounded by Douglas fir and western red cedar, about 2.7 km from the start. It is an excellent place for a rest before the final ascent to First Peak. When you look to the east from here, the pipe exiting from Buntzen Lake can be seen leading into the Buntzen 2 generating station, which currently operates by remote control from Burnaby.

Begin the last section of the climb, which involves numerous short, steep traverses and about 300 m elevation gain and leads to a trail into a small ravine behind The Face ridge. First Peak can now be seen ahead and to the left and can be reached in about 20 minutes. Although the climb to the top is on a narrow ridge, there usually is a well-carved trail to lead you safely upward to where a new sign on a post in the shape of a rustic pump indicates the elevation is 1407 m. Well done!

The trail to Second Peak is not marked by poles but descends on a northwest angle from the First Peak ridge towards a tree-lined gully which ascends to the top of the Second Peak ridge. It takes about 30 minutes to go from the First Peak ridge to the top of Second Peak. There are steep drop-offs to the north on the Second Peak ridge, so be careful here. Now Third Peak – the "real Mount Seymour," at a height of 1449 m – can be seen. The descent and ascent to gain Third Peak is not recommended as a snowshoe trip. It is often icy, has a VERY steep fall line along the north side of Second Peak, as well as technical sections, and adds at least another hour and anxiety to the trip.

Return by the same route you took to arrive at Second Peak.

Because many people take advantage of the steep terrain to bum-slide portions of the trail, there may be icy sections and some need for careful traversing on your descent. If snowshoeing slowly and peacefully downhill, be alert for the snowshoers hurtling along their self-made luge tracks and for backcountry skiers returning from their ascent of the peaks.

MOUNT SEYMOUR'S PEAKS

The first two peaks are sometimes called First and Second Pump because it is reported that at one time there was a twisted tree on First Peak that looked like a pump handle and base. GeoBC suggests that the first climbing party in 1908 gave Brockton Point its name from an association with the similarly named point in Stanley Park. That one was originally named after the engineer on Captain Richards's HMS *Plumper*. From First Peak a view of the expansiveness of Mount Seymour Provincial Park is available. The 3509 hectare park, established in 1936, was named for Frederick Seymour, the second governor of British Columbia, who was in office from 1864 to 1869.

The first climb to the top of Mount Seymour was made in 1908 by a group of BC Mountaineering Club members, but it was not until 1937 that a ski lodge opened, with a cafeteria and ski rental. The BC government purchased the business in 1949 but in 1984 it sold the ski operation and awarded a park use permit to Mount Seymour Resorts. The ski hill as been run as a private enterprise ever since. The annual average snowfall is 10 m, with 5 m at the Brockton Point weather station.

Thunderbird Ridge Trail

ACCESS: Take the Capilano Road exit from Marine Drive in North Vancouver and proceed for about 5 km to the Grouse Mountain Resort parking lots. Turn right, into the gravel lot to the east, where parking is less expensive.

RATING: easy to intermediate terrain, with many short steep pitches at start

SEASON: mid-December to April

MAP: 92G06 North Vancouver

BEGINNING ALTITUDE: 1095 m

DESTINATION ALTITUDE: 1257 m on Thunderbird Ridge; 1349 m on Dam Mountain

DISTANCE: 6.5 km round trip to Thunderbird Ridge, returning via base of Dam Mountain; add about 400 m for loop to viewpoint on Dam Mountain

TIME: 2½–3 hours round trip to Thunderbird Ridge, returning via lower Dam Mountain; add 20–25 minutes for Dam Mountain viewpoint loop

CELLPHONE ACCESS: yes

FOOD AND DRINK: Grouse Mountain: Lupins Café and The Observatory restaurant

WASHROOMS: Peak Chalet; wooden building at bottom of Peak ski run

DOGS: dogs are not allowed on the gondola

AVALANCHE CONDITIONS: **avalanche.ca**

NOTE: It is worthwhile to phone ahead for snow and avalanche conditions. Although this trail is within sight of the resort, it is in steep backcountry terrain that can easily have avalanche or severe ice conditions and be closed for all activities.

This trail is not for the money-challenged. It is accessible only by taking the Grouse Mountain Skyride to the main resort. An Annual Local's Pass should be considered – it allows access to the mountain for the year following the date of purchase and 50 per cent off for one-time round trips for two accompanying friends. The pass also allows free rides down to the base for snowshoers and Grouse Grind or BC *Mountaineering Club trail enthusiasts.*

Neither is this a hike for the lung-impaired. Although short in distance, it involves frequent and quite steep climbs at the beginning of the uphill section to Dam Mountain. However, during the winter school term, the satisfaction of passing young teenagers staggering up the hills as they make their first attempt at snowshoeing (and often their first at any self-propelled winter sport) may result in a feeling of pride for those who snowshoe more frequently. On the other hand, this is the route for the Grouse Snowshoe Grind, so snowshoe racers may pass you as they attempt to better their times for the 4.3 km (and 215 m elevation gain) round trip to the top of Dam Mountain and back to the resort.

Directions

After leaving the gondola, pass the skating rink on the left and go past three carved wooden statues. Head along a groomed road to the left of the ski runs. Grouse Mountain's Munday Alpine Snowshoe Park trails are on the left in the woods as the road passes under a chairlift. Go between the shorter chairlift and The Peak chairlift and head towards the grizzly bear viewing station close to the bottom of The Peak ski run. Stay on the left, then turn left onto a wide, groomed path that hugs steep rock walls on the right and falls away with precipitous inclines on the left. Sign in at Metro Vancouver's Lynn Headwaters Regional Park station before heading onto the path ("Metro Vancouver" was formerly called the "Greater Vancouver Regional District," or GVRD).

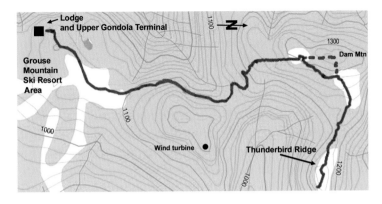

Continue for 20 minutes and about 1 km since the start to information signs that give current conditions and list the areas that are closed for backcountry activities. Grouse Mountain passes will be confiscated from those who require rescue after venturing beyond designated backcountry snowshoe areas.

A steep trail with pole markers can now be seen rising into the forest. About 7 more minutes of climbing brings into view an elevated wooden platform. When snowshoeing in the springtime, flying people can sometimes be seen. This is not a hallucination caused by lack of oxygen from the climb, and the people are not leaping snowboarders. They are individuals who paid for the excitement of riding a Grouse Mountain zipline at up to 80 km/h. The attraction runs three such lines near the resort.

Continue climbing steeply for 8 minutes to reach a small plateau where a loop trail leads to a GVRD area with a view over the Capilano River watershed. **NOTE:** This loop trail has neither tree markers nor marker poles, so unless the trail has previously been tramped it is easy to get lost in this terrain that has steep drop-offs at the viewpoint. The loop takes about 20–25 minutes and is approximately 800 m long. The loop exits just below the plateau at the southerly base of Dam Mountain. After approximately

2.1 km from the start, the highest part of the main trail is reached at about 1312 m on a plateau. Here the path divides, with the left trail leading upwards from the south to the top of Dam Mountain (1349 m), while the right branch heads to the easterly base of Dam Mountain and onwards to Thunderbird Ridge. From this vantage point Thunderbird Ridge looks like it is attainable by an easy downward trail through virgin snow directly over to it from the base of Dam Mountain. That terrain has steep fall lines, so stay on the track. After another 350 m, there is a junction where the trail again divides, going upward on the left to a northside ascent of Dam Mountain and straight ahead to Little Goat Mountain (often closed because of avalanche danger). To the east is an easy-to-follow trail heading downward for about 20 minutes and then rising to get to the modest high point near the end of Thunderbird Ridge.

The Eye of the Wind turbine atop Grouse Mountain can be clearly seen from the ridge. Also on this trail there are unimpeded views of the mountains behind Grouse – on the left is Crown Mountain (informally known as "The Sleeping Beauty") with a short notch separating it from "The Camel" formation to the east. In the centre is Goat Mountain and to the right, Mount Seymour. Snowshoe about 670 m along the undulating path that follows the ridge from the three-way intersection to the small summit at an elevation of 1255 m. In the steep valley to the left is Kennedy Lake. About 130 m farther, at approximately 3.2 km from the start at the Grouse Mountain resort, is the end of the ridge. Steep drop-offs are on every side. The little summit and ridge are named after the mythical First Nations Thunderbird, who is considered the most powerful of all the spirits, and it provides views in all directions. Looking southwest, you'll see the peak of Grouse Mountain, identified by the exit of skiers from the lift; south and east are the city of Vancouver, Mount Baker, Boundary

Bay and the Olympic Peninsula; and towards the west, Vancouver Island and the Gulf Islands.

Return the same way along the ridge, and upon rejoining the main trail and snowshoeing south for about 50 m you'll often see marker poles or tracks indicating a trail up the north side of Dam Mountain. **NOTE:** This trail is not suitable for children or those with a fear of heights. It is a steep and narrow path at the top with a drop-off to the west side. It is easier and safer to attain the top of Dam Mountain from the south side, used for the Snowshoe Grind.

This small peak with an elevation of 1349 m provides another view looking northwest towards the Lions and southwest to the Cypress downhill ski area and the Hollyburn cross-country and snowshoe area. Far below, the Capilano reservoir provides water to Vancouver. The dam that helps form the lake gives this small summit its name. The Peak Chalet can be seen clearly from this vantage point. The return to the lodge is a steep downhill journey that provides a visual explanation for why heavy breathing was heard on the way up. But no surprise hills occur on the way back, so it is down all the way, a fast return after a "Peak experience."

Before ending the adventure, exploration of the four woodland snowshoe trails to the west of the Peak Chalet in the Munday Alpine Snowshoe Park is fun. Tickets or extra fees are not necessary for use of these trails. Use the map available in the lodge for orientation to these paths.

GROUSE MOUNTAIN SIGHTS

In 2010 an intriguing visual addition to the Grouse Mountain skyline was built, in the form of a gigantic turbine – the Eye of the Wind. It is as tall as a 20-storey building and has three blades that are 37 m long. An elevator takes visitors up into a 360 degree observation pod – the first of its kind in the world – located just beneath the turbine, its massive blades rotating just 3 m outside the windows. Over 20 per cent of the resort's electricity is generated by this turbine, which is the largest one in Canada.

The large chainsaw-carved wooden sculptures that are seen on paths leading to the ski and snowshoe areas are of birds and animals native to British Columbia, as well as scenes of mining, lumbering and First Nations people. In the resort area there are 31 of the carvings with the theme of *Tribute to the Forest*, carved by First Nations artist Glen Greenside.

Cal-Cheak Recreation Site to Brandywine Falls

ACCESS: Drive north on Highway 99 (Sea to Sky) towards Whistler. For a one-way trip from the campground to Brandywine Falls, leave a car at the turnout at McGuire Forest Service Road (about 3 km north past the Brandywine Falls exit). During the winter months, Brandywine Falls has no parking area, but in the early winter and spring a car can be left in the pullout at Brandywine Falls if the space plowed there is big enough. Carpool and continue on Highway 99 to Cal-Cheak Recreation Site. For increased security, park in the pullout close to the Cheakamus Community Forest sign, where the car will be visible from the highway. Alternative parking is on the road at the start of the trail.

RATING: easy terrain

SEASON: December to mid-March

MAP: 92J03 Brandywine

BEGINNING ALTITUDE: 505 m at the yellow gate south entrance to the campground

DESTINATION ALTITUDE: 490 m at Brandywine Falls BC Parks sign

DISTANCE: 6 km one way (car left at either end)

TIME: 2½–3 hours; add about 1 hour for return from Brandywine Falls to McGuire FSR if a car is left there

CELLPHONE ACCESS: yes

FOOD AND DRINK: Squamish and Whistler

WASHROOMS: outhouses in Cal-Cheak campground (if not under snow) and Brandywine Falls Park

DOGS: yes, although in the Brandywine Provincial Park part of the trail dogs must be on leash

AVALANCHE CONDITIONS: **avalanche.ca**

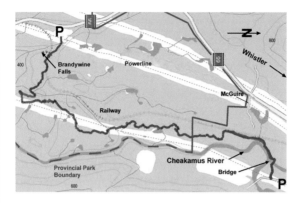

This generally low-level trail is suitable for families and beginner snowshoers who want an outdoor experience without a lot of elevation gain or steep inclines. In early winter and spring there may be patches of dirt and running water that have to be crossed because of the low-lying terrain and extensive runoff.

Directions

From the parking area by the Cheakamus Community Forest sign, walk about 800 m along the road to the far (south) end of the campground, passing a sign on the left that says NORTH SITE and points to the Sea to Sky trail. Close to the end of the campsite there is a sign indicating the SOUTH SITE. Pass by the stop sign and turn right at the locked yellow gate. Put on your snowshoes and go straight ahead, then curve slightly to the left through the forest for about 200 m to arrive at a suspension bridge. The bridge crosses the confluence of Callaghan Creek from the north and the Cheakamus River from the east – hence the Cal-Cheak name. After crossing the bridge, turn left and follow the next portion of the trail along the Cheakamus River and into the forest. After about 860 m from the start, the trail meets the McGuire Forest Service Road railway crossing (where the pickup car may have been left if there was no parking at Brandywine

Brandywine Falls in winter   PHOTOGRAPHER: CHRIS BARTON, SEATOSKY.500PX.COM

Falls pullout). Although there is an alternative route to Brandywine Falls by crossing the tracks and heading south along the Lava Lake trail, the present trail goes into the forest that is to your left when facing the track. After entering the forest, snowshoe straight ahead, then gradually turn left and cross a small bridge. At about 1 km and 25 minutes since the beginning, climb a short incline in a ravine and then traverse to the right. A small open area is at the top. Continue in a southerly direction, soon observing a Brandywine Falls Park boundary sign at about 1.5 km and after 40 minutes of snowshoeing. Curve to the right and continue, climbing up a slight slope that leads to a small lake on the left at about 1.6 km. Facing north, you'll see steep-sided rock on your left as well as snow shelves that may break off. Angle across the slope and upward on the right side of the rocky area. Once on flatter open ground at the top of the hill, walk forward and then curve around to the left to regain the path below.

At about 2.1 km and after more than an hour of snowshoeing, you will see a fairly large lake on the left. Stay midway along the slope. There are bog holes and standing water in ponds in this area, both of which could be disguised by a skim of ice and snow. Immediately before you descend back into the forest, a viewpoint gives a clear view of Black Tusk. This is the highest point on the trip. The route now follows a short valley, again with large wet areas and rocks on either side. Stay on the trail, which for a short time runs parallel with and in sight of the railway track.

At about 2.35 km there is a BC Parks sign saying the trail straight ahead is closed. This is to protect the unique wetland habitat of the rare red-legged frogs found here. Turn to the left and snowshoe through the forest on a wide path on a slight right diagonal.

At approximately 2.7 km emerge onto a BC Hydro right-of-way. Cross this, at first skirting the forest on the right, then heading diagonally upward to an orange flag on a tree midway across and then to a grove of conifers to the right of tall rock cliffs. Flagging marks the entrance to an old logging road. Snowshoe along this pleasant path and emerge once again onto the hydro right-of-way. Post signs now give directions to Whistler's Bungee Bridge (800 m to the south) and via that road back to Cal-Cheak Suspension Bridge (2.2 km). However, the path to Brandywine Falls is across the hydro right-of-way, curving slightly left to an opening in the forest and a moderately wide track. From here to Brandywine Falls the trail is often used by dog walkers, so it may be well tramped.

Continue along the path and emerge one more time to snowshoe a short distance on a diagonal left past the hydro tower. Then turn to the right close to its base and re-enter the forest, at a distance of approximately 3.7 km from the beginning. Soon there is a lookout – with a very steep drop-off. Examples of black basalt rock can be seen, as well as a view of Daisy Lake to the left. (Daisy Lake was enlarged by BC Hydro to supply water for its Cheakamus generating station on the Squamish River, via an 11 km tunnel drilled beneath Cloudburst Mountain.) At approximately 4.2 km there is a second lookout, with an even steeper drop-off.

Continue to snowshoe downward along the path for another 30 minutes, first heading north and then winding back south. The trail now has a long, shallow climb and at close to 5.45 km it intersects with the railway track. A directional post indicates that the Brandywine Falls are to the left. Making a side trip of about 200 m round trip to view the falls in winter is worthwhile. Return and cross the railway track and continue on a wide, easy trail. The Brandywine Falls parking lot is at approximately 6 km from the trailhead yellow gate (or 5.5 km if the falls are not viewed). A volunteer (or the whole group) will need to either snowshoe back by the trail, walk along the road (approximately 3 km) or return via the Lava Lake trail to get the car if it was left at McGuire Forest Service Road.

CAL-CHEAK TRAIL

This route was originally part of the historic Pemberton Trail connecting Squamish with Pemberton. The trail at one time was a popular route used by the early pioneers and First Nations people and for cattle drives to the Coast. Today the Cal-Cheak trail is the only maintained section of that bygone transportation route.

BRANDYWINE FALLS

It is suggested that this 70-metre cataract was named when two railway surveyors bet a bottle of brandy on who could accurately guess the height of the falls. The winning surveyor got the brandy and named the falls after their escapade.

ACCESS: Drive north along Highway 99 (Sea to Sky) towards Whistler. At the stop light at Function Junction turn right onto Cheakamus Lake Road. Cross the wide cement bridge and make a right turn onto Legacy Way. Drive straight ahead, pass the HI-Whistler Youth Hostel, turn right and park at the far end of the elevated parking lot. If you are parking in the Mt. Fee lot, you'll find it is approximately 1 km from there to the beginning of the trail. **NOTE:** There is no parking on municipal roads in the Whistler area during the winter.

RATING: easy terrain

SEASON: December to mid-March

MAP: 92J03 Brandywine

BEGINNING ALTITUDE: 605 m

DESTINATION ALTITUDE: 650 m high point

DISTANCE: 8.1 km loop trip

TIME: 3–3½ hours loop trip

CELLPHONE ACCESS: yes

FOOD AND DRINK: Cheaky's Café in the youth hostel on Legacy Way

WASHROOMS: Cheaky's Café

DOGS: yes

AVALANCHE CONDITIONS: **avalanche.ca**

This easy trail provides a variety of rolling terrain, and because it starts and ends at Cheakamus Crossing (formerly the site of the Olympic 2010 athletes village), it does not require a transfer car at the end. The counterclockwise direction is described, since this gives a forested trail for the morning trip and an open and generally downhill trail for the return, when participants may be cold and/

Basalt rocks along the trail

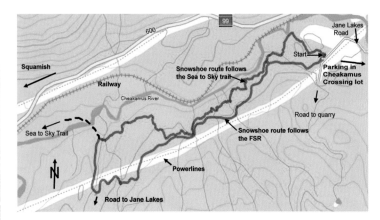

or tired. Hopefully snowshoers will be able to catch some afternoon sun on the way back to the trailhead. The route has several spots to make an early return and still complete a loop, so it is a good choice for families with young children.

Directions

From the parking area, snowshoe over the hill and slant right to get onto the road below. Snowshoe or walk south on Jane Lakes Road for about 400 m, passing a sign low on a post close to a large rock on the right indicating the Sea to Sky trail. On the left is a wide logging road often used by cross-country skiers; on the right is a forested trail with directional signposts. This snowshoe route departs via the forested Sea to Sky trail and returns by the logging road. Using the Sea to Sky in both directions is also an option if the weather is cold and windy or there is active logging in the area. The trail is frequently used for dog walking, so at least part of it should be well tracked. It spends part of its length meandering beside various streams and snow runoff channels racing to the Cheakamus River, so if these waters are not frozen a pleasing gurgle accompanies snowshoers. However, during early spring the low elevation and runoff rivulets create bare spots or spongy, decaying snow that may unexpectedly collapse under snowshoes.

Pass the Sea to Sky signage and go along the path into the woods. Continue on the path for about 25 minutes and approximately 900 m to the first bridge. The route continues with mild elevation gain until on the left it nears the wide Nordic track at about 1.2 km. If there are small children along or any of the party who need only a short outing, this is a good time to access the Nordic trail and head back to Cheakamus Crossing. Otherwise, continue along, crossing another short bridge and beginning a gentle ascent with winding switchbacks and several bridges to an open area. Follow the path to the right and continue on with slight elevation loss and gain. At about 2.6 km you reach another intersection with the Nordic trail/logging road, where once again there is the option to return to Cheakamus Crossing by way of a shorter loop. A large bridge follows and the trail ascends into sparser, younger trees. Views to the west and north now are prominent, and some flatter open areas are available for a lunch or snack spot. At about 3.4 km and approximately 70 minutes from the trailhead there is a viewpoint to the south and west. If the snow is low there is a stone seat to rest on. Follow the now wider and open way between small, self-seeded conifers. The path begins to descend, often with a rock sidewall on the left as it makes small traverses. It takes about another 15 minutes on short descending traverses to reach a small bridge and then the main logging road that is ascending from the Cal-Cheak Recreation Site beside Highway 99. This junction is approximately 4.1 km and 1½–2 hours from trailhead. (Our measurements consistently differed from the sign located just after the bridge crossing, which claims it is 3.2 km to Cheakamus Crossing where the trail began and 4.2 km to Function Junction.)

A decision can be made to turn right to go to the Cal-Cheak campground for lunch (about another 2.4 km one way) and return to complete the loop, or turn left immediately to go to the T junction of the wide Nordic ski track seen at the beginning of this trail. If turning left, it is a steady 20-minute climb and approximately 600 m to reach the Nordic trail. Turn left at the T junction and return in 80 minutes and about 3.5 km from the T junction to the trailhead.

VOLCANIC BASALT

Basalt rock is formed when lava pushes up from a volcano and rapidly cools. The lava meets either cold rocks or air as it ascends, and it shrinks as it cools, creating long columns of rock. Columnar basalt can have four-, five- and even eight-sided forms in its columns.

SEA TO SKY TRAIL

Once an off-road route for hardcore mountain bikers, this is now a multi-use, four-season trail that will eventually extend in an accessible manner from Horseshoe Bay to Lillooet. Many segments of the route have been surfaced with a 1.5 m width of crushed gravel, allowing cyclists, hikers and even wheelchair users to make use of it. In winter, cross-country skiers and snowshoers take advantage of this peaceful pathway. The Squamish Lillooet Regional District and numerous other partners have contributed funds to completing additional sections of the trail each year. See **seatoskytrail.ca** for maps and more information about the Sea to Sky trail.

Cheakamus Crossing to Cal-Cheak Recreation Site Trail

ACCESS: Drive north along Highway 99 towards Whistler and leave one car at the Cal-Cheak Recreation Site. At the first stop light at Function Junction turn right onto Cheakamus Lake Road. Cross the wide cement bridge and make a right turn onto Legacy Drive. Go straight ahead, pass the youth hostel and Cheaky's Café and park at the south end of the elevated lot on the right. **NOTE:** There is no parking on municipal roads in the Whistler area during the winter.

RATING: easy terrain

SEASON: December to mid-March

MAP: 92J03 Brandywine

BEGINNING ALTITUDE: 605 m at trailhead

DESTINATION ALTITUDE: 520 m (campground)

DISTANCE: 6.6 km one way from trailhead to campground

TIME: 2½–3 hours

CELLPHONE ACCESS: yes

FOOD AND DRINK: Cheaky's Café in youth hostel on Legacy Way

WASHROOMS: at youth hostel on Legacy Way; outhouse in Cal-Cheak campground

DOGS: yes

AVALANCHE CONDITIONS: **avalanche.ca**

This trail is often used in winter by cross-country skiers and in summer by bicyclists on the Sea to Sky route. This means it is fairly easy to follow, wide and of a moderate grade. It requires a car at the beginning and end unless the longer return loop (12.4 km) through the forest is used.

Descending the ramp

Directions

After parking, snowshoe over the hill and angle to the right to get onto the road below. Snowshoe left along Jane Lakes Road, passing a sign on the right, mounted low on a post, indicating the Sea to Sky trail. On the left is an open logging road, on the right a forested trail with additional signage for the Sea to Sky. For variety this route uses the logging road for the initial part and you can return by the forested (Sea to Sky) segment if a loop path is chosen. Snowshoe along the wide logging road as it gradually rises. The forested path will be on the right. After about 1 km there is an opening on the right where access to the forest track is easy if for some reason this is now preferred. After about 1.6 km and 25 minutes of snowshoeing from the trailhead the top of a

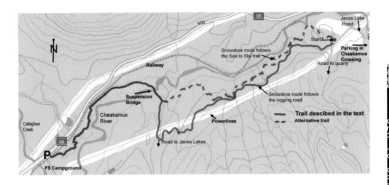

small incline is reached. Continue along the open path, and at approximately 2.3 km another access to the forested Sea to Sky trail can be seen, marked with an orange disc on a roadside tree at a bridge crossing a small river. Some of the towers and wires that bring power from northern BC to the Lower Mainland are now close by. At about 2.8 km from the beginning of the route there is a wooden sign on the right saying it is 3 km from the start of the road (perhaps from the junction of Jane Lakes and Legacy roads?).

About an hour from the start, at approximately 3.1 km, the way passes directly under the powerline and a panoramic view of the Tantalus range is provided. Soon the high point is reached at about 644 m. In about 5 minutes, at approximately 3.5 km, there is a T junction with a sign saying Function Junction is 3.5 km from here (possibly measured from the Jane Lakes Road inter-section) and that the Cal-Cheak suspension bridge is 4.5 km. The trail heading up the hill to the left is an enjoyable summer route to Jane Lakes but in winter it generally has so many bent bushes and small trees that it becomes impassable.

Take the downhill trail and continue for approximately 20 minutes and 600 m. On the right is a sign for the Sea to Sky/ Trans Canada Trail leading back to Cheakamus Crossing, with a bridge to cross the small river. Continue on the main logging road trail for another 8 minutes or so until the new Cheakamus River Suspension Bridge appears at approximately 4.4 km from trailhead. Cross the bridge and go to the left onto the path bordered by the river on the left and at times by views of the railway on the right. The trail gradually ascends to a wide open area that overlooks Highway 99 and a basalt landform commonly known as Sugarcube Hill. It is named this because of the multi-sided sugar-cube-shaped rocks of basalt found in this region. With a bit of imagination the sloping sides of a basalt teapot might be seen on the west side of the way. The path winds and descends through these formations, passing a small tarn and then ascending gradually. At the top of the ascent, take a sharp right towards a tree with an orange disc on it (rather than going straight ahead on the more obvious Sea to Sky trail). This avoids a long, steep, exposed slope that is dangerous in the winter. Snowshoe along a short ridge that has a small tarn on the left and a steep slope on the right. Soon a wooden ramp leading downwards appears. Early and late in the season the side railings provide protection, but if there have been heavy snowfalls the walk often is filled to the top of the railings and requires very careful descent. Turn left at the bottom and make several traverses to gain the lowest ground. Head east to the largest trees and stay to the left at the edge of the slope to avoid bog holes and wet spots on the right. After passing a large tree with an orange disc on it, turn right and continue on a trail that shows some flagging as it heads southwest. Descend to the road that leads to the bungee jumping site. The trail leaves the forest and ends after about 6.6 km at a sign and map describing the Cheakamus Community Forest.

If a car was left here the snowshoe trip is finished. If not, this is a good spot for getting a ride from friendly locals or returning bungee jumpers back to Cheakamus Crossing to pick up the car.

If a snowshoeing loop was chosen, return on the same trail. After passing the new suspension bridge, turning left and walking for a short time up the hill, turn left at the Sea to Sky sign and cross the small bridge. (See Cheakamus Crossing Loop Trail for a description of the rest of the return loop using the forest part of this route.)

CHEAKAMUS COMMUNITY FOREST

This one of more than 50 community managed forests in British Columbia. Managing and operating the forest is done by the equal partners of the Lil'wat and Squamish First Nations and the Resort Municipality of Whistler (RMOW). The management includes harvesting on about 15,000 hectares in the over 30,000 hectares of forest surrounding Whistler. The independent not-for-profit Cheakamus Community Forest Society oversees the three managing organizations during their 25-year tenure of the area. See **cheakamuscommunityforest.com** for more information on this initiative and trails development.

Garibaldi Lake and Taylor Meadows Trails

ACCESS: Drive Highway 99 (Sea to Sky) to just before Daisy Lake. Be alert for the BC Parks sign for Garibaldi Provincial Park saying 2.5 km. The road is immediately after this sign. The summer parking lot is 2.5 km from here on a paved road, but during the winter the road is not plowed, so it may need to be snowshoed. Park away from the driveways of homeowners.

RATING: easy terrain with some narrow sections on the Garibaldi Lake portion and overall very long if you do the loop

SEASON: mid-December to mid-March

MAP: 92G14 Cheakamus River

BEGINNING ALTITUDE: 580 m at summer parking lot

DESTINATION ALTITUDE: 1476 m at Garibaldi Lake; 1500 m at shelter cabin in Taylor Meadows

DISTANCE: 18 km round trip to Garibaldi Lake outlet; 15 km round trip to Taylor Meadows; 19 km loop trip; distances are from summer parking lot

TIME: 6–6½ hours round trip to Garibaldi Lake; 5½–6 hours round trip to Taylor Meadows; 7–8 hours loop trip to Taylor Meadows and Garibaldi Lake

CELLPHONE ACCESS: no

FOOD AND DRINK: Squamish

WASHROOMS: summer parking lot; Taylor Meadows and Garibaldi Lake (but they may be under snow)

DOGS: dogs are NOT ALLOWED AT ALL in Garibaldi Provincial Park

AVALANCHE CONDITIONS: **avalanche.ca**

In 2015 The Economist *magazine shocked Vancouverites by describing the city as "mind-numbingly boring." We of course totally disagree but after snowshoeing the more than 40 long and short*

Martin high above Garibaldi Lake   PHOTOGRAPHER: ANNE BREVIG, 1985

switchbacks on the trail leading to Taylor Meadows or Garibaldi Lake, that phrase may drift through your mind. So it is up to each snowshoer to find a way to make the first part of the trip interesting as the trail climbs through western red cedar and Douglas fir. Time will then pass quickly until you reach the winter playground of Taylor Meadows. For example, think of all the words that have snow in them; develop new ideas for using pine beetle infested trees; think of new ways to conserve water; sing all the snow songs you know; etc.

Directions

After you leave the parking area by Rubble Creek, an interesting geological formation that can be seen on the right is The Barrier, made of red and grey volcanic rock. The trail continues as a steady slog up switchbacks for the first approximately 6.5 km until a junction is reached. Kilometre posts can be seen along the

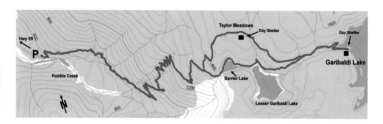

trail if the snow is not too deep. At the junction a BC Parks map will help provide orientation. At this point a decision must be made. Straight ahead the trail will lead shortly to a good viewpoint for a close-up inspection of The Barrier. Pass by Barrier Lake and Lesser Garibaldi Lake and after another approximately 2.5 km the trail leads to the outlet of Garibaldi Lake. The lake often remains frozen (but not safe to snowshoe on) until the end of June. The last part of the trail to Garibaldi Lake is quite narrow with steep sides above and below and a traverse down to the bridge that leads to the lakeside ranger cabin, so place your snowshoes carefully.

From the BC Parks map at the junction the trail to the left heads to Taylor Meadows, reaching it after another approximately 150 m elevation and 1.5 km. The Meadows offer a clear view of the imposing Black Tusk surrounded by snow. As well, there is an opportunity to be a kid again and play the snow games listed in the chapter on Snowshoeing with Children or create giant snow art such as the designs placed by British artist Simon Beck on snowscapes throughout the world.

Either Taylor Meadows or Garibaldi Lake is by itself a worthy destination. If late spring days are long and there is still a good snow layer, a loop trip can be completed by going to the meadows and then on to Garibaldi Lake. After entering the Meadows, snowshoe to the shelter and washroom. Continue on as though heading to Black Tusk. Turn right at the ranger storage shed (identified by the wire on all the windows) and leave the Meadows in a southeasterly direction. The trail down to the intersection with the lake trail is not marked where it enters the woods, but it is gained by taking a few short switchbacks, a bridge across a creek, several switchbacks up a short slope and then a trail winding through woods. After descending on the trail for a bit over 1 km the junction with the Garibaldi Lake trail is reached. Turn left and after about another 600 m you'll come to the Garibaldi Lake outlet. It is about 9 km to the summer parking lot via the lake trail from this point (add another 2 to 2.5 km to where cars park in winter), so it is best not to linger but to start the trip back down the trail.

RUBBLE CREEK

The bed of the stream that today races below The Barrier was once filled with a glacier, and when molten lava met the ice The Barrier was formed as the lava cooled. The rock face now acts as a dam to contain the waters flowing from Garibaldi Lake. The most recent collapse of lava rock from the face was in 1885–86. The rock rubble seen in the creek is from this avalanche. The Barrier is over 300 m thick and about 2 km wide, and no one can predict whether or when more (or all) of the rock will break off. The area below The Barrier has been declared unsafe and no construction is allowed in the possibly devastating path of the water if this natural dam should break.

ACCESS: Drive north on Highway 99 (Sea to Sky) towards Whistler and park at the Brandywine Falls winter pullout in front of the yellow locked gate and cement blocks. Be sure to park out of the way of cars and snowplows using the pullout to turn around. This is usually only possible in early or late winter. If there is not adequate space, park on McGuire Forest Service Road and begin and end the trail there, still completing the loop in a clockwise direction.

RATING: easy terrain

SEASON: late December to mid-March

MAP: 92J03 Brandywine

BEGINNING ALTITUDE: 490 m at Brandywine Falls BC Parks sign

DESTINATION ALTITUDE: 490 m

DISTANCE: 8.6 km round trip

TIME: 3–3½ hours round trip

CELLPHONE ACCESS: yes

FOOD AND DRINK: Squamish; Whistler

WASHROOMS: outhouses at Brandywine Falls Park

DOGS: yes, although they must be on leash in the Brandywine Provincial Park part of the route

AVALANCHE CONDITIONS: **avalanche.ca**

This wide, low-level trail is suitable for families and beginning snow-shoers. Since much of the trail is also part of the Sea to Sky summer cycling and hiking route, it has a raised gravel surface that ensures a solid base for the snow trail. The route has several view spots and passes by many small ponds that, depending on the time of winter or early spring, may present icy mirrors, snow-covered surfaces or tranquil water.

Directions

Walk towards the picnic tables, BC Parks maps and the First Nations interpretive information kiosk. Cross Brandywine Creek on the bridge and immediately turn left at the directional signpost.

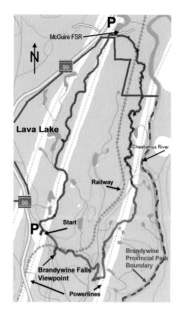

Trail-breaking may be required, since the most popular route for tourists and snowshoers is the one on the right towards Brandywine Falls. It is worth the effort, though, so continue up the slight incline of a long hill to reach the top and a view of... hydro wires and pylons. Cross under these and head into the forest. Follow the wide path through the trees, exit from the woods, cross the right-of-way under the wires again and re-enter the woods on the west side. Continue on the treed path in a northerly direction, passing (or snowshoeing to view) Lava Lake on the left at about 1.3 km. At approximately 2 km turn right where usually there is a large pond on either side of the path. Bear left when a hydro pylon is immediately ahead and continue on the trail in the forest, eventually emerging into the hydro right-of-way and a short walk in the open to a yellow gate and road.

This is McGuire Forest Service Road, at about 2.8 km from the trailhead. If parking was unavailable at Brandywine Falls, this is the spot to start the snowshoe trail and return in a clockwise loop to this point. Turn right, walk to the stop sign, turn right again and follow the path to the railway. Cross carefully to a directional signpost at about 3.3 km and after an hour of snowshoeing from the start (more if breaking trail). The route from McGuire going south is the same one used for the Cal-Cheak campground to Brandywine Falls route. It is repeated here to avoid having to flip back and forth between two different descriptions.

Facing east, enter the forest to the right and snowshoe southward, through private property, along a trail that occasionally is marked with tape. Gradually turn left and cross a small bridge. Climb a short incline in a ravine and then traverse to the right. A small open area is at the top. Continue in a southerly direction, soon arriving at a Brandywine Falls Park boundary sign at about 3.9 km and after 1¾ hours of snowshoeing. Turn right and continue, climbing a slight slope that leads to a small lake on the left at about 4.2 km. Facing north, you will see steep-sided rock on your left. Head around the hill by angling across the slope on the right side to avoid snow shelves on the left that may break off. Once on flatter open ground at the top of the hill, curve around to the left and regain the path below. Continue on and soon a fairly large lake at approximately 4.8 km can be seen on the left. Stay on the path, midway along the slope. There are bog holes and standing water in ponds along here, both of which can be disguised by a skim of ice and snow. Just before you descend back into the forest, an open viewpoint gives a clear outlook toward Black Tusk. The trail now follows a short valley, again with large wet areas and rocks on either side. For a short time the route follows parallel and in sight of the railway track.

At about 5.1 km there is a BC Parks sign saying the trail straight ahead is closed. This is to protect the unique wetland habitat of the rare red-legged frogs found here. Turn to the left and snowshoe through the forest on a wide path on a diagonal leading slightly to the right.

At approximately 5.5 km, emerge into the hydro right-of-way. Cross this area (about 200 m) at first fairly close to the forest on the right and then heading diagonally upward to a tape on a bush midway across that leads to a grove of conifers to the right of tall rock cliffs. Here the entrance to an old logging road can be found. Snowshoe along this pleasant path and emerge once again onto the hydro right-of-way at about 6.1 km from the trailhead. A signpost now gives directions to the bungee jumping bridge (800 m) and via the bungee jump access road back to the Cal-Cheak suspension bridge (2.2 km). However, the path to Brandywine Falls is across the hydro right-of-way, curving slightly to the left to an opening in the forest and a moderately wide track. From here to Brandywine Falls the trail is often used by dog walkers, so it may be well tramped. The route continues south, leading to a lookout with a very steep drop-off. Examples of black basalt rock can be seen, as well as Daisy Lake to the left. (Daisy Lake was enlarged by BC Hydro to supply water for its Cheakamus generating station on the Squamish River, via an 11 km tunnel drilled beneath Cloudburst Mountain.) Continue and emerge once again onto the hydro right-of-way. Cross diagonally southward toward a hydro tower, passing around it on the left close to its base, and then head west towards the forest. Enter and shortly after there is a second lookout with an even steeper drop-off.

Walk downward along the path for about another 30 minutes, first heading north and then winding back south. A long, gentle climb follows. The trail then parallels the railway, and at close to 7.8 km (8 km if visiting the falls), intersects with it. A directional post indicates that Brandywine Falls is 100 m to the left. Making a side trip to view this 70 m cataract surrounded by lacy ice and long icicles is worthwhile. Carefully cross the railway tracks and continue on the wide, easy path back to the trailhead at about 8.6 km.

Mount Atwell from Red Heather Meadows   PHOTOGRAPHER: CLIFF KELSEY

The original Diamond Head Lodge ca. 1979   PHOTOGRAPHER: ANNE BREVIG

ACCESS: Drive north on Highway 99 (Sea to Sky) to Squamish and turn right at Mamquam Road (just before the Canadian Tire). Follow signs marking the way to Garibaldi Park (Diamond Head), which leads through a housing area and past the private Quest University campus. The route turns into a gravel-based logging road. Snow tires are required here, and to advance to the summer parking lot chains are mandatory. Without tire chains there will be an additional about 1.9 km trek on the road before starting.

FEES: $15 per person if staying overnight in the Elfin Lakes cabin.

RATING: easy to Red Heather Meadows; moderate from Meadows to Elfin Lakes because of total distance and terrain

SEASON: late November to April

MAPS: 92G14 Cheakamus River; 92G15 Mamquam Mountain

BEGINNING ALTITUDE: 955 m at parking lot

DESTINATION ALTITUDE: 1407 m at Red Heather Meadows; 1565 m at Paul Ridge; 1485 m at Elfin Lakes

DISTANCE: 9.2 km round trip to Red Heather Meadows; 11.6 km round trip to Paul Ridge; 22 km round trip to Elfin Lakes

TIME: 3–3½ hours round trip to Red Heather Meadows; add 1½ hours to Paul Ridge and back to the Meadows; 7–8 hours round trip to Elfin Lakes, depending on snow conditions

CELLPHONE ACCESS: yes

FOOD AND DRINK: Squamish

WASHROOMS: outhouse at summer parking lot and at Red Heather Meadows and Elfin Lakes

DOGS: dogs are NOT ALLOWED AT ALL in Garibaldi Park

AVALANCHE CONDITIONS: **avalanche.ca**

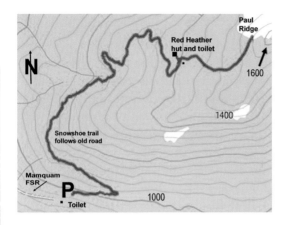

This popular route located in Garibaldi Provincial Park is an easy, steady uphill snowshoe along an old access road that once led to the now removed Diamond Head Lodge at Elfin Lakes. Depending on your energy or ambition it can provide access to the cozy Red Heather day shelter and its wood burning stove, the mellow, open terrain of Paul Ridge or a hard-earned rest in the Elfin Lakes shelter.

Directions

About 20 minutes after leaving the summer parking lot, there is one view looking back over the town of Squamish and towards the islands in Howe Sound. From then on, the beauty is in the surrounding snow-covered trees, spiders on the snow and tracks of animals until another view over the Squamish River estuary can be seen at about 3.7 km. In early winter and spring, at about 2.4 km and an hour along the trail, a waterfall with icicles and ice formations over large slabs of rock can be seen on the right-hand side. Approximately 1¾ hours of snowshoeing leads to a tight bend in the trail and, on the left, ski tracks and (sometimes) marker poles heading into the trees. Either stick to the easy-to-follow roadbed for another 10–15 minutes or, if marker poles are in place, take the slightly shorter track through the woods to the warming hut. After approximately 2 hours of snowshoeing on the road trail, you will see the warming hut, with the outhouse a short bit farther along. The warming hut is just that – no camping or sleeping is allowed. However, there is a wood stove for drying wet clothes and usually gas for a hotplate to make soup or hot chocolate. There is no water source at the hut.

Beginning just beyond the Red Heather shelter, BC Parks marks the winter route to Elfin Lakes via Paul Ridge with orange-topped poles. The track starts off heading east for about 500 m before making a sharp switchback left and cutting back to hug the west side of the ridge well above the summer trail and the avalanche terrain in that area. Look behind you while climbing up to the ridge – the majesty of the surrounding mountains can be seen from the warming hut onwards. If the weather co-operates, a preferred lunch spot is about 1.2 km along this trail to the high point on Paul Ridge, where the views include the downward route to Elfin Lakes, as well as Columnar Peak, the Gargoyles, Opal Cone, Mount Atwell (the diamond-shaped mountain beside the Garibaldi Massif) to the northwest and Mamquam Mountain to the east. During weekdays and after new snowfall this trail to the ridge may involve breaking track – take turns with everyone in the group leading this strenuous activity.

Elfin Lakes Trail

The next approximately 5 km from Paul Ridge to Elfin Lakes (originally called Crystal Lakes) is in high alpine terrain. Weather can change quickly, with rapid accumulation of deep snow and whiteout conditions so that marker poles are not visible, and off the track there is very steep terrain. When snowshoeing to Elfin Lakes it is best to make the trip as an overnighter – especially from December to late February, when daylight hours are short.

Directions

Follow the orange markers steadily downward, passing by the swimming lake and the water supply lake just before reaching the ranger cabin and the outhouse, to arrive at the Elfin Lakes cabin. Here you can sleep, eat and enjoy. Although there is capacity for 33 people in bunk beds in the upper level, places fill up fast on sunny weekends. Many people prefer to make use of the cooking area and tables on the main floor before retreating to their tents or snow caves for a quiet night's sleep.

Return by the same route as you came up.

GARIBALDI PARK AND DIAMOND HEAD CHALET

Garibaldi Provincial Park is a 194,676 hectare wilderness established in 1927 as the second provincial park in BC. When he surveyed the area in 1860, Captain Richards in HMS *Plumper* named the area after Giuseppe Garibaldi, a 19th-century Italian general and statesman who was a pivotal military figure in the creation of Italy and engaged in a lifelong fight against oppression of his countrymen. With over 90 km of marked summer hiking trails, Garibaldi Provincial Park also provides numerous additional snowshoeing possibilities.

Up until 2009 when the last decaying remnants were removed because of safety issues, a piece of history was standing beside the two Elfin Lakes. Diamond Head Chalet was built in 1945 by Ottar and Emil Brandvold and Joan Mathews. It was the first high-altitude ski lodge to be developed in BC north of Vancouver. Access to the chalet required a four-hour ferry trip to Squamish, followed by a six- or seven-hour hike to the lodge. A corner of the old lodge has been retained as a historical artifact. Learn more about the history of the lodge at this Hollyburn Heritage Society page: **is.gd/WwP2x8**.

Tetrahedron Provincial Park: Edwards Cabin Trail

ACCESS: Drive Highway 101 (Sunshine Coast Highway) to Sechelt. At the first traffic light turn north to Wharf Avenue and then to East Porpoise Bay Road, which becomes Sechelt Inlet Road. Follow this for about 9.5 km. Cross Gray Creek, and after about 300 m, soon after a "Truck Crossing 150 m" sign, turn right onto Todd Road (also called the Gray Creek logging road). Drive about 11 km to the lower parking lot. The road is usually plowed as far as the lower parking area, but taking an AWD with high clearance and winter tires is still essential, or, even better, take a four-wheel-drive equipped with tire chains and know how to use them.

RATING: easy terrain

SEASON: mid-December to March

MAP: 92G12 Sechelt Inlet

BEGINNING ALTITUDE: 840 m at lower parking lot

DESTINATION ALTITUDES: 1125 m at Edwards Cabin; 1060 m at Batchelor Cabin

DISTANCE: 12.2 km round trip to Edwards; 6.8 km round trip to Batchelor; (both are from lower parking lot)

TIME: 4½–5 hours round trip to Edwards; 2–2½ hours round trip to Batchelor

CELLPHONE ACCESS: no

FOOD AND DRINK: Sechelt

WASHROOMS: outhouses at summer trailhead and at cabins

DOGS: Dogs are NOT ALLOWED AT ALL in this provincial park, which has within its boundaries the main water supply for local communities

AVALANCHE CONDITIONS: **avalanche.ca**

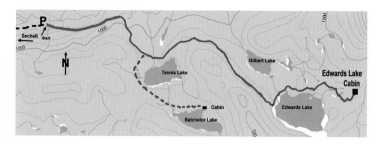

The winter snowshoe trails that go directly to either Edwards Cabin or Batchelor Cabin offer a view of valleys, mountains and open terrain. Close to each cabin is a lake that is part of the Sunshine Coast drinking water system. The trip to Batchelor makes an easy family trip for young children and could be used as their first overnight winter snowshoe/camping experience, since it is a short distance for parents to backpack all the overnight gear. There is a fee for staying at either the Batchelor or the Edwards cabin. See **tetoutdoor.ca/park--cabin-info.html** *for details.*

In winter the trip to either Edwards or Batchelor begins at the lower parking lot. Although there are winter trails shown on the pdf map linked from the BC Parks webpage for Tetrahedron Provincial Park, they make use of trails that cross lakes (Gilbert and Edwards lakes to Edwards Cabin and Tannis Lake to Batchelor Cabin). Given the wide variation in winter temperatures related to climate change, both BC Parks and we strongly recommend using the summer overland routes if you are at all unsure of the ice conditions on these lakes.

Directions

Pass by the locked yellow gate and snowshoe for about 1 km along the logging road to the summer parking lot. The winter trail via Gilbert Lake begins to the left. The trail described here goes past a signpost saying it is 4.9 km to Edwards Cabin and

Edwards Cabin, New Year's Day 2016   PHOTOGRAPHER: PATRICK NOLAN

2.4 km to Batchelor Cabin. The route continues up a gradual hill for about 660 m. After about 45 minutes from the start, the trail forms a Y junction with the path to Batchelor Cabin. For the trail to Edwards, continue to the left and follow the winding road for about another 900 m, with a gradual elevation gain to about 1084 m that gives greater views in all directions. Pass by large boulders at Victor's Landing at about 2.4 km and continue to the right along the slope of the hill. With steep rocks above and clear-cuts below, check this area for snow stability before crossing. At approximately 4.2 km the trail enters the woods and progresses to Edwards Lake. High orange winter markers help trace the path, which continues along the edge of the lake to a signpost indicating the cabin is 1.7 km away. The next part of the trail leaves the lakeshore and begins a climb through forest. On the left, about 100 m from the signpost and marked by flagging tape, faded markers and a large standing hollow snag, is the exit (or return trail) for the winter trail via the lake.

Upon reaching Edwards Cabin after approximately 6.1 km from the lower parking lot, a view can be seen to the northeast of part of the steep area to be climbed if Mount Steele Cabin is a destination – a suitable overnight backpack stay for energetic and experienced snowshoers. Edwards Cabin has tables, a stove and cooking area and sleeping accommodations upstairs. It also is reported to have mice and squirrels as cohabitants. Enjoy the warmth, eat your lunch and in the journal write a thank-you to the Tetrahedron Outdoor Club members who built the Tetrahedron Park cabins in 1987 and continue to maintain them.

Return on the same land trail as the one used to arrive at the cabin, a faster trip now with the majority of it on a downward slope.

NOTE: If you plan to go beyond Edwards Cabin you'll need good map-reading and route-finding skills. Do not go if avalanche ratings are high. The Tetrahedron Outdoor Club warns: "High winds create unstable slabs all around Mt. Steele and its interconnecting ridges. A very significant avalanche hazard exists in the west-facing bowl between Mt. Steele and its lesser peak to the southwest."

Tetrahedron Provincial Park: Batchelor Cabin Trail

For Batchelor Cabin turn right at the signposted junction reached after about 45 minutes from the start. Continue to snowshoe for about 430 m, then turn left at a sign close to a gravel pit. Tannis Lake will be below on the left as the trail continues, and soon Batchelor Lake will be on the right. Snowshoe for another approximately 1.4 km to the cabin, located at 1060 m elevation by the edge of Batchelor Lake.

TETRAHEDRON PROVINCIAL PARK

In 1995 Tetrahedron Provincial Park was one of several created under the Lower Mainland Nature Legacy. Within its 6000 hectares it contains Tetrahedron Peak (1727 m), Panther Peak (1681 m) and Mt. Steele (1651 m). Although logged in a number of sections before being designated as a provincial park, the area represents the only old-growth forest larger than 1000 hectares on the lower Sunshine Coast. Mountain and western hemlock and yellow cedar forests ranging from 300–1,000 years in age are found in the park.

ACCESS: Drive west on the Sunshine Coast Road (Highway 101) towards Powell River. Take Dixon Road north (opposite Langbay Store) to the E Branch turnoff. See more detailed directions below. A four-wheel-drive vehicle with high clearance is recommended. Chains are useful in heavy snow. These logging roads are restricted from 5 a.m. to 8 p.m. weekdays but check about weekend logging traffic as well.

RATING: easy terrain

SEASON: December to late March

MAP: 92F16 Haslam Lake

BEGINNING ALTITUDE: 676 m at pullout at the bridge

DESTINATION ALTITUDE: 1075 m at E Branch cabin; 1210 m at A Branch cabin

DISTANCE: 12.2 km round trip to E Branch cabin

TIME: 4–4½ hours round trip to E Branch cabin

CELLPHONE ACCESS: intermittent

FOOD AND DRINK: prepare your own at the cozy E Branch cabin with the gas stove (bring your own canister) and wood-pellet stove

WASHROOMS: environmentally considerate use of forest; outhouse at each cabin

DOGS: yes

AVALANCHE CONDITIONS: **avalanche.ca**

LOGGING ROAD INFORMATION: Western Forest Products 24/7 Road Access Hotline 604-485-3132 or office 604-485-3100 ext 0. In order to access the roads during weekdays you must have a radio programmed with the appropriate channels.

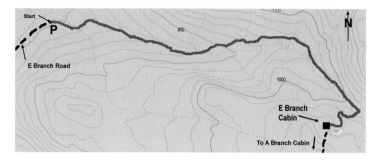

Don't let the distance from the Lower Mainland put you off from visiting the Sunshine Coast and Knuckleheads Winter Recreation Area. Some of the most enjoyable snowshoeing opportunities in southwestern BC are here. Cozy cabins, easy access to the alpine, and multiple routes with stunning views make this an excellent destination for a single- or multi-day trip.

This peaceful logging road trail, with a gentle upward grade through a forest, leads to a small cabin rebuilt on a site where once a ski lodge and tow shed stood. Getting to this cabin on the logging roads is half the adventure, and with any luck on the drive in or out the resident herd of 10 to 12 elk may be seen taking a leisurely stroll across the road and munching their way through the clear-cut areas.

The approach to both E Branch and A Branch cabins is initially the same. Note that these roads are in active logging areas and so there are some one-way ones. Contact the Road Access Hotline noted opposite for any closures and current logging work, which occurs 7 days a week from 5 a.m. to 8 p.m. On weekends there may be less truck traffic. Caution should be taken at all times when driving.

Directions

Reset your odometer at the beginning of Dixon Road (opposite Langbay Store). At approximately 3.9 km is Goat Lake Hookup

Road. Go left on the one-way system, staying on the main road. Continue on past a sign for Goat Lake Main and Tin Hat Junction at about 4.7 km. Stay on the main road to 12 km, turning right at the sign for Stillwater Main. (A wooden sign also indicates that the direction is indeed towards the Knuckleheads.) At approximately 12.8 km turn left at Tin Hat Junction onto the continuation of Stillwater Main and continue on past the Horseshoe Creek sign. Soon after, on the right, there is a sign for the portage that is part of the Powell Lake canoe route to Lois Lake. At Freda Main, at about 17.1 km, continue on the right to approximately 19.7 km, where the road takes a left turn at the fork. Additional wooden signs point the way to the Knuckleheads, Mount Freda and Alpha, Beta and Gamma lakes. This road continues to be Stillwater Main. At marker 14, about 21.8 km, hydro lines can be seen to the right, and at about 24 km the A Branch marker occurs. Stay to the left on a road that continues to run parallel to the hydro lines slash. At 25.3 km turn right on E Branch, crossing under the power lines, and drive towards a stand of trees. **NOTE:** From here on, it is essential to have a four-wheel-drive vehicle with high clearance, since this track is a decommissioned forest road with numerous deep dips and some small stream crossings. Depending on snowfall and time of year, the wide areas at about 28 km from the start and at 28.4 km where there is a bridge on the left may be the best places to park. At 29.9 km there is a second bridge, and even if the route has continued to be passable, parking here is definitely recommended, since after the bridge the road rapidly deteriorates into a rocky stream bed.

Now the snowshoe trail begins (after the second bridge), winding gently uphill on the continuation of the logging road. Even with heavy snowfalls there may be numerous dips that have to be traversed down and up – look for the lowest level of snow without running water under it and cross there. Although some

The big broom will help to leave E Branch cabin clean

of these areas have log bridge crossings, those can be deceptive. It is easy to misjudge how wide they are – possibly OK for hiking boots but too narrow for snowshoes. As the cabin gets closer, there are several wide and substantial bridges that make crossing the dips safe and fast.

After about two hours (longer if breaking track) and about 3.65 km of snowshoeing, a large orange marker can be seen on a tree, with a metal bridge to the right of the sign. You have reached

Water Can Junction, a place where in early skiing days a water can was left to be filled from Alpha Creek and carried up to the lodge. This creek continues to be the main source of water other than melted snow if plans include staying overnight at the cabin.

Cross the bridge, turn right and walk uphill for about 10 minutes. Turn left and climb for another 25 minutes, following the cleared trail, and the cabin will soon appear at about 6.1 km. This was the original lift shack for the Mount Diadem Ski Club. It can accommodate 6–8 people for sleeping and has a wood-pellet stove, picnic table and a propane gas stove for cooking (bring your own canisters). For an overnight stay, individuals need to bring their own sleeping pads, sleeping bags, food, dishes, cutlery, pots and pans. The outhouse is 30 m northeast of the cabin.

Once at the cabin, a view of the Knuckleheads can be seen to the north. If they are not completely covered with snow, the Knuckles do indeed look like a closed fist, with the small lump on the right resembling the thumb. So those early Knucklehead skiers who built the ski tow and lodge here weren't just "stupid or dull-witted" (the *Canadian Oxford Dictionary* definition of "knucklehead"); they were identified by the geography of their ski hill.

Return on the same trail as the ascent.

Additional trails

There are numerous options for additional exploration by snowshoe. There is a summer marked trail from E Branch cabin to join up with the route to A Branch cabin. New markings are planned for this roughly 1.6 km trail so it will be clearly marked for winter travel.

Logging Road E400 from E Branch towards A Branch is 1.5 km; the old clear-cut area has 2 km of roads; A700 is 1.5 km long; A900 is 3 km; and there is a 6-foot-wide trail between the end of E400 into the clear-cut area that has a steep beginning then levels out.

Additional trails being cleared are a switchback of 2 km on the old road for E Branch towards Alpha Lake and the peaks at the Mount of the Moon, and a path down from Mount of the Moon to Alpha Lake. A paper map showing many of these decommissioned logging roads is available from Powell River Tourism, **powellriver. info/tourism**.

Remember that any slope can potentially become an avalanche – especially open, steep ones – and that by staying within treed areas and on logging roads, some protection is afforded but not assured.

A Branch cabin
The road to A Branch cabin, the one that was passed on the right at about 24 km when approaching E Branch road, may be decommissioned in 2016 due to persistent vandalism by a few irresponsible locals. At present, and depending on snow depth, the road can be driven for 6 km to a locked gate. From here it is about 2.5 km to get to A Branch cabin, which is in a clearing at about 1210 m elevation with wonderful views (especially from the no-door outhouse!).

To find out the status of this cabin and road for winter use from 2016 onwards, get in touch with Knuckleheads Winter Recreation Association at **theknuckleheads.wordpress.com/contact-us**.

KNUCKLEHEADS
The Knuckleheads Recreation Area is located in the Pacific Coast Range and is approximately 4.8 km by 3.2 km in size, with the ridge from the Knuckleheads extending in a westerly direction. Although recent recognition of its potential as a backcountry destination has seen more support for outdoor recreation development, it has a history of community use and facility construction. The Mount Diadem Ski Club was formed

in 1959 by a group of climbers. (The climbers mistakenly identified Mount Freda as Mount Diadem – or perhaps just liked the name better.) By the 1960s the Knucklehead location was well frequented by local cross-country and downhill skiers. A lodge was built by volunteers and a tow shack constructed to take skiers to the top of the area at the end of E Branch. The roads that were left after the end of extensive logging provided the trails for cross-country skiers. Although a core group of volunteers did all the construction and maintenance, the lodge was used by many outdoors people and families. Unfortunately it was also a destination for vandals. While the fire that destroyed it in 1977 was not deliberately set, no plans were made to rebuild the lodge and the ski club was dissolved by its discouraged participants.

However, the area continued to remain popular as a backcountry destination, and the little tow hut (E Branch cabin) was used as a shelter. In 2002 a group consisting of members of the Sunshine Coast Forest District Local 2171 of the loggers union, Sliammon First Nation, Weyerhaeuser's Stillwater Division, the Powell River Rotary Club and Knuckleheads Winter Recreation Association joined together to build A Branch cabin. Materials were donated by forest product companies and local Powell River businesses. Members of the Knuckleheads Association take primary responsibility for maintaining these cabins and are developing plans for future ones in various areas such as near the peak called The Sentinel.

WHISTLER INTERPRETIVE FOREST TRAILS

WHISTLER INTERPRETIVE FOREST

The 3000 hectare Whistler Interpretive Forest encompasses a variety of trees, geological formations and terrain. It is co-operatively managed by the BC Ministry of Forests, the Resort Municipality of Whistler and Pacific Forest Products Ltd. The area is used to explore sustainable forestry practices and biodiversity in the forest setting. As an extra there is a wide array of well-marked trails on old logging roads that wind throughout the forest and are used for walking, biking, cross-country skiing and snowshoeing. See **whistler.com/pdf/maps/interpretive-forest-map.pdf** for a map.

ACCESS: Drive north on Highway 99 (Sea to Sky) to the Function Junction stoplight. Turn right onto Cheakamus Lake Road. Cross over the wide cement bridge and turn right on Legacy Way. Turn left to Mount Fee Road, go to its end and park in the Mount Fee lot. **NOTE:** Parking on streets in Whistler during the winter is prohibited.

RATING: easy terrain but a long distance if going to the park boundary

SEASON: mid-December to mid-March

MAP: 92J03 Brandywine

BEGINNING ALTITUDE: 634 m

DESTINATION ALTITUDE: 1030 m at park boundary; 1060 m at trail high point

DISTANCE: 14.6 km round trip to Garibaldi Park boundary

TIME: 4½–5 hours round trip

CELLPHONE ACCESS: yes

FOOD AND DRINK: Cheaky's Café at the youth hostel on Legacy Way

WASHROOMS: Cheaky's Café

DOGS: yes

AVALANCHE CONDITIONS: **avalanche.ca**

This snowshoe trail is a steady upward walk on a forestry access road that is used for servicing the microwave relay tower below Black Tusk. The trail makes a very good dog-walking path, and if snow conditions are good, friends who cross-country ski may enjoy the terrain (and break a trail) as well. When it leaves the side of the Cheakamus River and turns to the right to the locked yellow gate it may require breaking trail unless the maintenance

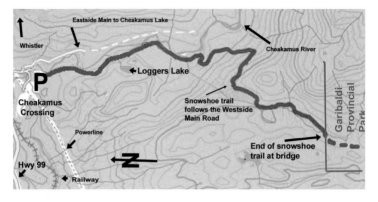

snowmobile has been in to service the microwave. The best un-impeded views of Black Tusk are at about 7.3 km, where the beginning of Garibaldi Provincial Park is indicated on a signpost south of a large new bridge.

Directions

To begin, cross over the snowbanks at the northeast end of the Mount Fee parking lot to reach the Westside Main Road. Turn right and begin snowshoeing along a gently rising trail that leads to a rather steep hill. The road levels out as it reaches the Logger's Lake parking lot and information board after about 1.8 km. The road now is fairly level as it follows along the course of the Cheakamus River. Just before a right-angle turn, the road meets the river again at its edge after about 3.4 km and one hour of snowshoeing.

Make a right turn and begin a steady upward ascent. Soon, at about 4 km, a yellow locked gate comes into view. Pass beside it and continue snowshoeing upwards. And upwards and upwards – generally a gentle elevation gain with long switchbacks followed by long straight (still upward) sections. The views are of forest scenes, wildlife tracks, and sun and shadows on the snow. At about 6.4 km, on the right-hand side, there are flagging tapes

Black Tusk in winter   PHOTOGRAPHER: CLIFF KELSEY

and signs in the forest indicating the trail to the eastern Jane Lakes. The access to these lakes is across a fast-flowing river on a rounded, slippery log. Even in summer it is quite sketchy to use this, but then, in summer with low water, wading is an option. Just not today, thanks.

Continue for about another 900 m to reach the destination – a wide new bridge crossing a tumbling, icy river fed by the glaciers surrounding the Tusk. Eat lunch while looking at the volcanic cone that creates Black Tusk.

The northern boundary of Garibaldi Provincial Park is immediately south of the bridge.

Return on the same trail – generally much faster with only a few gentle ups on the way down.

An alternative to snowshoeing on the road along the Cheakamus River for the return is to take the forest Riverside Trail (indicated by a blue sign on the left of the downward trail) before reaching the yellow gate. It runs parallel to Westside Main Road and intersects with Basalt Spur Trail at 400 m (where it is easy to return to Westside Main Road). The forest path continues, to come out close to the Loggers Lake information map and Westside Main Road after about 2 km from the intersection sign. This trail is not marked in winter and may need trail-breaking but it is a pleasant alternative to road-walking and is about the same distance.

THE TUSK

Black Tusk – a favourite photo op for visitors to Whistler – is the hard lava-core remains of a stratovolcano that was built up from layers of various materials ejected from the centre. It was formed about 1.1 to 1.3 million years ago. The summit was created about 170,000 years ago after glaciation and more cinder and lava production. The softer cinder easily wore away, leaving the core. The peak of the Tusk is at 2319 m, while the microwave relay tower is at about 1800 m.

The Squamish First Nations name for the Tusk is "landing place of the Thunderbird." The Thunderbird is often given the characteristics of power, vengefulness and intelligence. In Squamish legend about the Tusk, it is said the peak's black colouring and jagged shape were created by the Thunderbird's lightning.

ACCESS: Drive Highway 99 (Sea to Sky) to the Function Junction traffic light and turn right on Cheakamus Lake Road. Park to the left in the lot by the Whistler Interpretive Forest sign. If this lot is full, cross the wide cement bridge, turn right onto Legacy Way, then left onto Mount Fee Road and park in the lot at the end of the road. **NOTE:** No parking is allowed on municipal roads in Whistler during the winter.

RATING: easy terrain but long distance

SEASON: December to mid-March

MAPS: 92J02 Whistler; 92J03 Brandywine

BEGINNING ALTITUDE: 618 m

DESTINATION ALTITUDE: 853 m (at day use area at lake)

DISTANCE: 14 km round trip to summer parking lot; 18 km round trip to day use area at lake

TIME: 4–4½ hours round trip to summer parking lot; 6–6½ hours round trip to day use area

CELLPHONE ACCESS: yes

FOOD AND DRINK: Cheaky's Café at the youth hostel on Legacy Way; Olives at Function Junction

WASHROOMS: Cheaky's Café at the youth hostel; trailhead to the lake; day use area by the lake

DOGS: all dogs must be on leash in provincial parks

AVALANCHE CONDITIONS: **avalanche.ca**

This easy trail begins at the sign indicating Eastside Main Road, which is to the left of the main Cheakamus Lake road and before the bridge leading to Cheakamus Crossing.

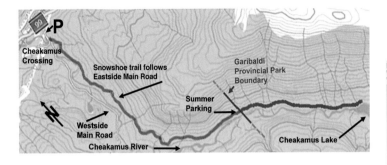

Directions

After parking at the Whistler Interpretive Forest sign, walk along Valley Trail to Eastside Main Road on the left. Put your snowshoes on and begin a gentle upward stretch of about 7 km towards the Cheakamus Lake trailhead. The road to the trailhead may be used by snowmobilers, who provide the service of packing down new snow. However, for a snowmobiler it is a short trip, so there are generally few vehicles on the road. There will be several signs on the right along the way for loop trails in the Interpretive Forest and one trail sign on the left at approximately 2.3 km (opposite Crater View Lookout) indicating Highline Trail. At about 3.9 km on the left there is a small sign that may cause laughter: "See colours and puke." This is the exit to a mountain-biking route that is steep (300 m elevation gain in 2 km) and has numerous hairpin turns – hence the graphic title.

After several hours of walking along the road, you reach the wide summer parking area. On sunny winter days the place is often filled with sparkling snow and the view opens to the south hills and mountains. For short winter days or tired legs this may become the destination of choice. The outdoor toilet can be found across the parking lot, on the left just after the trailhead to the lake.

The way to the lake runs parallel to the Cheakamus River and is blazed with orange tree markers and high tagging ribbon, so trail finding should not present a problem. It is a favourite with cross-country skiers, whose tracks may also provide a path. The trail begins on the other side of a rockslide chute (which needs to be assessed for snow stability before crossing, since this is a significant avalanche zone) and then heads into mixed deciduous and coniferous forest. After 20 minutes of snowshoeing and about 7.9 km from the start, the deep forest of cedar, Douglas fir and western hemlock begins. From here to the lake there are numerous large trees of all three varieties to marvel at. After some 40 minutes of snowshoeing, a sign at about 8.4 km indicates the trail to a bridge over the river and southwest to Helm Lake Trail. Continue winding through the tall trees and eventually the trail emerges to again parallel the Cheakamus River. To reach the first day use area located by the lake, it is a total of approximately 9.1 km one way from the start at Eastside Main and over 3 to 3½ hours of snowshoeing. Add at least another 2 hours round trip if progressing to Singing Creek campground (7 km from the summer parking area). The day use area is the most popular stopping place, so the trail on to Singing Pass Creek may need the trail broken – adding even more time. This distance is not advisable for a day trip when winter light is briefer.

Return the same way – much easier and faster now with a generally downward direction to reach the trailhead.

While this trail is straightforward, it is long at approximately 18 km round trip to the lake, so it requires a very early start even when winter days begin to lengthen. However, there is a reward for planning to go the extra approximately 2 kilometres through the forest to the day use area (especially on a sunny day): the frozen lake with the winter vista of white-clad mountains, glaciers and trees presents a memorable image.

ACCESS: Travelling north along Highway 99 (Sea to Sky) to Whistler, turn right at the first stoplight at the outskirts of Whistler (Function Junction) to Cheakamus Lake Road. Continue for about 300 m, crossing a cement bridge, and turn right on Legacy Way towards Cheakamus Crossing (the former 2010 Olympics Athletes Village). Turn left onto Mount Fee Road and park at the end in a small lot. This area is often rutted and good snow tires are needed to get in and out of it. If parking is not available here, there may be additional space immediately to the left after turning onto Cheakamus Lake Road, in a lot to the north of the Whistler Interpretive Forest sign. **NOTE**: in winter no parking is allowed on municipal roads in Whistler.

RATING: easy terrain but may be untracked on Highline section

SEASON: mid-December to late March

MAP: 92J02 Whistler

BEGINNING ALTITUDE: 618 m

DESTINATION ALTITUDE: 770 m

DISTANCE: 6.4 km loop trail (6.9 km back to Mount Fee)

TIME: 2½–3 hours (more if breaking trail)

CELLPHONE ACCESS: yes

FOOD AND DRINK: Cheaky's Café in the youth hostel on Legacy Way; Function Junction; Whistler Creekside and Village

WASHROOMS: Cheaky's Café – opens at 7 a.m. on weekdays, 9:00 a.m. on weekends

DOGS: yes

AVALANCHE CONDITIONS: **avalanche.ca**

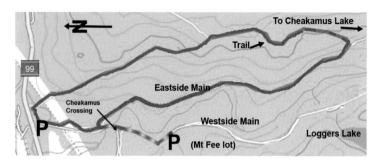

This trail provides a short experience of snowshoeing in Whistler Interpretive Forest and begins and ends close to bus stops at Function Junction and Cheakamus Crossing (former site of the Olympic athletes village) for those vacationing at Whistler without a car. It is easy terrain – initially following the well-used Eastside Main, frequented by dog-walkers, cross-country skiers and snowshoers. This may require speedy evasive action on the part of snowshoers who might experience a skier hurtling towards them on a narrow track. However, the Highline cross trail will provide a contrast to the more popular initial part of the trail. It often requires breaking track if there is new snow, so progress may be slower, but this provides extra exercise and the novelty of walking in untracked snow.

Directions

If parking in the Mount Fee lot, turn left on the snow-covered Westside Main road that parallels the Cheakamus River and walk back towards Cheakamus Lake Road for about 15 minutes. Cross a small bridge with green metal railings. Turn right and walk to the stop sign. A sign indicates Eastside Main, the road that eventually leads to the Cheakamus Lake trail. Highline Trail begins partway along this logging road. An alternative trail, so that backtracking is not needed, is to turn right on Westside Main Road after leaving the Mount Fee parking lot and walk across

"CHEAKAMUS"

The word Cheakamus is said to be from the Squamish word "ch'iyákmesh," "people of the fish weir," an indication of the salmon habitat and fishing that the lower Cheakamus River provides. Cheakamus Lake has catch and release, a bait ban and a single barbless hook restriction for fishing the rainbow trout and Dolly Varden char found in its glacial waters.

the suspension bridge to reach Eastside Main Road shortly before it intersects with Highline Trail. If parking in the lot by the Whistler Interpretive Forest sign, walk on Valley Trail until the cement bridge, go down the embankment to the left of the bridge and turn left to approach the stop sign at the intersection with Eastside Main Road.

After walking along Eastside Main for approximately 15 minutes, the first of several Farside Trail signs can be seen. This trail provides an option of walking closer to the Cheakamus River and under the trees parallel to the road rather than on the road trail. After approximately 1.4 km the Farside river trail emerges at the suspension bridge, where a left turn brings snowshoers back to the trail on Eastside Main Road.

For those who chose to stay on the Eastside Main Road trail, after about 40 minutes of snowshoeing and approximately 2.0 km on the road, a sign for Cross Valley Trail gives directions to the suspension bridge.

At about 2.4 km and 1 hour of gradual uphill walking since the beginning on Eastside Main, a sign on the right indicates a Valleyview lookout area (and trail back to the suspension bridge). On the left of the road is a sign to Highline Trail.

Turn left and walk along a wide cut with both deciduous and coniferous trees on either side. After approximately 2.8 km (from the beginning of the trail at the stop sign on Eastside Main Road), a large swamp to the right can be seen below a cliff. From this point the trail for a short while often has running water in small streams under or beside it that creates deep depressions or wet spots that need to be crossed. Carefully explore the solidity of the base of snow or depth of water before stepping on any snow bridge or crossing a puddle. After another 100 m there is a small clearing and a sign saying it is 1.2 km to return to Valleyview Lookout close to where the Highline trail began. Continue upwards on the trail and after approximately 2.7 km of walking on the Highline (according to the signpost), emerge to intersect with Microwave Hill Road. This intersection is about 3.6 km from the Mount Fee parking lot. With any luck this road will have been packed by the snowmobile that takes workers up to service the microwave tower, saving a lot more trail-breaking. Walk about 1.4 km down the road past a large cement water tank on the left that has samples of colourful graffiti. Continue to where the road intersects under the powerlines with Valley Trail. Walk about 150 m straight ahead to the bottom of the hill or turn left and then right, following the S trail downwards for approximately 300 m towards Highway 99. Turn left to reach the parking lot by the Whistler Interpretive Forest sign. Part of the return to the cement bridge and then to the Mount Fee parking lot can be done by entering the forest at this point and following the Interpretive Forest signs. An alternative is to walk along the well-maintained Valley Trail and the Westside Main snow path for about another 20 minutes and about 1.3 km.

ACCESS: Travelling north along Highway 99 (Sea to Sky) towards Whistler, at the first stoplight on the outskirts of town (Function Junction), turn right onto Cheakamus Lake Road. Cross a cement bridge and turn right on Legacy Way towards Cheakamus Crossing (the former 2010 Olympics athletes village). Turn left onto Mount Fee Road and park at the end in a small lot. This lot is often rutted and good snow tires are needed to get in and out of it. If parking is not available here, there may be additional space immediately to the left after turning onto Cheakamus Lake Road, in a lot to the north of the Whistler Interpretive Forest sign. **NOTE:** in winter no parking is allowed on municipal roads in Whistler.

RATING: easy to moderate terrain

SEASON: mid-December to late March

MAP: 92J03 Brandywine

BEGINNING ALTITUDE: 634 m

DESTINATION ALTITUDE: 755 m at lake; 806 m at high point

DISTANCE: 5.1 km loop trail

TIME: 2½–3 hours

CELLPHONE ACCESS: yes

FOOD AND DRINK: Cheaky's Café in the youth hostel on Legacy Way; Function Junction; Whistler Creekside and Village

WASHROOMS: Cheaky's Café – opens at 7 a.m. on weekdays, 9:00 a.m. on weekends

DOGS: yes

AVALANCHE CONDITIONS: **avalanche.ca**

The loop trail to Logger's Lake and back by way of Ridge Trail offers a variety of terrain and exercise opportunities with some short upward and downward grades and some fantastic views. It is easily accessible by bus from Whistler Village and generally needs little trail-breaking, since it is a favourite of both locals and visitors.

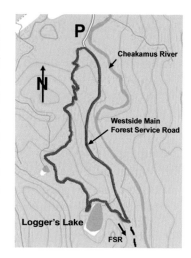

P

Cheakamus River

N

Westside Main
Forest Service Road

Logger's Lake

FSR

Directions

Start at the Mount Fee parking lot and climb over the bank to reach Westside Main Road. If parked in the lot beside the Whistler Interpretive Forest sign, walk along Valley Trail until the concrete bridge on Cheakamus Lake Road. Go over the bank to the road and cross the narrow bridge with green railings. This is the start of the Westside Main road, which gradually increases in elevation as it goes along the Cheakamus River. There is one steeper hill and then the road levels out until it arrives at the Logger's Lake parking lot at approximately 1.8 km. A sign says it is another 350 m to the lake, which is reached after a steep upward journey beside a rock bluff, arriving at the shore after about 2.2 km since the beginning. At an elevation of about 755 m and surrounded by the cone of a volcano, the lake makes an attractive lunch spot on a sunny day. Continue counterclockwise around the lake until you reach a sign indicating Ridge Trail, Crater Rim Trail and Lava Lookout. Turn to the right on Ridge Trail and snowshoe in a northwesterly direction on a gentle upward track. There may be small bushes and trees bent over through the snow but they usually are easy

Looking north from Logger's Lake and Ridge Loop Trail

to pass through. Just before the trail gradually turns north there is a sign marking Crater Rim Trail to the left. While interesting in summer, this is not a safe trail to do in the winter since it has very narrow ridge paths in places and very steep sides. At about 4 km the bushes and trees open up to allow a view of Whistler and Wedge mountains. The trail now begins to descend with traverses through forested terrain for about 900 m. A T junction occurs just before the exit to Westside Main Road, where a left turn will take you back to the parking lot. The right-hand trail from the T leads back to Westside Main Road, while the left-hand option passes through the forest and exits past condominium housing close to the Mount Fee parking lot. Usually the latter route has enough local foot traffic that it is well tracked. With either return trail choice, the total distance is about 5.1 km.

Ancient Cedars Grove Trail

ACCESS: Drive Highway 99 (Sea to Sky) to Whistler and go about 7 km past the resort area. Emerald Estate is the last big development sign on the left. Shortly after, there is a sign on the left indicating Cougar Mountain. Turn onto the road to Cougar Mountain – the Soo River FSR/16 Mile Creek road – and park in the general lot, making sure to avoid the snowmobile unloading zone.

RATING: easy terrain but long distance

SEASON: late December to April

MAP: 92J02 Whistler

BEGINNING ALTITUDE: 683 m at Adventure Centre parking lot

DESTINATION ALTITUDE: 1025 m at Ancient Cedar Grove

DISTANCE: 12.6 km round trip using summer trail; 13.5 km round trip using summer trail out and upper logging road loop back

TIME: 5–6 hours round trip

CELLPHONE ACCESS: no

FOOD AND DRINK: Whistler Village; Nesters complex

WASHROOMS: Whistler Village; Adventure Centre; outhouse at summer parking area

DOGS: yes (but because of snowmobiles, keep dogs on a leash for safety on the main road)

AVALANCHE CONDITIONS: **avalanche.ca**

This snowshoe route is best done in the spring when the days are longer, and on weekdays when there are fewer snowmobile tours on their way into the Soo Valley. Despite the intermittent buzz of

these machines, the trail is quiet for the most part and provides river, valley and mountain views.

Directions

Begin the trail by passing the office of the snowmobile tour company The Adventure Group. While their business adds occasional noise to the valley, their employees and snowmobiles do keep the roads packed and sometimes they track (by foot) the trails into the Ancient Cedars. However, unless backcountry skiers or snowshoers have gone on the summer trail and into the grove, new tracks may have to be broken and this will add to the time to complete the trip.

Continue walking on the road for approximately 3.7 km and to about 852 m elevation to a small wooden building that is the horse barn for summer trail rides. While carrying your snowshoes on this packed road may seem an option, wearing them will provide more traction on the slight upward grade, particularly in the spring when the snow is sugary in texture and boot grip is variable.

Pass by the right side of the cabin and walk along the road, staying to the right at a Y junction.

At about 4 km there is the summer parking area, with the summer trail on the right side. An outhouse is in the woods to the left of the parking lot. The marked trail passes through the forest and exits at about 5.3 km where a right turn leads to the base of the final hill and the beginning of a switchback ascent to the forest entrance. While climbing, look back for a view over the river valley and towards the hills where the more adventurous snowmobilers have left their trails.

The snowshoe trail that now enters the forest to go to the Ancient Cedars may be well tracked by The Adventure Group staff and other snowshoers or a trail may have to be forged through

A long-time tree hugger in the Ancient Cedar Grove

deep snow. There are faded orange streamer tags high in trees to show the trail that runs along a ledge high above the creek and leads to a bridge. Cross the bridge, turn left and then right (to avoid a bog hole) and follow the trail tags to arrive, after a total of approximately 6.3 km, at the centre of the cedar grove. Walk among the trees and feel their energy, enjoy their beauty and marvel at their age. This is a peaceful spot to enjoy lunch.

The return trip can be the same as the ascent trail, or an alternative choice can be to follow the wide forestry road straight

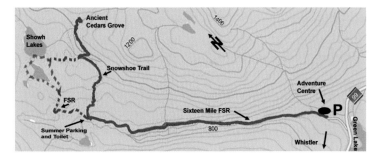

ahead instead of turning left at the exit from the summer trail. The forestry road winds towards the Showh Lakes and passes a direction post for the Showh Lake loop, which you come to after snowshoeing from the Ancient Cedar Grove on the return trip. The Showh Lake loop does not have any markings to assist in winter exploration. Continue on the road until it intersects with the road to the Soo Valley that is used by the snowmobilers. Turn left and snowshoe back to the summer parking lot and from there begin the 4 km of road back to the start.

THE BIG TREES

After seeing such magnificent ancient trees up close, it is easy to become a fan of hiking or snowshoeing to see more of the "big trees" found throughout British Columbia. There are a number of books that give the locations of the groves, notably *Hiking the Ancient Forests of British Columbia and Washington* and *Hiking Guide to the Big Trees of Southwestern British Columbia*, both by Randy Stoltmann. Organizations that focus on saving these groves also provide directions for finding additional ones, for example, the Ancient Forest Alliance, **ancientforestalliance. org**. Also involved with the Alliance's mission are the ancient forest committees of students at UBC, UVic and SFU.

Mid-Flank Trail

ACCESS: Drive north on Highway 99 (Sea to Sky) towards Whistler and turn left at the Function Junction traffic light. Continue to the end of the short road, turn left and park in the lot to the left of or behind Olives Community Market. If planning to leave a pickup car at the Rainbow Lake trailhead, have two vehicles go to the end by turning left on Alta Lake Road, cross the railway tracks and continue for about 7 km, passing the Whistler cemetery, to the parking area by the trailhead sign. Return in one car to the Function Junction parking lot.

RATING: easy terrain with numerous long switchback ascents and descents

SEASON: late December to mid-March

MAPS: 92J02 Whistler; 92J03 Brandywine

BEGINNING ALTITUDE: 605 m

DESTINATION ALTITUDE: 1020 m (high viewpoint on trail); 1029 m high point in woods

DISTANCE: 9.4 km one way

TIME: 4½–5 hours from Function Junction to Rainbow Lake trailhead; 3½–4 hours round trip to high point

CELLPHONE ACCESS: yes

FOOD AND DRINK: Function Junction; Olives Community Market close to the trailhead; Whistler Creekside and Village

WASHROOMS: key for outside toilet at Olives Community Market; gas station in Creekside

DOGS: yes

AVALANCHE CONDITIONS: **avalanche.ca**

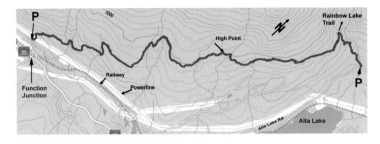

This trip provides an opportunity to go on a trail that traverses the side of Mount Sproatt and provides panoramic views of both Blackcomb and Whistler ski hills. Portions of the route may require breaking track, so depending on the snow conditions this may increase the time it takes. Reaching the high point from either the Function Junction or the Rainbow Lake trailhead makes a good day trip during the winter. Completing the entire trip is possible with an early start in spring when days are getting longer.

Directions

Start at the Function Junction parking lot, where the first challenge is to climb over the gigantic wall of snow on the south side of the lot that is deposited by snowplows. At the edge of the forest is a map of the trail and area. Pass by it on the right and walk a short way through the woods to a junction that usually has a path well trodden by dog owners. The left-hand part of Flank Trail leads 21 km to Alexander Falls. Continue straight ahead, then angle slightly to the left across a flat area with some short bushes and trees poking through the snow. After about 130 m there is an opening in the forest, usually marked with flagging tape. The ascent begins with short traverses to gain the first 100 m of elevation up to a wider path. After about 15 minutes of climbing and some 400 m distance, the trail levels out and then descends briefly. At about 500 m a fork splits

View from Mid-Flank Trail

off to the right – stay to the left. As it continues, the way becomes less obvious, and in heavy snow years the well-defined summer bicycle and hiking path is obscured by bent trees and deep snow. Follow intermittent orange tape on trees until you come to the main logging road trail. The bridges on the way may be piled high with snow with steep sides, making for a narrow base for crossing. Walk slowly and carefully, using your poles to probe snow depth. At about 660 m there is Van West Creek. Along the trail, several creeks and small waterfalls create an opportunity for winter pictures, whether running or frozen. The wide logging road leads to the first viewpoint after about 900 m of snowshoeing. Rocks from a long-ago slide in the open area above and below confirm this is a place where nature has readjusted the landscape at least once before. Assess the snow conditions and practise wise avalanche precautions by walking across this area one person at a time. From the north side of the opening admire the view overlooking the lower part of Whistler Mountain and the village. Sometimes there are plastic lawn chairs here for those who want a seat to rest briefly.

The deceptively gradual ascent continues as you walk along the forest road. By the time the second lookout is reached – an opening created by a large rocky area – more direct views of Whistler Mountain, Creekside and Black Tusk can be seen.

As you snowshoe farther along the road, the sides become steeper and the new trailhead for the Sproatt alpine trail can be seen. Later, one exit for a lower loop for this new trail occurs on the left, while another exit is in the Callaghan Valley. About 1¾ hours after departing from Function Junction, you reach the first high point, 1020 m, at about 5.7 km. A rock cairn is usually here but may not be visible under heavy snow. The main viewpoint is close to the high point and again overlooks the ski runs of Blackcomb and Whistler and to the north, Wedge Mountain. While viewing these two successful commercial resorts and outdoor adventure playgrounds, a feeling of freedom may overcome snowshoers who are enjoying their own low-cost day of winter adventure.

After briefly descending on the trail, several upward traverses lead to the next high point, in the forest at around 1029 m. While walking along the rocky ridge follow tape and orange markers, as this terrain can be confusing. A gradual descent leads to a wide, open area and a trail on the left that begins a steady, narrow, winding descent. At a point where there is a choice to go straight ahead or to the right down a winding, steeper path, take the steep right path. The left one is narrow even in the

Myrtle Philip, Whistler pioneer and co-owner of Rainbow Lodge on Alta Lake ca. 1930
WHISTLER MUSEUM AND ARCHIVES, P86 1319 WMA

summer and may have ledges with steep drop-offs after snow accumulates. A wider logging road continues downward (sometimes quite steeply), followed by a brief upward climb leading to a viewpoint towards Alta Lake. Now a gentle downward path leads to the intersection with the Rainbow Lake trail after about 8.5 km from Function Junction. Turn right, passing the snow-covered outhouse on the left, and continue past the water treatment building. Enter the forest straight ahead to find the path that descends for about 900 m to the Rainbow Lake trailhead. If you follow the wide service road down instead of the forest route, you'll find it emerges close to the Whistler cemetery and about 400 m from the Rainbow Lake trailhead. Return to pick up your car at Function Junction and indulge in a pastry at Olives Community Market, open daily 8:30 to 7:00.

Rainbow Falls Loop

Begin on the far side of the Rainbow Lake trailhead parking lot, where the sign indicates the Flank Trail. This is also the trailhead for the northern part of Flank Trail that leads to Alpine Meadows and is seldom used by snowshoers. Enter the woods and begin a steady climb. At a possible turn to the right, go to the left. Continue until you come to a log gate on the left restricting access by motorized vehicles. Go through the gate and follow the path, which leads to a view high above the falls. After viewing the falls, continue to the right until you reach the bridge. Ensure that the bridge is clear enough of snow to have sides for a safe crossing before using it as part of the loop. Otherwise, return on the ascent trail. If the bridge is safe, cross over and snowshoe briefly to the right, climb up a short hill on a left traverse and arrive at the top, where there is one end of the service road from the road below. Go to the left (the right leads to more water service buildings and has no access) and exit at the largest water building. Here a choice can be made to either take the forest path to the left to the Rainbow Lake trailhead and your car or take the service road downhill. By using the service road to descend to the cemetery gates it is approximately a 2.4 km loop and 1 hour of snowshoeing.

This trail can be done in a clockwise manner by starting at the Rainbow Lake trailhead sign.

FLANK TRAIL

The entire Flank Trail is called Rainbow–Sproatt Flank Trail and is divided into three parts: Alexander Falls to Function Junction; Function Junction to Rainbow Lake Trailhead; and Rainbow Lake Trailhead to Alpine Meadows. Located on the "flank" of Mount Sproatt and Rainbow Mountain, the trail makes an easy traverse for any season of the year and is used by mountain bikers, dog walkers, hikers and snowshoers.

The north end of Flank Trail overlooks Alta Lake, the site of Rainbow Lodge built by Whistler pioneers and visionaries John and Myrtle Philip in 1914. The original lodge burned down in 1977 but several of the cabins and information about the early history of the region can be seen in Rainbow Park, situated on Alta Lake.

Parkhurst Ghost Town Loop

ACCESS: Drive north to Whistler on Highway 99. Pass Village Gate Boulevard and go about 11.4 km farther to the Wedgemount Lake turnoff on the right. Cross Green River on the bridge and turn right into the plowed parking area.

RATING: easy to moderate with several steep areas and narrow trails; parts of the trail may need to be tracked

SEASON: December to mid-March

MAP: 92J02 Whistler

BEGINNING ALTITUDE: 607 m

DESTINATION ALTITUDE: 671 m at Parkhurst Ghost Town; 740 m at high point

DISTANCE: 8.5 km loop to Parkhurst Ghost Town with return via Sea to Sky trail; 8.2 km loop via early cut-off

TIME: 4½–5 hours

CELLPHONE ACCESS: yes

FOOD AND DRINK: Whistler; stores in the Nesters subdivision

WASHROOMS: environmentally considerate use of the forest

DOGS: yes

AVALANCHE CONDITIONS: **avalanche.ca**

This trail starts at the north end of the Green Lake section of the Sea to Sky trail and leads to the last remaining semi-intact house and other artifacts in the Parkhurst Ghost Town. If it has not been tracked it is a good trail to get your backcountry ski friends to break for you.

Directions

Take the wide road leading south from the parking area. On the left a small sign on a tree indicates the end of the Green Lake

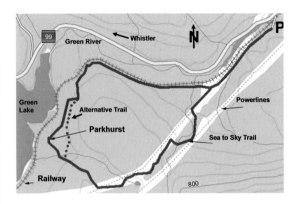

section of the Sea to Sky Trail. Follow a logging road up a hill, past a sign warning about a 20 per cent grade. This is to alert drivers heading for Whistler Paintball's summer playground. Continue on this road, eventually descending to a wide flat area where there's an abandoned camper van. Cross the Bethal Creek bridge and go past the first and second yellow gates on the left. Here a decision can be made depending on weather and time and the energy and skill of the participants.

Clockwise on Sea to Sky trail

This trail is easier for beginning snowshoers. By passing beside the yellow gate and using the Sea to Sky trail to reach the ghost town in a clockwise direction, you'll encounter terrain that will have gradual steep hills to the cross trail and then be mainly flat into the townsite. This trail may not need tracking. It generally runs through open terrain under the hydro right-of-way and does not require walking along narrow paths on the sides of hills. Head south and cross over to the left under the power lines. Follow the Sea to Sky trail upward along an access road, cross a bridge and then re-enter the forest, taking short traverses to gain altitude. After exiting from the forest and leaving the marked Sea to Sky trail, turn left and then either go straight ahead past a small hill on the right or climb briefly and to the right to arrive close to hydro tower 522. Descend a small hill on a left diagonal and continue on the left side of the hydro right-of-way. The turnoff to the ghost town can be found farther south by snowshoeing along on the flat past the (frozen) water and log hollow on the left and looking south. Two hydro towers appear, side by side on a small rise. Turn right at the base of this rise and head towards the forest, a wide opening and the cross trail leading to the ghost town.

Counterclockwise on forest trail

This route is more challenging for the last half, where snowshoeing on forest hillsides and tracking the path may be required. It will take longer, so start early in the day. However, it provides an interesting and peaceful forest trail, so pass both yellow gates, walk straight ahead and then turn left and walk carefully across a car bridge that has no supporting sides. There are boards where car tires would travel and this is where the snowshoe path needs to follow; on either side and in the middle there are wide gaps between the logs. Keep the railway to your right through a wide, flat meadow that is actually a siding for trains. Just before the rail line makes a right-hand bend at about 2.3 km there is a small, colourful railway sign. A few metres ahead, on a tree to the left, is a sign that says GREEN LAKE LOOP/PARKHURST.

Enter the woods and snowshoe along a wide path with a tree-covered slope on the left and trees and the railway below to the right. After about 600 m there is a Y junction.

NOTE: The following information is for interest/information only. It is illegal to walk on or near CN railway property and this section of track is especially dangerous because of the sharp C

Town of Parkhurst, BC, photographed from the mill ca. 1938 or later   P90_003_CHESLEY WMA

A haunting face on the sole remaining Parkhurst house

curve of the tracks. The area below the tracks is easily and safely accessed by canoe during the summer.

To the right, down a slope and across the tracks, is a tract of land on Green Lake where part of a mill was situated. Rusting water tanks, old vehicles and machinery are scattered everywhere. Roadways now overgrown with deciduous scrub trees lead to the river's edge.

Choose safety and take the left path to begin a gradual ascent of the ridge by following the scattered tapes on the trees. A turn to the left leading to steeper terrain has an open area on the right but the only views are of more trees.

For a shorter, more direct way to the old townsite, continue on the rising and falling path along the side of the ridge. This stretch may need to be tracked and some of it requires traversing the ridge hill and kicking-in the track. At about 3.6 km watch for flagging on the right. Follow the tree flags down a short hill and along a path for about 700 m to the one house still standing, which has the compelling blue face of a woman painted on it.

For a slightly longer and more challenging trail, after passing the open area noted above, continue climbing on the path in a southeasterly direction. Pass the shortcut trail on the right. Similar to trail conditions noted previously, this section may need to be tracked and some portions may require snowshoeing along narrow shelves kicked into the side of the hill. After turning southwest, descend through thinning forest and flatter terrain. The exit from this slightly longer route – about 4.35 m from the beginning – is marked by a tree encircled in pink ribbon. To see the last remains of the old Parkhurst townsite, turn right and follow the wide biking path for a short distance to another broad track on the right. The trail now returns through forest for about 300 m to the main Parkhurst townsite, on a small ridge overlooking Green Lake. The location was chosen because it was a bit more remote from the smoke and noise of the mill. Depending on snow cover, you may see a vehicle and other artifacts throughout the site. Farther west on the lakeside (along the east–west Sea to Sky trail), an old caterpillar tractor used in some aspects of lumbering rests on a point overlooking the north end of Green Lake.

Take (or retrace) the trail that led into the townsite from the Sea to Sky cross trail and turn left at the junction with the cross trail. Follow this about 500 m east to its intersection with the BC Hydro right-of-way. Cross under the wires and turn left. Continue north, staying to the right and passing through a narrow path between short coniferous trees. On the left is a hollow, often filled with logs and water. At the base of a small hill, either go straight ahead to the right of the hill or begin a gradual ascent while crossing on a diagonal to the left. At the top of the hill on the left is hydro tower 522. Turn right and descend to the wide access road that leads on the left to the marked forest path of the Sea to Sky trail. A relatively steep downhill path with short traverses awaits and then this narrow trail meets up again with the wide access road. Turn right and continue to descend. After a sharp right turn, there is a left turn across a wide bridge. Continue on the road and then on a diagonal crossing under the hydro lines to the other side of the right-of-way. Then aim north to reach the yellow gates that mark the road to the Bethal Creek bridge. Cross the bridge and retrace the road to the trailhead.

PARKHURST GHOST TOWN

What is now called the Parkhurst Ghost Town was once a small logging town on the ridge above the north end of Green Lake. Industrial activity began in an organized fashion in 1926 when Barr Brothers Logging Co. purchased the land from a widow named Mrs. Parkhurst, who with her husband had pre-empted the property in 1902. The Barr bothers kept the Parkhursts' original cabin and added bunkhouses for the over 70 loggers who felled trees in the area and operated the steam-powered mill. Workers were paid $1 a day to cut logs around the lake and boom them to the mill. When the Depression-era struggling economy and low lumber prices caused a slowdown, the operation went into receivership in 1930 and was purchased by Northern Mills in 1932. When the mill burned in 1938 the business floundered again. Not to be defeated, the loggers first moved the enterprise to Lost Lake and then back again to Parkhurst, where it continued operating until 1956. Although the town had a store, family houses and by 1956 a small school, it was abandoned in the 1960s. Some use was made of the buildings in the early years of Whistler by "alternative lifestyle individuals." Today, parts of several of the old collapsed houses can be seen through the snow, and if the snow is low at least one rusting vehicle, cans and household appliances. Please help preserve this historic place.

Tumbler Ridge Shipyard–Titanic Trail   PHOTOGRAPHER: BIRGIT SHARMAN, 2015

MORE SNOWSHOE ADVENTURES IN BRITISH COLUMBIA

This chapter will help you find new places throughout British Columbia to extend your exploration of snowshoe trails. All of these possibilities are located close to a Nordic and/or downhill ski venue or in a provincial park or protected community area, and many of them have marked trails.

Snowshoe trails have been developed at most of the major and smaller ski resorts. The larger commercial venues often require paid tickets for the use of their trails, but they do provide a safe, mapped environment in unfamiliar terrain. Cost of trail tickets varies for each resort. At a number of the smaller, local Nordic ski venues that also have marked snowshoe trails, the cost is often covered by contribution, which provides the funds necessary for maintaining the trails and warming huts.

NOTE: When snowshoeing on trails that intersect cross-country trails, do not go on or beside any trackset trails. Stay to the outside edges of any track, and cross only at designated locations.

An additional possible location to find trails is in the provincial parks using the summer trail maps. As noted elsewhere in this book, however, in winter the familiar well-trodden summer paths are covered with snow; bushes are often bent over paths; landmarks such as bridges, streams or falls are frozen and filled in with snow; and the whole terrain may appear bewildering and have hidden danger zones. Places that are safe to cross in summer may be avalanche-prone in winter. Use these trails only if you have a topographic map and good map-reading skills as well as suitable wilderness survival equipment and avalanche safety knowledge. Always check the avalanche status and terrain for the area in which you plan to snowshoe.

The information given here about each of these ski centres and clubs was summarized from their various websites and direct contact with them during completion of this guidebook in September 2016. We recommend you check for maps, the current status of trails, and weather and road conditions before planning your trip.

SOUTH COASTAL MOUNTAINS

Mount Seymour

mountseymour.com • Guest services 604-986-2261 • Snow report 604-986-2261 ext 1

NEAREST CITY/TOWN: North Vancouver

DISTANCE FROM NEAREST CITY/TOWN: 17 km from downtown Vancouver

RESORT/LODGE: Mount Seymour Resort lodge

LOCAL NORDIC SKI CLUB: n/a

EXTENT OF TRAILS: 10+ km marked and ticketed on the Discovery Snowshoe Trails

TICKETS: at Snowshoe Adventure Centre rental office (trails in the provincial parks are free)

TRAIL MAP: at Snowshoe Adventure Centre for pay trails and at **mountseymour.com/snowshoe-trail-status-map**

GUIDED TOURS: guided and group tours; Baby and Me tours; fondue evening tours; snow-fit

RENTALS: at Snowshoe Adventure Centre

SHUTTLE SERVICE: Mt. Seymour shuttle bus from Lonsdale Quay and Parkgate Village. Park on residential streets, not in the shopping centre parking lots.

Hollyburn Mountain

cypressmountain.com • 604-926-5612

NEAREST CITY/TOWN: West Vancouver

DISTANCE FROM NEAREST CITY/TOWN: 27 km from downtown Vancouver

RESORT/LODGE: Hollyburn day lodge

LOCAL NORDIC SKI CLUB: Hollyburn Nordic Ski Club, **hollyburnxc.ca**

EXTENT OF TRAILS: 10 km of ticketed snowshoe trails

TICKETS: available at the Nordic ticket booth

TRAIL MAP: **cypressmountain.com**; ticket office

GUIDED TOURS: guided and group tours; cheese and chocolate fondue tours

RENTALS: at Nordic ski/ticketed snowshoe area

SHUTTLE SERVICE: **cypresscoachlines.com**

Grouse Mountain

grousemountain.com • 604-980-9311 • Snow phone 604-986-6262

NEAREST CITY/TOWN: North Vancouver

DISTANCE FROM NEAREST CITY/TOWN: 14 km from downtown Vancouver

RESORT/LODGE: Grouse Mountain Resort

LOCAL NORDIC SKI CLUB: n/a

EXTENT OF TRAILS: 9.4 km in Munday Alpine Snowshoe Park and Snowshoe Grind to top of Dam Mountain

TICKETS: cost of gondola ride to peak

TRAIL MAP: pdf linked from **grousemountain.com/ mountain-map/winter**; at resort

GUIDED TOURS: as part of specific programs

RENTALS: at Fireside Hut by the skating pond

SHUTTLE SERVICE: TransLink bus 232 Grouse Mtn/Phibbs Exchange; details at **translink.ca**

Squamish Sea to Sky Gondola

seatoskygondola.com/adventures/snowshoeing • 1-855-732-8675

NEAREST CITY/TOWN: Squamish

DISTANCE FROM NEAREST CITY/TOWN: 65 km from downtown Vancouver

RESORT: Summit Lodge (day only), Summit Restaurant, Edge Bar and Summit Tea House

LOCAL NORDIC SKI CLUB: Sea to Sky Nordics, **seatoskynordics.ca**

EXTENT OF TRAILS: over 30 km, both groomed and backcountry

TICKETS: **seatoskygondola.com/visit/tickets-and-passes**

TRAIL MAP: **seatoskygondola.com/adventures/trail-maps** and at ticket booth

GUIDED TOURS: available in area of lodge

RENTALS: Vancouver; Squamish; Summit Lodge

HOURS: December 1 to April 30, 10 a.m. to 5 p.m. daily

SHUTTLE: from three Vancouver locations, **seatoskygondola. com/visit/shuttle**

Whistler/Blackcomb

whistlerblackcomb.com • 1-800-766-0449

Lost Lake Trails • crosscountryconnection.ca/lost-lake

NEAREST CITY/TOWN: Whistler

DISTANCE FROM NEAREST CITY/TOWN: 127 km from downtown Vancouver

RESORT/LODGE: Whistler Blackcomb

LOCAL NORDIC SKI CLUB: Whistler Nordics Ski Club **whistlernordics.com**; Pemberton Spud Valley Nordic Ski Association, **spudvalleynordics.com**; Sea to Sky Nordics, **seatoskynordics.ca**

EXTENT OF TRAILS: 13.8 km plus Fairmont Chateau Whistler and Nicklaus North golf courses and around Green Lake

TICKETS: Cross Country Connection, 604-905-0071, open 8:00 a.m. to 8:00 p.m.

TRAIL MAP: **crosscountryconnection.ca/snowshoe**

GUIDED TOURS: nature, cookout, fondue, eagle and First Nations cultural, **whistler.com/snowshoeing**

RENTALS: Cross Country Connection, **crosscountryconnection.ca,** at beginning of trails; Sportstop near the Conference Centre in Village

SHUTTLE SERVICE: free village shuttle

Whistler Olympic Park

whistlersportlegacies.com • 1-877-764-2455, 604-964-2455

NEAREST CITY/TOWN: Whistler

DISTANCES FROM NEAREST CITIES/TOWNS: 16 km southwest of Whistler; 50 km north of Squamish; 115 km north of Vancouver

RESORT/LODGE: day lodge

LOCAL NORDIC SKI CLUBS: Whistler Nordics Ski club, **whistlernordics.com**; Pemberton Spud Valley Nordic Ski Assn., **spudvalleynordics.com**; Sea to Sky Nordics, **seatoskynordics.ca**

EXTENT OF TRAILS: 40+ km (7.5 km dog friendly)

TICKETS: available at day lodge

TRAIL MAP: **whistlersportlegacies.com**; at lodge

GUIDED TOURS: private and group tours

RENTALS: Whistler; Squamish; day lodge

SHUTTLE SERVICE: From Whistler Village 604-964-0060, **info@whistlerolympicpark.com**

Callaghan Country

callaghancountry.com • 1-877-938-0616 • Information also available at Olympic Park Lodge

NEAREST CITY/TOWN: Whistler

DISTANCES FROM NEAREST CITIES/TOWNS: 16 km southwest of Whistler; 115 km north of Vancouver

RESORT/LODGE: Journeyman Lodge

LOCAL NORDIC SKI CLUB: Callaghan Valley Nordic Ski Club, **callaghanxcski.ca**; Pemberton Spud Valley Nordic Ski Association, **spudvalleynordics.com**; Sea to Sky Nordics, **seatoskynordics.ca**

EXTENT OF TRAILS: 15 km of lower trails with route flags; 12.5 km to lodge, which has meadow and forest trails that are unmarked

TICKETS: at Olympic Park day lodge and Callaghan Country base warming cabin

TRAIL MAP: pdf from **is.gd/XODHGK**; paper from Olympic Park day lodge and Alexander Falls Touring Centre

GUIDED TOURS: weekend snowshoe tours

RENTALS: Callaghan Country base warming cabin

SHUTTLE SERVICE: snowcat from Callaghan Country base to lodge

Hemlock Ski Resort

hemlockvalleyresort.com • 1-866-567-6866

NEAREST CITY/TOWN: Mission

DISTANCES FROM NEAREST CITIES/TOWNS: Mission, 55 km; Abbotsford, 67.4 km; Vancouver, 128 km
NOTE: to use the Hemlock Valley resort road, all vehicles must carry chains or tire cables throughout the winter.

RESORT/LODGE: small day lodge at ski hill

LOCAL NORDIC SKI CLUB: n/a

EXTENT OF TRAILS: 9 km plus guided wilderness trails

TICKETS: available at lodge and necessary for use of lift or any trek trails

TRAIL MAP: **hemlockresort.ca/snowshoeing-at-hemlock-valley-resort**; at lodge

GUIDED TOURS: at lodge; also guided cardio workouts

RENTALS: at lodge
SHUTTLE: n/a

SUNSHINE COAST
Dakota Ridge

dakotaridge.ca • Sunshine Coast Regional District 604-885-6802

NEAREST CITY/TOWN: Sechelt

DISTANCES FROM NEAREST CITIES/TOWNS: 14 km of
4WD (with chains) serviced road from Sechelt; 84 km and
less than 2 hours (plus ferry time) from Vancouver; refer to
dakotaridge.ca for road and snow conditions

RESORT/LODGE: day warming hut

LOCAL NORDIC SKI CLUB: Tetrahedron Outdoor Club,
tetoutdoor.ca

EXTENT OF TRAILS: 8 km for beginners plus ungroomed
wilderness trails

TICKETS: at warming hut

TRAIL MAP: **dakotaridge.ca** and at warming hut

GUIDED TOURS: Alpha Adventures, 604-885-8838
or 1-877-43-KAYAK, **outdooradventurestore.ca/
snowshow-ski/guided-snowshoe-tours**

RENTALS: Alpha Adventures, **outdooradventurestore.ca/
snowshow-ski/snowshoe-rentals**

SHUTTLE SERVICE: Alpha Adventures, **is.gd/lltgGP**

Knuckleheads Winter Recreation Area

Knuckleheads Winter Recreation Society • theknuckleheads.wordpress.com/cabins-2 •
(no phone number published)

NEAREST CITY/TOWN: Powell River

DISTANCES FROM NEAREST CITIES/TOWNS: 37 km from
Powell River + 28 km from turnoff on Dixon Road; 102 km +
28 km from Sechelt

NOTE: check status of logging roads; active logging occurs daily. Western Forest Products 24/7 hotline 604-485-3132 or office 604-485-3100 ext 0

RESORT/LODGE: n/a; overnight huts accessible by A Branch and E Branch

LOCAL NORDIC SKI CLUB: Knuckleheads Winter Recreation Society

EXTENT OF TRAILS: all trails are unmarked

TICKETS: n/a

TRAIL MAP: pdf linked from **powellriver.info/ Tourism-Powell-River**

GUIDED TOURS: n/a

RENTALS: Powell River, **canoeingbc.com/snowshoe-rentals**

SHUTTLE SERVICE: n/a

NOTE: Winter roads need four-wheel drive with chains

Tetrahedron Provincial Park

www.env.gov.bc.ca/bcparks/explore/parkpgs/tetrahedron

NEAREST CITY/TOWN: Sechelt

DISTANCE FROM NEAREST CITY/TOWN: about 21 km from Sechelt (snow tires, 4WD and chains are needed to get to park)

RESORT/LODGE: n/a (four sleeping huts available at various spots in the park)

LOCAL NORDIC SKI CLUB: Tetrahedron Outdoor Club, **tetoutdoor.ca**

EXTENT OF TRAILS: all trails are intermediate (ski) trails with some steep sections; (ski) trail to Mt. Steele is considered advanced

DOGS: dogs are NOT ALLOWED AT ALL in this provincial park – it is a watershed

TICKETS: n/a

TRAIL MAP: pdf at **tetoutdoor.ca/maps.html**

GUIDED TOURS: Alpha Adventures Sechelt,
info@outdooradventurestore.ca

RENTALS: Alpha Adventures Sechelt, **outdooradventurestore.ca/snowshow-ski/snowshoe-rentals**

SHUTTLE SERVICE: Alpha Adventures Sechelt, **info@outdooradventurestore.ca**

NOTE: winter roads need four-wheel drive with chains

THOMPSON/OKANAGAN

Big White Ski Resort

bigwhite.com • 250-765-3101

NEAREST CITY/TOWN: Kelowna

DISTANCE FROM NEAREST CITY/TOWN: 56 km from Kelowna

RESORT/LODGE: Big White Ski Resort

LOCAL NORDIC SKI CLUB: Kelowna Nordic Ski & Snowshoe Club, **kelownanordic.com**

EXTENT OF TRAILS: 25 km of combined Nordic and wilderness trails

TICKETS: Happy Valley Day Lodge; Village Centre Mall

TRAIL MAP: **bigwhite.com/events-and-activities/on-the-mountain/snowshoeing**

GUIDED TOURS: variety of tours bookable on website

RENTALS: Kelowna; Big White Ski Resort

SHUTTLE SERVICE: on mountain throughout the day; shopping shuttle to Kelowna Superstore; Kelowna Airport shuttle

McCulloch Nordic Area

NEAREST CITY/TOWN: Kelowna

DISTANCE FROM NEAREST CITY/TOWN: 35 km southeast of Kelowna

RESORT/LODGE: small day lodge; three trail shelters

LOCAL NORDIC SKI CLUB: Kelowna Nordic Ski Club
kelownanordic.com

EXTENT OF TRAILS: about 80 km, all named with variations on "snow" or "snowy"

TICKETS: at trailhead

TRAIL MAP: pdf from **kelownanordic.com/index.php/trail-info/snowshoeing**

GUIDED TOURS: available through Kelowna Nordic Club and Monashee Adventure Tours, **monasheeadventuretours.com**

RENTALS: Kelowna

SHUTTLE SERVICE: n/a

Crystal Mountain

crystalresort.com • 250-768-5189 • Crystal Mountain was closed for the 2015/2016 winter season but hopes to open for 2016/2017

NEAREST CITIES/TOWNS: Westbank; Kelowna

DISTANCE FROM NEAREST CITY/TOWN: 14 km from Westbank; 28 km from Kelowna

RESORT/LODGE: day lodge (when open)

LOCAL NORDIC SKI CLUB: Kelowna Nordic Ski Club, **kelownanordic.com**

EXTENT OF TRAILS: 12 km of packed trail at periphery of ski hill; not accessible except with a tour until hill reopens

TICKETS: nominal fee

TRAIL MAP: available at **crystalresort.com**

GUIDED TOURS: available from Selah Outdoor Adventures 250-768-4961 Discovery Tours, Winterwoods and Starlight tours

RENTALS: Kelowna

SHUTTLE SERVICE: n/a

Silver Star Mountain Resort

250-542-0224 • 1-800-663-4431 • snow phone 250-542-1745 • skisilverstar.com

Sovereign Lake Nordic Centre

250-558-3036 ext 203 • 1-877-768-5253 • snow phone 250-260-5335 • sovereignlake.com

NEAREST CITY/TOWN: Vernon

DISTANCE FROM NEAREST CITY/TOWN: 28 km from Vernon

RESORT/LODGE: Silver Star Mountain Resort; Sovereign Lake day lodge

LOCAL NORDIC SKI CLUB: Sovereign Lake Nordic Club, **sovereignlake.com/club**

EXTENT OF TRAILS: 16 km in Silverstar's lower Nordic area; 14 km in Sovereign Lakes Nordic trail system

TICKETS: Silver Star Mountain Resort ticket office; Sovereign Lake day lodge

TRAIL MAP: **skisilverstar.com** or Silver Star ticket office; **sovereignlake.com** or Sovereign Lake day lodge

GUIDED TOURS: volunteer tours available

RENTALS: Sovereign Lake day lodge; Silver Star Mountain Resort ski rental shop

SHUTTLE SERVICE: n/a

Nickel Plate Nordic Centre

nickelplatenordic.org

NEAREST CITY/TOWN: Penticton

DISTANCE FROM NEAREST CITY/TOWN: about 44 km from Penticton and 7 km from Apex Mountain Resort

RESORT/LODGE: day lodge

LOCAL NORDIC SKI CLUB: Nickel Plate Nordic ski club, **nickelplatenordic.org**

EXTENT OF TRAILS: 25 km of marked snowshoe trails

TICKETS: at ticket office

TRAIL MAP: **nickelplatenordic.org/trails**; at ticket office

GUIDED TOURS: group leaders Tuesdays at 10 a.m.

RENTALS: at ticket office

SHUTTLE SERVICE: n/a

Sun Peaks (Kamloops)

sunpeaksresort.com • (250) 578-5474 • 1.800.807.3257 • snow phone (250) 578-7232

NEAREST CITY/TOWN: Kamloops

DISTANCE FROM NEAREST CITY/TOWN: 50 km from Kamloops

RESORT/LODGE: Sun Peaks Resort

LOCAL NORDIC SKI CLUB: Overlander Ski Club, **overlanderskiclub.com**

EXTENT OF TRAILS: 15.5 km

TICKETS: at resort

TRAIL MAP: **sunpeaksresort.com/winter/interactive-maps/ nordic** and at resort

GUIDED TOURS: from resort – moonlight, marshmallow roast, valley of the lynx, winter wonderland and snowshoe golf

RENTALS: at resort

SHUTTLE SERVICE: n/a

Stake Lake

overlanderskiclub.com • snow phone 250-372-5514

NEAREST CITY/TOWN: Kamloops

DISTANCE FROM NEAREST CITY/TOWN: 25 km south of Kamloops

RESORT/LODGE: day lodge

LOCAL NORDIC SKI CLUB: Overlander Ski Club, **overlanderskiclub.com**

EXTENT OF TRAILS: 13 km of marked snowshoe trails

TICKETS: at day lodge

TRAIL MAP: pdf linked from **overlanderskiclub.com/ enjoy-our-trails**

GUIDED TOURS: n/a
RENTALS: on site; Kamloops
SHUTTLE SERVICE: n/a

Kane Valley

sonotek.com/kane_snowshoe.html

NEAREST CITY/TOWN: Merritt
DISTANCE FROM NEAREST CITY/TOWN: 18 km south of Merritt
RESORT/LODGE: shelters with fire pits
LOCAL NORDIC SKI CLUB: Nicola Nordic Ski Club, **nicolanordic.ca**
EXTENT OF TRAILS: 11.5 km of ungroomed trails that may
   have blowdowns. Do not snowshoe in the Nordic trail areas.
   Access is from several of the parking lots.
TICKETS: donation
TRAIL MAP: **sonotek.com/kane_snowshoe.html** has brief
   written trail descriptions with links to GPX data and Google
   Earth KMZ data; you'll still need a map and adequate
   route-finding/map-reading skills
GUIDED TOURS: n/a
RENTALS: Kamloops; Kelowna
SHUTTLE SERVICE: n/a

Mount Baldy

skibaldy.com • Office 250-485-7593

NOTE: Mount Baldy was in receivership for winter 2015/16; the new owners anticipate the mountain will be open for the 2016/17 season.

NEAREST CITY/TOWN: Oliver
DISTANCE FROM NEAREST CITY/TOWN: 35 km from Oliver
RESORT/LODGE: day lodge
LOCAL NORDIC SKI CLUB: n/a
EXTENT OF TRAILS: 10 km
TICKETS: at ticket booth

TRAIL MAP: at day lodge

GUIDED TOURS: n/a

RENTALS: at day lodge

SHUTTLE SERVICE: n/a

Wells Gray Provincial Park (Info Centre)

wellsgraypark.info/snowshoeing • 250-674-3334

NEAREST CITY/TOWN: Clearwater

DISTANCE FROM NEAREST CITY/TOWN: 35 km from Clearwater

RESORT/LODGE: Helmcken Falls Lodge, **helmckenfalls.com**

LOCAL NORDIC SKI CLUB: Wells Gray Outdoors Club,
wellsgrayoutdoorsclub.ca

EXTENT OF TRAILS: numerous trails from lodge are shared
with Nordic skiers; also use of summer hiking trails in park

TICKETS: n/a

TRAIL MAP: lodge staff will direct you; brief trail descriptions
at **wellsgraypark.info/snowshoeing**

GUIDED TOURS: combined snowshoeing/snowmobiling,
**bcbackcountryadventures.com/mushing/canadianclassic
.htm**

RENTALS: n/a

SHUTTLE SERVICE: n/a

Larch Hills

skilarchhills.ca

NEAREST CITY/TOWN: Salmon Arm

DISTANCE FROM NEAREST CITY/TOWN: 24 km east of
Salmon Arm

RESORT/LODGE: n/a

LOCAL NORDIC SKI CLUB: Larch Hills Nordic Society

EXTENT OF TRAILS: 14 km

TICKETS: at trailhead

TRAIL MAP: **skilarchhills.ca/maps**; at chalet
RENTALS: Salmon Arm
SHUTTLE SERVICE: n/a

Logan Lake

loganlake.ca

NEAREST CITIES/TOWNS: Merritt; Kamloops
DISTANCE FROM NEAREST CITIES/TOWNS: 48 km from Merritt; 60 km from Kamloops
RESORT/LODGE: no lodge or warming huts
LOCAL NORDIC SKI CLUB: n/a, but see **kamloopshikingclub.net**; **highlandvalleyoutdoorassociation.com**
EXTENT OF TRAILS: 14 km snowshoeing (7.5 km shared with Nordic skiing); plus summer trails in Tunkwa Lake Provincial Park 16 km away
TICKETS: at trailhead
TRAIL MAPS: pdf from **visitloganlake.com/things-to-do/trails**
RENTALS: Merritt; Kamloops
SHUTTLE SERVICE: n/a

KOOTENAY ROCKIES

Kimberley Alpine Resort

skikimberley.com • 1-800-258-SNOW (7669)

NEAREST CITY/TOWN: Kimberley
DISTANCE FROM NEAREST CITIES/TOWNS: 30 km from Cranbrook; 2 km from Kimberley
RESORT/LODGE: day lodge
LOCAL NORDIC SKI CLUB: Kimberley Nordic Club, **kimberleynordic.org**
EXTENT OF TRAILS: The resort does not have set trails but offers two tours descending through trees from the top of the ski lift.

TICKETS: tour tickets
TRAIL MAP: n/a
GUIDED TOURS: daily
RENTALS: at resort lodge
SHUTTLE SERVICE: n/a

Kimberley Nordic Centre

kimberleynordic.org

NEAREST CITY/TOWN: Kimberley

DISTANCE FROM NEAREST CITIES/TOWNS: 30 km from Cranbrook; 2 km from Kimberley; trails are near Kimberley ski hill

RESORT/LODGE: day lodge

LOCAL NORDIC SKI CLUB: Kimberley Nordic Club, **kimberleynordic.org**

EXTENT OF TRAILS: The Nordic Centre offers access to Kimberley Nature Park and adjacent Crown land.
NOTE: the trails are neither marked nor patrolled and are user-maintained

TICKETS: at trail kiosk

TRAIL MAP: map of Kimberley Nature Park available at city hall, chamber of commerce and tourist bureau in Kimberley; for suggested trails see **kimberleynordic.org/map**

GUIDED TOURS: n/a

RENTALS: Kimberley Alpine Resort

SHUTTLE SERVICE: n/a

Panorama Mountain

panoramaresort.com • 250-342-6941 • Snow phone 250-342-6941 ext. 3

NEAREST CITY/TOWN: Invermere

DISTANCE FROM NEAREST CITY/TOWN: 18 km west of Invermere

RESORT/LODGE: Panorama Mountain Village, Grey Wolf
Nordic Centre, 250-341-4100

LOCAL NORDIC SKI CLUB: Toby Creek Nordic Ski Club
tobycreeknordic.ca

EXTENT OF TRAILS: 4 km; shared trails may also be available
at Nordic ski areas of Lake Windermere, Whiteway, Hale
Hut, Baptiste Lake at Edgewater, The Radium Course golf
links. Check before going.

TICKETS: unknown

TRAIL MAP: at resort

GUIDED TOURS: by request

RENTALS: Greywolf Nordic Centre

SHUTTLE SERVICE: Mountain and Valley shuttle connects
Panorama with Invermere

Mount Macpherson

revelstokemountainresort.com • 1-866-373-4754

NEAREST CITY/TOWN: Revelstoke

DISTANCE FROM NEAREST CITY/TOWN: 7 km south of
Revelstoke

RESORT/LODGE: Revelstoke Mountain Resort

LOCAL NORDIC SKI CLUB: Revelstoke Nordic Ski Club,
revelstokenordic.org

EXTENT OF TRAILS: unmarked trails close to ski trails 4.5 km
of marked trail

TICKETS: at day lodge or trailhead honesty box

TRAIL MAP: on sign at trailhead; smaller maps at trail
junctions; **revelstokenordic.org**

GUIDED TOURS: n/a

RENTALS: Revelstoke

SHUTTLE SERVICE: n/a

Paulson Nordic Ski Area

NEAREST CITY/TOWN: Castlegar

DISTANCE FROM NEAREST CITY/TOWN: 32 km west of Castlegar

RESORT/LODGE: Viking Centre day lodge and three warming huts

LOCAL NORDIC SKI CLUB: Castlegar Nordic Ski Club
castlegarnordic.ca

EXTENT OF TRAILS: 45 km of tracked trails for Nordic skiing
NOTE: seek permission first before snowshoeing beside the
ski trails: **castlegarnordicski@gmail.com**

TICKETS: donation

TRAIL MAP: pdf from **castlegarnordic.ca/trails-map-0**

GUIDED TOURS: n/a

RENTALS: Rossland

SHUTTLE SERVICE: n/a

Fernie Trails

NEAREST CITY/TOWN: Fernie

DISTANCE FROM NEAREST CITY/TOWN: 96 km from
Cranbrook

RESORT/LODGE: n/a; trails are close to Fernie town amenities

LOCAL NORDIC SKI CLUB: Fernie Nordic Society,
fernienordic.com

EXTENT OF TRAILS: 12 km on golf course; Fernie dike has
additional multi-use trails in Montane Nordic ski area; no
snowshoeing at Elk Valley Nordic Centre

TICKETS: lock box in Fernie Golf & Country Club parking lot
or Island Lake Lodge lower parking lot; online via PayPal at
fernienordic.com

TRAIL MAP: **fernienordic.com/visitor_info**

GUIDED TOURS: n/a

RENTALS: downtown Fernie; Fernie Alpine Resort

SHUTTLE SERVICE: n/a

Fernie Alpine Resort

skifernie.com • 1-800-258-7669

NEAREST CITY/TOWN: Fernie

DISTANCE FROM NEAREST CITY/TOWN: 7 km from Fernie

RESORT/LODGE: Fernie Alpine Resort

LOCAL NORDIC SKI CLUB: Fernie Nordic Society,
fernienordic.com

EXTENT OF TRAILS: 12 km

TICKETS: unknown

TRAIL MAP: **fernie.com/activities/winter-activities/
cross-country-skiing**

GUIDED TOURS: Wild Nature Tours, **wildnaturetours.ca**

RENTALS: Fernie; Lizard Creek Lodge

SHUTTLE SERVICE: daytime shuttle from Fernie to the
Fernie Alpine Resort

Red Mountain Resort

redresort.com • 1-800-663-0105 or 250-362-7384

NEAREST CITY/TOWN: Rossland

DISTANCE FROM NEAREST CITY/TOWN: 9 km from Trail;
37 km from Castlegar; 4 km from Rossland

RESORT/LODGE: Red Mountain Resort

LOCAL NORDIC SKI CLUB: Blackjack Ski Club, **skiblackjack.ca**

EXTENT OF TRAILS: 1 km marked loop at base of mountain,
with 4 new loops added in 2015/16. **NOTE:** No snowshoeing
is allowed at Blackjack Nordic area.

TICKETS: unknown

TRAIL MAP: pdf linked from **redresort.com/mountain/
stats-map**

GUIDED TOURS: fondue tour with **lepetitfromage.ca**; tours
at Red Mountain Resort and Nancy Green Summit with
kootenaysnowshoeing.com

RENTALS: Red Mountain Resort; Rossland; Trail
SHUTTLE SERVICE: free between Rossland and resort; fares
from Trail, Castlegar, Kelowna and Cranbrook airports

Jack Rabbit Trail (Nakusp Community Forest Trail)

NEAREST CITIES/TOWNS: Nakusp; Nelson; Revelstoke
DISTANCE FROM NEAREST CITY/TOWN: 3 km from Nakusp
RESORT/LODGE: warming hut along Wensley Creek
cross-country trail, but **NOTE** that no snowshoeing is
allowed along the trail to this hut
LOCAL NORDIC SKI CLUB: Arrow Lakes Cross-country Ski
Club, **is.gd/eS0w4c**
EXTENT OF TRAILS: 4 km one-way interpretive trail starting just
east of Arrow Lakes Cross-country Ski Club equipment shed
in Upper Brouse, accessible from each end of the trail (Upper
Brouse or Wilson Lake); other routes are Peter Roulston Trail off
the Nakusp Hot Springs road, 8.5 km one way; and unmarked
trails around Nakusp Hot Springs. Check avalanche areas.
TICKETS: n/a
TRAIL MAPS: pdf from **nakuspcommunityforest.com/
projects/jackrabbit**
GUIDED TOURS: n/a
RENTALS: n/a
SHUTTLE SERVICE: n/a

Summit Lake Ski & Snowboard Area

skisummitlake.com • 250-265-3312

NEAREST CITY/TOWN: Nakusp
DISTANCE FROM NEAREST CITY/TOWN: 15 km
RESORT/LODGE: day lodge
LOCAL NORDIC SKI CLUB: Arrow Lakes Cross-country Ski
Club, **is.gd/eS0w4c**

EXTENT OF TRAILS: Rails to Trails – Nakusp to Summit Lake, about 16 km

TICKETS: n/a

TRAIL MAP: pdf at **nakusptrails.ca/wp-content/uploads/nakusp-to-rosebery-railway-trail.pdf**

GUIDED TOURS: n/a

RENTALS: n/a

SHUTTLE SERVICE: n/a

Whitewater Winter Resort

skiwhitewater.com • 250-354-4944 or 1-800-666-9420

NEAREST CITY/TOWN: Nelson

DISTANCE FROM NEAREST CITY/TOWN: about 22 km from Nelson

RESORT/LODGE: Whitewater day lodge

LOCAL NORDIC SKI CLUB: Nelson Nordic Ski club, **nelsonnordicski.ca**

EXTENT OF TRAILS: 10 km at Nordic Centre plus 5 km mixed use

TICKETS: day lodge and Nordic Centre

TRAIL MAP: **skiwhitewater.com/whitewater_nordic_centre.php**; at kiosk

GUIDED TOURS: lessons available on request

RENTALS: Nelson; day lodge

SHUTTLE SERVICE: morning departure from various points in Nelson; afternoon return; fare

Creston Valley Wildlife Management Area

crestonwildlife.ca/recreation/trails

NEAREST CITIES/TOWNS: Cranbrook; Nelson

DISTANCE FROM NEAREST CITIES/TOWNS: 105 km southwest of Cranbrook; 124 km southeast of Nelson

RESORT/LODGE: town amenities

LOCAL NORDIC SKI CLUB: n/a

EXTENT OF TRAILS: about 30 km on dike paths through Creston Valley Wildlife Management Area, plus unmarked trails requiring route finding and map reading in Stagleap Provincial Park about half an hour west of town (at the top of Salmo–Creston Pass)

TICKETS: n/a

TRAIL MAP: **crestonwildlife.ca/recreation/trails**

GUIDED TOURS: n/a

RENTALS: Creston

SHUTTLE SERVICE: n/a

Kicking Horse Mountain Resort

kickinghorseresort.com • 1-866-ski-kick (754-5425)

NEAREST CITY/TOWN: Golden

DISTANCE FROM NEAREST CITY/TOWN: 14 km west of Golden

RESORT/LODGE: Kicking Horse Mountain Resort

LOCAL NORDIC SKI CLUB: Golden Nordic Ski Club, **goldennordicclub.ca**

EXTENT OF TRAILS: loops of 2 or 4 km at resort; also 4.6 km weaving among Dawn Mountain Nordic ski trails (13 km from Golden) and Golden golf course (6 km from Golden): **goldennordicclub.ca/directions**

TICKETS: Dawn Mountain Nordic Centre

TRAIL MAPS: **kickinghorseresort.com/winter-main/the-resort/things-to-do/snowshoeing; goldennordicclub.ca/descriptions-maps**

GUIDED TOURS: Dawn Mountain Ski School

RENTALS: Kicking Horse lodge; Dawn Mountain Chalet

SHUTTLE SERVICE: n/a

Emerald Lake Lodge in Yoho National Park

pc.gc.ca/eng/pn-np/bc/yoho/index.aspx

NEAREST CITY/TOWN: Lake Louise or Golden

DISTANCE FROM NEAREST CITY/TOWN: about 30 km west of Lake Louise

RESORT/LODGE: Emerald Lake Lodge; Emerald Sports & Gifts for purchased food

LOCAL NORDIC SKI CLUB: Kicking Horse Ski Club, **khsc.ca**

EXTENT OF TRAILS: 20+ km wilderness trails: Hamilton Falls, Lake O'Hara, Emerald River to the meeting of the Kicking Horse and Amiskwi rivers.

TICKETS: by donation

TRAIL MAP: **khsc.ca/trail-maps**; Emerald Sports & Gifts

GUIDED TOURS: Great Divide Nature Interpretation tours in Lake Louise area, **greatdivide.ca/snowshoeing.html**

RENTALS: Emerald Lake Lodge; Lake Louise; Emerald Sports & Gifts in Field

SHUTTLE SERVICE: n/a

Nipika Mountain Resort

nipika.com • 1-877-647-4525

NEAREST CITIES/TOWNS: Radium Hot Springs; Invermere

DISTANCE FROM NEAREST CITIES/TOWNS: 35 km from Radium Hot Springs; 51 km from Invermere

RESORT/LODGE: Nipika Mountain Resort

LOCAL NORDIC SKI CLUB: Toby Creek Nordic Ski Club, **tobycreeknordic.ca**

EXTENT OF TRAILS: 50 km of shared Nordic from resort; 9 km Columbia Valley Greenways Trail Alliance Old Coach Trail, **cvtrails.ca/trails/104**

TICKETS: at lodge

TRAIL MAP: **nipika.com/eco-resort-rocky-mountain-cabins/ nipika-resort-rocky-mountain-trails**

GUIDED TOURS: on request at lodge

RENTALS: at resort; in Invermere

SHUTTLE: to White River bridge; back to Nipika from Canal Flats

99 Mile Ski Trails and Nordic Day Lodge

NEAREST CITY/TOWN: 100 Mile House

DISTANCE FROM NEAREST CITY/TOWN: 5 km south of 100 Mile House

RESORT/LODGE: day lodge

LOCAL NORDIC SKI CLUB: 100 Mile Nordic Ski Society, **100milenordics.com**

EXTENT OF TRAILS: 7.5 km

TICKETS: at day lodge

TRAIL MAP: **100milenordics.com/trail-maps.html**

GUIDED TOURS: reserve-and-pay special-focus tours

RENTALS: at day lodge

SHUTTLE SERVICE: n/a

Spruce Hills Resort & Spa at 108 Mile House

sprucehillresort.com • 1.800.668.2233

NEAREST CITY/TOWN: 100 Mile House

DISTANCE FROM NEAREST CITY/TOWN: 8 km north of 100 Mile House

RESORT/LODGE: private resort lodge

LOCAL NORDIC SKI CLUB: 100 Mile Nordic Ski Society, **100milenordics.com**

EXTENT OF TRAILS: 20 km of snowshoe trails; extensive wilderness trails

TICKETS: day use tickets at lodge; free for guests

TRAIL MAP: at lodge

GUIDED TOURS: at lodge, by reservation

RENTALS: n/a

SHUTTLE SERVICE: n/a

Wells/Barkerville Mountain Trails

wellsbarkervilletrails.com

NEAREST CITY/TOWN: Quesnel

DISTANCE FROM NEAREST CITY/TOWN: 74 km from Quesnel; additional 7 km to Barkerville

RESORT/LODGE: n/a

LOCAL NORDIC SKI CLUB: Wells and Area Trails Society

EXTENT OF TRAILS: 49.6 km of ungroomed trails that make up the Barkerville Boneshaker mountain bike event; additional trails in adjacent areas

TICKETS: n/a

TRAIL MAP: **wellsbarkervilletrails.com/trails/wells/#tab5**

GUIDED TOURS: n/a

RENTALS: Quesnel

SHUTTLE SERVICE: n/a

Williams Lake Bull Mountain Trails

bullmountain.ca/ski-area.html

NEAREST CITY/TOWN: Williams Lake

DISTANCE FROM NEAREST CITY/TOWN: 16 km north of Williams Lake

RESORT/LODGE: warming hut

LOCAL NORDIC SKI CLUB: Williams Lake Cross-Country Ski Club, **bullmountain.ca**

EXTENT OF TRAILS: 4.3 km of beginner and intermediate loops

TICKETS: at warming hut

TRAIL MAPS: **bullmountain.ca/downloads.html**

GUIDED TOURS: n/a

RENTALS: Williams Lake
SHUTTLE SERVICE: n/a

Tweedsmuir Provincial Park South, East Branch

www.env.gov.bc.ca/bcparks/explore/parkpgs/tweeds_s

NEAREST CITIES/TOWNS: Anahim Lake; Bella Coola
DISTANCE FROM NEAREST CITIES/TOWNS: 45 km west of Anahim Lake; 95 km east of Bella Coola
RESORT/LODGE: warming hut/day lodge at ski hill, 3.5 km from parking; overnight cabin by reservation
LOCAL NORDIC SKI CLUB: Tweedsmuir Ski Club, **tweedsmuirskiclub.com**
EXTENT OF TRAILS: 30 km of mixed use ski trails
TICKETS: make a contribution by joining Tweedsmuir Ski Club
TRAIL MAP: **tweedsmuirskiclub.com/cross-country-information**
GUIDED TOURS: n/a
RENTALS: n/a
SHUTTLE SERVICE: n/a

NORTHERN BRITISH COLUMBIA

Smithers and Burns Lake

NEAREST CITIES/TOWNS: Smithers; Burns Lake
DISTANCE FROM NEAREST CITIES/TOWNS: Bulkley Valley Nordic Centre is 12 km southwest of Smithers on Hudson Bay Mountain Road; Omineca Ski Club is 8 km south of Burns Lake on Highway 35
RESORT/LODGE: Bulkley Valley Nordic Centre's Buchfink Lodge; Omineca's Jean Paulson Lodge (not always open but the heated wax cabin is)
LOCAL NORDIC SKI CLUBS: Bulkley Valley Cross Country Ski Club, **bvnordic.ca**; Omineca Ski Club, **ominecaskiclub.ca**

EXTENT OF TRAILS: Bulkley Valley has shared Nordic trails as well as snowshoe-only ones, plus 5.5 km of lighted routes and 7 km of dog-friendly trails; Omineca has 45 km shared with Nordic skiers as well as two snowshoe-only trails of 1.7 and 3 km

TICKETS: self-ticketing is available at the wax cabin near the upper parking lot and at Buchfink Lodge; also in downtown Smithers at McBike & Sport and at Winterland Ski.

TRAIL MAP: **bvnordic.ca/trails-and-facilities/maps**; **ominecaskiclub.ca/trails/trail-maps-and-routes** and at Buchfink Lodge

GUIDED TOURS: n/a

RENTALS: Smithers

SHUTTLE SERVICE: n/a

Babine Mountains Provincial Park

www.env.gov.bc.ca/bcparks/explore/parkpgs/babine_mtn

NEAREST CITY/TOWN: Smithers

DISTANCE FROM NEAREST CITY/TOWN: 6 km northeast of Smithers

RESORT/LODGE: day lodge; overnight shelters available for longer snowshoeing trips

LOCAL NORDIC SKI CLUBS: Bulkley Valley Cross Country Ski Club, **bvnordic.ca** and Omineca Ski Club, **ominecaskiclub.ca**

EXTENT OF TRAILS: 6 km to Sunny Point; skiers and snow-shoers may travel on the snowmobile trails. Snowshoeing is best explored throughout the Silver King and Cronin Creek basins or by following Lyon Creek Trail and Harvey Mountain Trail. Map reading will be necessary.

TICKETS: n/a

TRAIL MAP: pdf at **is.gd/8F5sj8**

GUIDED TOURS: n/a

RENTALS: Smithers: McBike & Sport; Winterland Ski

SHUTTLE SERVICE: n/a

Howson Hut Wilderness Retreats (privately owned)

NEAREST CITY/TOWN: Telkwa; Smithers

DISTANCE FROM NEAREST CITY/TOWN: 20 km from Smithers

RESORT/LODGE: log cabin and sauna at McDowell Lake

LOCAL NORDIC SKI CLUBS: Bulkley Valley Cross Country Ski Club, **bvnordic.ca**; Omineca Ski Club, **ominecaskiclub.ca**

EXTENT OF TRAILS: 25–30 km track-set ski trails – unknown whether these are shared; there are also unmarked wilderness trails

TICKETS: n/a

TRAIL MAP: guided tours by request; information available from lodge

RENTALS: Smithers: McBike & Sport; Winterland Ski

SHUTTLE SERVICE: n/a

Eskers Provincial Park

www.env.gov.bc.ca/bcparks/explore/parkpgs/eskers

NEAREST CITY/TOWN: Prince George

DISTANCE FROM NEAREST CITY/TOWN: 40 km northwest of Prince George

RESORT/LODGE: picnic shelter

LOCAL NORDIC SKI CLUB: Caledonia Nordic Ski Club, **caledonianordic.com**

EXTENT OF TRAILS: 4.6 km mapped snowshoe trail; about 12 km using summer trails in Eskers park; also routes in Giscome Portage Trail Protected Area, about 40 km north of Prince George

TICKETS: n/a

TRAIL MAP: pdf at **is.gd/Q3itQ5**
GUIDED TOURS: n/a
RENTALS: Prince George
SHUTTLE SERVICE: n/a

Powder King Resort
powderking.com • 1-866-769-5464

NEAREST CITY/TOWN: Prince George
DISTANCE FROM NEAREST CITY/TOWN: 184 km north of Prince George
RESORT/LODGE: Powder King Mountain Resort
LOCAL NORDIC SKI CLUB: Caledonia Nordic Ski Club, **caledonianordic.com**
EXTENT OF TRAILS: approximately 13 km for snowshoeing
TICKETS: free
TRAIL MAP: from website eventually
GUIDED TOURS: reserve by phone
RENTALS: at lodge
SHUTTLE SERVICE: PK Express from Prince George

Otway Nordic Ski Centre
250-564-3809; snowphone 250-649-1144

NEAREST CITY/TOWN: Prince George
DISTANCE FROM NEAREST CITY/TOWN: about 5 km north-west of Prince George
RESORT/LODGE: Nordic Centre
LOCAL NORDIC SKI CLUB: Caledonia Nordic Ski Club, **caledonianordic.com**
EXTENT OF TRAILS: 30 km of snowshoe trails and 18 km along greenway from UNBC to Otway
TICKETS: from office and rental shop at Nordic Centre

TRAIL MAP: **caledonianordic.com/trails-facilities/maps/ snowshoe-trails**; at Nordic Centre

GUIDED TOURS: n/a

RENTALS: at Nordic Centre

SHUTTLE SERVICE: n/a

Giscome Portage Trail Protected Area

www.env.gov.bc.ca/bcparks/explore/parkpgs/giscome

NEAREST CITY/TOWN: Prince George

DISTANCE FROM NEAREST CITY/TOWN: 46 km north of Prince George

RESORT/LODGE: n/a

LOCAL NORDIC SKI CLUB: Caledonia Nordic Ski Club, **caledonianordic.com**

EXTENT OF TRAILS: 8.5 km one way, using a summer trail

TICKETS: n/a

TRAIL MAP: pdf at **is.gd/5wTpXH**

GUIDED TOURS: n/a

RENTALS: Prince George

SHUTTLE SERVICE: n/a

Bear Mountain Ski Hill

NEAREST CITY/TOWN: Dawson Creek

DISTANCE FROM NEAREST CITY/TOWN: about 11 km south-west of Dawson Creek

RESORT/LODGE: warm-up shelters and a cabin

LOCAL NORDIC SKI CLUB: Bear Mountain Nordic Ski Association, **nordicski.ca**

EXTENT OF TRAILS: 10 km snowshoe; 26 km ski

TICKETS: day pass at trailhead

TRAIL MAP: **nordicski.ca/maps.php**

GUIDED TOURS: by appointment

RENTALS: Dawson Creek (sales)
SHUTTLE SERVICE: n/a

Tumbler Ridge

visittumblerridge.ca/Tumbler-Ridge/Activities • 1-877-729-3466 • 250-242-3123 (tourism information)

NEAREST CITIES/TOWNS: Tumbler Ridge

DISTANCE FROM NEAREST CITY/TOWN: (numerous venues in region)

RESORT/LODGE: shops and accommodation in town

LOCAL NORDIC SKI CLUB: Wolverine Nordic and Mountain Society, **wnms.ca**

EXTENT OF TRAILS: no marked snowshoe routes but summer hiking trails can be used, as well as sides of Nordic tracks leaving from golf course

TICKETS: n/a

TRAIL MAP: route descriptions booklet (pdf) from **wnms. ca/?page_id=57**; Tumbler Ridge Community Centre

GUIDED TOURS: n/a

RENTALS: Tumbler Ridge Community Centre (four pairs of snowshoes)

SHUTTLE SERVICE: n/a

Beatton Provincial Park

www.env.gov.bc.ca/bcparks/explore/parkpgs/beatton

NEAREST CITY/TOWN: Fort St. John

DISTANCE FROM NEAREST CITY/TOWN: 13 km northwest of Fort St. John

RESORT/LODGE: picnic shelter

LOCAL NORDIC SKI CLUB: Whiskey Jack Nordic Ski Club: Eliza Stanford, **whiskeyjacknsc@gmail.com**

EXTENT OF TRAILS: approximately 12 km

TICKETS: n/a

TRAIL MAP: pdf at **is.gd/9CdLbM**
GUIDED TOURS: n/a
RENTALS: Fort St. John
SHUTTLE SERVICE: n/a

Onion Lake Ski Trails

NEAREST CITIES/TOWNS: Kitimat; Terrace
DISTANCES FROM NEAREST CITIES/TOWNS: about 31 km
from either city
RESORT/LODGE: clubhouse
LOCAL NORDIC SKI CLUB: Snow Valley Nordic Ski Club,
snowvalleynordics.com
EXTENT OF TRAILS: 6 km mixed use on dog-run trail
TICKETS: at ticket booth facing parking lot
TRAIL MAP: **snowvalleynordics.com**
GUIDED TOURS: n/a
RENTALS: Terrace
SHUTTLE SERVICE: n/a

VANCOUVER ISLAND

Mount Cain

mountcain.com • 1-888-668-6622 • snow phone 250-949-snow (7669)
NEAREST CITIES/TOWNS: Port McNeil; Sayward
DISTANCES FROM NEAREST CITIES/TOWNS: about 91 km
southeast of Port McNeil; 77 km southwest of Sayward; near
Schoen Lake Provincial Park
RESORT/LODGE: day lodge
LOCAL NORDIC SKI CLUB: Mount Cain Alpine Park Society,
mountcain.com
EXTENT OF TRAILS: no marked trails; route finding needed;
head for the meadows and make your own trail
TICKETS: n/a

TRAIL MAP: pdf at **mountcain.com/about-cain/trail-map. html** (downhill ski map, for general orientation only)

GUIDED TOURS: n/a

RENTALS: n/a

SHUTTLE SERVICE: from lower parking lot

Mount Washington Alpine Resort

mountwashington.ca • 250-338-1386 • 1-888-231-1499

recipient of a Best Snowshoeing award from Ski Canada magazine

NEAREST CITIES/TOWNS: Courtenay; Comox; Nanaimo

DISTANCES FROM NEAREST CITIES/TOWNS: 18 km west of Courtenay and Comox; 100 km north of Nanaimo

RESORT/LODGE: Raven Nordic Lodge

LOCAL NORDIC SKI CLUB: Strathcona Nordic Ski Club, **strathconanordics.com**

EXTENT OF TRAILS: 16 km close to Raven Lodge, plus trails in Paradise Meadows in Strathcona Park

TICKETS: at Raven Lodge on Nordic Road

TRAIL MAP: pdf at **mountwashington.ca/downloads/re- sort/Nordic-Snowshoe-13.pdf**; Nordic Raven Lodge

GUIDED TOURS: Discover Snowshoeing package; Snowshoe Tour and Fondue Dinner; customized tours

RENTALS: Raven Lodge

SHUTTLE SERVICE: **mountwashington.ca/travelling-by-bus.html**

USA DESTINATIONS

For those wishing to explore the snowshoe trails in the United States close to the lower mainland, there are several websites available. Although these sites are primarily addressed to downhill skiers, the individual resorts often also describe Nordic ski and snowshoe trails in their area: **skiwashington.com**, **skioregon.org** and **visitidaho.org/winter**. As well, there are numerous guidebooks covering snowshoe trails in many of the US states.

PART 3

SNOWSHOEING RESOURCES

Once you discover how enjoyable trail snowshoeing can be, you may want to extend the activity as part of a cross-training regime or enter competitions involving snowshoe races. There are opportunities to meet new people through outdoor groups that hike in the summer and snowshoe in the winter. Activities such as fondue or full moon snowshoe trips planned by various organizations or ski hills are fun and can add romance to the activity. Increasingly, snowshoe trips are being organized for families and seniors through community centres.

Jack gets an early start on training for a snowshoe race

SNOWSHOE RACING

Grouse Mountain provides a clinic to prepare athletes of any level to compete in snowshoe races. There is also the annual Grouse Mountain Snowshoe Grind Challenge, **grousemountain.com/events**.

The World Snowshoe Federation's Snowshoe World Championships took place as part of the Quebec Winter Carnival in 2015. The race was held at Vezza d'Oglio, Italy, in 2016 and at Saranac, NY, in 2017. (**snowshoerunning.org**)

The North Face Dirty Feet Snowshoe Fun Run and Walk occurs at Stake Lake, Silver Star, Big White and Sun Peaks. Check **dirtyfeet.ca** for dates.

The Comox Valley Snow to Surf event has a snowshoe leg as part of the activities.

SNOWSHOE LESSONS AND TOURS IN THE LOWER MAINLAND

Cypress Mountain: guided tours on snowshoe trails within paid Nordic area, **cypressmountain.com**

Grouse Mountain: Boomers and Zoomers 50+, Ladies Only, Baby & Me, Beginner Clinics and private tours,
grousemountain.com/snowshoe

Hemlock Valley: lift-accessed tours along alpine snowshoe trails,
hemlockresort.ca/snowshoeing-at-hemlock-valley-resort

Hope Mountain Centre for Outdoor Learning: guided snowshoe trips to Manning and Coquihalla destinations,
hopemountain.org/programs

Manning Park: guided snowshoe tours,
manningpark.com/snowshoeing

Mount Seymour: Discovery Snowshoe guided tours within paid snowshoe area, **mountseymour.com/snowshoe-tours**

Powell River: tours to the Knuckleheads area by Mitchell's, **canoeingbc.ca**

Sechelt: tours to Dakota Ridge area by Alpha Adventures, **outdooradventurestore.ca**

Whistler: guided snowshoe tours, **canadianwilderness.com/snowshoe**; **tagwhistler.com/activity/snowshoe-tours**

SELECTED INDIVIDUAL OR GROUP OUTINGS

Cypress Mountain: Girls Night Out snowshoe tour **cypressmountain.com**

Grouse Mountain: Baby and Me Clinic, **grousemountain.com/snowshoe-clinics/baby-me**

Grouse Mountain: Snowshoe Grind – get a Grind timer chip to track your progress and time in completing the Dam Mountain Loop, Boomers and Zoomers 50+ group, **grousemountain.com/snowshoe**

Hope Mountain Centre for Outdoor Learning: family and women-only snowshoe outings, **hopemountain.org**

Manning Park: Snowshoe Stomp, **manningpark.com/event-calendar**

Mount Seymour: Baby and Me, **mountseymour.com/snowshoe-tours**

Mount Seymour: Snow Fit, **mountseymour.com/snowshoe-tours**

Vancouver Snowshoe Meet-up groups, **snowshoeing.meetup.com/cities/ca/bc/vancouver/**

ADVENTURES FOR EXPERIENCED SNOWSHOERS

Wells Gray Provincial Park, **www.env.gov.bc.ca/bcparks/explore/parkpgs/wells_gry** for trails in the park. For guided and self-catered cabin rental for backcountry skiers, cross-country skiers and snowshoers, visit **skihike.com**

Snowshoe racing up the Grouse Snowshoe Grind
PHOTO COURTESY OF GROUSE MOUNTAIN RESORT

LEARN HISTORY/CULTURE WHILE SNOWSHOEING

Cypress Mountain: Hollyburn Meadows Tour,
cypressmountain.com/snowshoe-tours

Mount Seymour: Legends and Lanterns tour,
mountseymour.com/snowshoe-tours

Whistler: Natural Mystic, Winter Wonderland and others,
tagwhistler.com/activity/snowshoe-tours

Whistler: The Medicine Trail,
  canadianwilderness.com/snowshoe

SNOWSHOEING AND FOOD

Cypress Mountain: Music Night Snowshoe Tour (Nordic
  Hollyburn Lodge access only with tour tickets); Cheese and
  Chocolate Dinner Fondue Tour; Chocolate Fondue Tour,
  cypressmountain.com/snowshoe-tours

Grouse Mountain: private evening snowshoe tour followed
  by cheese, broth and chocolate fondue in Altitudes Bistro,
  grousemountain.com/snowshoe-fondue

Mount Seymour: Chocolate Fondue Tour,
  mountseymour.com/snowshoe-tours

Disclaimer: Inclusion of the names of private companies, tours,
goods or services does not imply endorsement of them by the authors. It is the responsibility of each individual to assess the goods,
services, safety procedures, liability and costs from the company
or person offering the merchandise, event or service.

APPENDIX A: NAVIGATION

NTS MAPS

National Topographic System (NTS) maps at 1:50,000 scale show ground relief (landforms and terrain), drainage (lakes and rivers), forest cover, administrative areas, populated areas, transportation routes and facilities (including roads and railways) and other man-made features. A 1:50,000 scale map covers approximately 1000 square kilometres. These are the maps to use for accurate location finding. For complete details, see **nrcan.gc.ca/earth-sciences/geography/topographic-information/maps/9767**.

Particular NTS maps are searchable at Natural Resources Canada's GeoGratis site, **geogratis.gc.ca/geogratis/en/search** ...

... and can be purchased at physical stores such as MEC (**mec.ca**) and MapTown (**maptown.com**) and online stores such as YellowMaps (**canmaps.com**). See also the BC government service GeoBC (**geobc.gov.bc.ca**).

Trails alphabetically grouped by NTS map

92F16 Haslam Lake

　　Knuckleheads E Branch Cabin (p. 240)

92G06 North Vancouver

　　Black Mountain Loop Trail (p. 166)

　　Bowen Lookout Trail (p. 174)

　　Hollyburn Mountain Trail (p. 184)

　　Howe Sound Crest East Trail Loop (p. 190)

　　Thunderbird Ridge Trail (p. 201)

92G07 Port Coquitlam

　　Burke Ridge via Old Harper Road Trail (p. 131)

　　Dog Mountain and First Lake Loop Trail (p. 179)

　　Mount Seymour First Peak Trail (p. 195)

92G12 Sechelt Inlet

Tetrahedron Provincial Park: Edwards Cabin Trail (p. 235)

92G14 Cheakamus River

Garibaldi Lake and Taylor Meadows Trails (p. 222)

Red Heather Meadows Trail (p. 231)

92G15 Mamquam Mountain

Red Heather Meadows Trail (p. 231)

92H02 Manning Park

Cambie Creek Loop Trail (p. 135)

Fat Dog Ridge Trail (p. 139)

Lightning Lake Loop Trail (p. 142)

Monument 78 Trail (p. 147)

Poland Lake Trail (p. 151)

Windy Joe Trail (p. 160)

92H03 Skagit River

Skagit River Trail (p. 155)

92H06 Hope

Portia to Iago Station Trail (p. 123)

92H10 Tulameen

Mount Henning Cabin Loop Trail (p. 110)

92H11 Spuzzum

Falls Lake Trail (p. 107)

Mount Henning Cabin Loop Trail (p. 110)

Mount Ottomite Trail (p. 115)

Needle Peak Ridge Trail (p. 118)

Portia to Iago Station Trail (p. 123)

Zoa Peak Trail (p. 127)

92J02 Whistler

Ancient Cedars Grove Trail (p. 262)

Cheakamus Lake Trail (p. 252)

Highline Loop Trail (p. 255)

Mid-Flank Trail (p. 266)

Parkhurst Ghost Town Loop Trail (p. 273)

92J03 Brandywine

Black Tusk Microwave Road Trail (p. 248)

Cal-Cheak Recreation Site to Brandywine Falls Trail (p. 207)

Cheakamus Crossing Loop Trail (p. 212)

Cheakamus Crossing to Cal-Cheak Recreation Site Trail (p. 217)

Cheakamus Lake Trail (p. 252)

Lava Lake Loop Trail (p. 226)

Loggers Lake and Ridge Loop Trail (p. 259)

Mid-Flank Trail (p. 266)

Trail finders

Trailpeak route database: **trailpeak.com**

Vancouver Trails (includes a forum and a blog):
vancouvertrails.com

OTHER NAVIGATIONAL AIDS

Smartphone maps for local areas are helpful but should not be your only source for trail and location finding. Some apps suggested to us by MEC staff are Topomaps Canada for iOS and Mapstogo for Android. However, the MEC people we spoke with said they continue to prefer the paper topo maps.

Many of the trails described here are in provincial parks, and park summer trail maps may give a general sense of direction. But be aware that in winter the all-white landscape can be quite disorienting, so take along a topo map as well. Comprehensive information for the provincial parks is at **env. gov.bc.ca/bcparks/visiting**.

APPENDIX B: SAFETY

ALWAYS CHECK BEFORE YOU GO

Roads

Google Maps is useful for calculating approximate distances from your home to snowshoeing areas: **maps.google.ca**.

For current road conditions, consult **drivebc.com**.

BC Highways webcams are at **images.drivebc.ca**.

Logging road information

>Western Forest Products:
>
>24/7 Road Access Hotline 604-485-3132
>
>office 604-485-3100 ext 0
>
>In order to use logging roads during weekdays you must have a radio programmed with the appropriate channels.

Weather

Obtain up-to-date reports and forecasts for the areas to and through which you will be driving:

weather.gc.ca

theweathernetwork.com

Snow and avalanche conditions

Make sure to check snow and avalanche conditions for **every trip**:

>Avalanche Canada's Public Avalanche Bulletins, **avalanche.ca**.
>
>ACMG Mountain Conditions Report, **mountainconditions.com**.

Snow phones at the various parks and resorts can give you an idea of local conditions. For example:

>Cypress Mountain: **cypressmountain.com;** 604-419-SNOW (7669); snowshoe line 604-922-0825
>
>Mount Seymour: **mountseymour.com;** 604-986-2261 ext 1

Whistler: **whistlerblackcomb.com**; 604-932-4211

Grouse Mountain: **grousemountain.com**; 604-986-6262

See also ATES, the Avalanche Terrain Exposure Scale, available in printable pdf from Parks Canada at **is.gd/NBsJPq**.

AVALANCHE COURSES

Lower Mainland ski resorts Mount Seymour, Grouse, Cypress and Whistler offer two- to four-day avalanche skills training courses.

Hope Mountain Centre for Outdoor Learning, **hopemountain.org**, offers similar, three-day courses.

Other avalanche course providers include:

Altus Mountain Guides, **altusmountainguides.com**

Canada West Mountain School, **themountainschool.com**

Coast Mountain Guides, **coastmountainguides.com**

Mountain Skills Academy & Adventures, **mountainskillsacademy.com**

Powder Guides Inc., **powderguides.com**

BC Parks, partnering with Avalanche Canada, Canadian Pacific and others, sponsors Avalanche Awareness Days at numerous venues in the Lower Mainland. Check **avalanche.ca** under the News&Events/News tab for announcements like this: **avalanche.ca/news/avalanche-awareness-days-primer**.

Disclaimer: Inclusion of the named organizations and companies providing avalanche training does not imply endorsement of them by the authors. It is the responsibility of each individual to compare curriculums and ensure that the instructors are certified and that the course includes both classroom and snow field instruction. Classroom and outdoors simulated accidents that might occur in a wilderness setting are an essential part of the curriculum for wilderness first aid training.

GUIDE SERVICES

Association of Canadian Mountain Guides (ACMG): **acmg.ca**

Altus Mountain Guides: **altusmountainguides.com**

Coast Mountain Guides: **coastmountainguides.com**

Powder Guides Inc.: **powderguides.com**

APPENDIX C: OTHER
USEFUL RESOURCES

Clubs

Cross-Country BC has a listing of all the cross-country ski clubs in the province: **crosscountrybc.ca/club-directory**

Hope Mountain Centre for Outdoor Learning:
hopemountain.org

Inquiry BC: 604-660-2421 toll-free from Lower Mainland; 1-800-663-7867 if phoning from outside the Lower Mainland

Knuckleheads Winter Recreation Assn.:
theknuckleheads.wordpress.com

Sea to Sky Trail: **seatoskytrail.ca**

Snowshoe Canada: **snowshoecanada.com**

Snowshoe magazine has a listing of snowshoe clubs across Canada and the US, plus tips on how to start your own club: **snowshoemag.com**

Sunshine Coast Central:
suncoastcentral.com/outdoor-reports.asp

Tetrahedron Outdoor Club: **tetoutdoor.ca**, 604-740-3030

Traditional Mountaineering, a website by Robert Speik:
traditionalmountaineering.org

US Snowshoe Assn.: **snowshoeracing.com**

"How-to" videos

A Googled list of YouTube clips is at **is.gd/ljAFFt**

Also search "snowshoeing" at **search.aol.com/aol/video** and likewise at **ehow.com**

MISCELLANEOUS

Animal tracks identification

Beartracker's Animal Tracks Den: **bear-tracker.com**

Geographical name authorities

Canadian Geographical Names Database: **is.gd/Zx0HAD**

GeoBC: **apps.gov.bc.ca/pub/bcgnws**

Historical resources

The Canadian Register of Historic Places: **historicplaces.ca**

Hollyburn Heritage Society: **hollyburnheritage.ca**

North Vancouver Museum & Archives: **nvma.ca**

Whistler Museum: **whistlermuseum.org**

Tourism information

Destination BC: **hellobc.com**

Tourism Whistler: **whistler.com**

Whistler Hiatus: **whistlerhiatus.com**

See also the various municipalities' websites.

APPENDIX D: EQUIPMENT

RENTALS

When you first start snowshoeing, renting gear from a sports shop is often an economical option, and over several rentals this enables you to try different types of snowshoes. Some rental shops have longer return times, which allows more flexibility in your plans.

For instance, snowshoes can be rented from MEC and picked up between 3 p.m. and store closing the day before your trip and returned before 1 p.m. the day after you return. MEC also has a weekend special that allows you to pick up after 3 p.m. on a Thursday to return the following Monday morning, or alternatively from Friday to Tuesday, but in either case you pay only for the Saturday and Sunday. And if you purchase snowshoes from MEC within 30 days of a rental, you can deduct one day's rent. Membership in MEC (lifetime membership is still only $5) and your copy of the rental agreement are needed in order to receive the discount on the purchase. Check with your local sports store to see if they have similar options. Here are some examples:

Chilliwack: Mt. Waddington's Outdoors sales and rental,
   mtwaddingtons.com
Cypress Mountain: Nordic Rentals,
   cypressmountain.com/nordic-rentals
Grouse Mountain: Fireside Hut rental,
   grousemountain.com/snowshoe
Manning Park: Nordic Centre rental,
   winter.manningpark.com/snowshoeing
Mount Seymour: Snowshoe Adventure Centre rental,
   mountseymour.com/snowshoe-rates
Powell River: Mitchell's sales and rental,
   canoeingbc.com/snowshoe-rentals

Sunshine Coast: Alpha Adventures Sechelt sales and rental,
outdooradventurestore.ca

Vancouver, North Vancouver, Langley, Kelowna, Victoria: MEC
(Mountain Equipment Co-op) sales and rental,
mec.ca/en/explore/gear-rental

Vancouver: many sports shops, e.g., Atmosphere, **en.atmosphere.ca**

Whistler: Cross Country Connection at Lost Lake rental,
crosscountryconnection.ca/rentals

Whistler and Squamish: Escape Route product rental,
escaperoute.ca

COMPARISONS

Mountain Equipment Co-op, **mec.ca**

ORS Snowshoes Direct (Vermont), **orssnowshoesdirect.com**

Recreational Equipment, Inc. (USA), **rei.com**

TRADITIONAL WOODEN SNOWSHOES

Canadian sources

The Canadian Outdoor Equipment Co., Mississauga, Ont.:
canadianoutdoorequipment.com

Faber & Co., Quebec City, Que.: **fabersnowshoes.com**

GV Snowshoes, Wendake, Que.: **gvsnowshoes.com**

Total Snowshoes, Sturgeon Falls, Ont.: **totalsnowshoes.com**

US sources

The United States Snowshoe Association provides a list of
American manufacturers, some of whom make traditional snowshoes: **snowshoeracing.com/equipment.htm**.

For a fascinating look at the variety of antique snowshoe
styles, visit eBay's antique snowshoes pages:
ebay.com/bhp/antique-snowshoes.

Disclaimer: Please note that all of the equipment providers mentioned in this appendix are listed here for information purposes only. The authors take no responsibility for the quality of any equipment purchased through eBay or any commercial website or from any physical store.

REFERENCES

Baldwin, John. *Exploring the Coast Mountains on Skis: A Guide to Ski Mountaineering*. 3rd ed. Vancouver: J. Baldwin, 2009.

Bryceland, Jack, David Macaree and Mary Macaree. *103 Hikes in Southwestern British Columbia*. 6th ed. Vancouver: Greystone Books, 2008.

Christie, Jack. *The Whistler Book: An All-season Outdoor Guide*. Rev. ed., expanded and updated. Vancouver: Greystone Books, 2009.

Cyca, Robert, and Andrew Harcombe. *Exploring Manning Park*. Vancouver: Gundy's and Bernie's Guidebooks, 1972.

Hanna, Dawn. *Best Hikes and Walks of Southwestern British Columbia*. Vancouver: Lone Pine Publishing, 1997.

Jamieson, Bruce. *Backcountry Avalanche Awareness*. 8th ed. Revelstoke, BC: Canadian Avalanche Association, 2011.

Kingloff, Amanda, and Lauren Debellis. "20+ Fun Activities to Do in the Snow." *Parents* magazine, January 2010. Accessed August 25, 2016, at **parents.com/fun/activities/outdoor/snow-activities-kids**.

Langford, Dan, and Sandra Langford. *Cycling the Kettle Valley Railway*. 3rd ed. Calgary: Rocky Mountain Books, 2002, reprinted 2008.

Litzenberger, Lyle. *Burke and Widgeon: A Hiker's Guide*. Port Coquitlam, BC: Pebblestone Publishing, 2013.

Macaree, David, and Mary Macaree. *109 Walks in B.C.'s Lower Mainland*. Seattle: Mountaineers, 1976.

Merry, Wayne. *Official Wilderness First Aid Guide*. Toronto: St. John Ambulance, 1997.

Petersen, Florence. *First Tracks: Whistler's Early History*. Whistler Museum and Archives Society, 2012.

Prater, Gene, edited by Dave Felkley. *Snowshoeing from Novice to Master*. 5th ed. Seattle: The Mountaineers Books, 2002.

Shewchuk, Murphy. *Coquihalla Trips and Trails: A Guide to BC's North Cascade Mountains and Nicola Valley*, Toronto: Fitzhenry & Whiteside, 2007.

St. John Ambulance. *First Aid First on the Scene Activity Book*. Ottawa: St. John Ambulance, 2000.

Statham, Grant, et al., *The Avalanche Terrain Exposure Scale*. Proceedings of the International Snow Science Workshop, Telluride, Colo., 2006.

Stoltmann, Randy. *Hiking Guide to the Big Trees of Southwestern British Columbia*. 2nd ed. Vancouver: Western Canada Wilderness Committee, 1991.

————. *Hiking the Ancient Forests of British Columbia and Washington*. Vancouver: Lone Pine, 1996.

Wright, Richard, and Rochelle Wright. *British Columbia Cross-Country Ski Routes*. Vancouver: Douglas & McIntyre, 1983.

INDEX OF TRAILS

99 Mile Ski Trails and Nordic Day Lodge, 304
A Branch cabin, 245
Ancient Cedars Grove Trail, 262
Babine Mountains Provincial Park, 307
Batchelor Cabin Trail, 239
Bear Mountain Ski Hill, 310
Beatton Provincial Park, 311
Big White Ski Resort, 289
Black Mountain Loop Trail, 166
Black Tusk Microwave Tower Road Trail, 248
Bowen Lookout Trail, 174
Boyd's Meadow, 164
Burke Ridge Trail via Harper Road, 131
Burns Lake. See Smithers and Burns Lake.
Cal-Cheak Recreation Site to Brandywine Falls, 207
Callaghan Country, 285
Cambie Creek Loop Trail, 135
Cascade Lookout, 164
Cheakamus Crossing Loop Trail, 212
Cheakamus Crossing to Cal-Cheak Recreation Site Trail, 217
Cheakamus Lake Trail, 252
Creston Valley Wildlife Management Area, 301
Crystal Mountain, 290
Dakota Ridge, 287
Dog Mountain Trail, 179
Eagle Bluffs, 171
E Branch cabin, 240
Edwards Cabin Trail, 235
Elfin Lakes Trail, 233
Emerald Lake Lodge in Yoho National Park, 303

Eskers Provincial Park, 308
Falls Lake Trail, 107
Fat Dog Ridge Trail, 139
Fernie Alpine Resort, 299
Fernie Trails, 298
First Lake Loop Trail, 179
Flash Lake Loop Trail, 145
Garibaldi Lake Trails, 222
Giscome Portage Trail Protected Area, 310
Grouse Mountain, 283
Harper Road. See Burke Ridge Trail via Harper Road.
Hemlock Ski Resort, 286
Highline Loop Trail, 255
Hollyburn Mountain, 282
Hollyburn Mountain Trail, 184
Howe Sound Crest East Trail Loop, 190
Howson Hut Wilderness Retreats, 308
Jack Rabbit Trail (Nakusp Community Forest Trail), 300
Kane Valley, 293
Kicking Horse Mountain Resort, 302
Kimberley Alpine Resort, 295
Kimberley Nordic Centre, 296
Knuckleheads Winter Recreation Area, 287
    A Branch cabin, 245
    E Branch cabin, 240
Larch Hills, 294
Lava Lake Loop Trail, 226
Lightning Lake Loop Trail, 142
Logan Lake, 295
Logger's Lake and Ridge Loop Trail, 259
McCulloch Nordic Area, 289
Memaloose Trail, 164
Mid-Flank Trail, 266

Monument 78 Trail, 147
Monument 83 Trail, 163
Mount Baldy, 293
Mount Cain, 312
Mount Henning Cabin Loop Trail, 110
Mount Macpherson, 297
Mount Ottomite Trail, 115
Mount Seymour, 282
Mount Seymour First Peak Trail, 195
Mount Washington Alpine Resort, 313
Nakusp Community Forest Trail, 300
Needle Peak Ridge Trail, 118
Nickel Plate Nordic Centre, 291
Nipika Mountain Resort, 303
Onion Lake Ski Trails, 312
Otway Nordic Ski Centre, 309
Panorama Mountain, 296
Parkhurst Ghost Town Loop, 273
Paulson Nordic Ski Area, 298
Poland Lake Trail, 151
Portia to Iago Station Trail, 123
Powder King Resort, 309
Rainbow Falls Loop, 271
Red Heather Meadows, 231
Red Mountain Resort, 299
Ridge Loop Trail. *See* Logger's Lake and
    Ridge Loop Trail.
Silver Star Mountain Resort, 290
Skagit River Trail, 155
Smithers and Burns Lake, 306
Sovereign Lake Nordic Centre, 291
Spruce Hills Resort & Spa at 108 Mile
    House, 304
Squamish Sea to Sky Gondola, 283
Stake Lake, 292
Summit Lake Ski & Snowboard
    Area, 300

Sun Peaks (Kamloops), 292
Taylor Meadows Trails, 222
Tetrahedron Provincial Park, 288
    Batchelor Cabin Trail, 239
    Edwards Cabin Trail, 235
Thunderbird Ridge Trail, 201
Tumbler Ridge, 311
Tweedsmuir Provincial Park South,
    East Branch, 306
Wells/Barkerville Mountain Trails, 305
Wells Gray Provincial Park
    (Info Centre), 294
Whistler/Blackcomb, 284
Whistler Interpretive Forest Trails, 247
Whistler Olympic Park, 285
Whitewater Winter Resort, 301
Williams Lake Bull Mountain Trails, 305
Windy Joe Trail, 160
Zoa Peak Trail, 127

ABOUT THE AUTHORS

Aileen Stalker is a retired occupational therapist who, as her fifth career (having been a teacher, OT, mother and dyslexia tutor), began writing books on topics as varied as sensory regulation, public art, and kayaking. Writing about snowshoe trails has allowed her to do what she loves best: activities with friends and family in the wonderful parks and wilderness areas of BC. When not writing, Aileen enjoys travel, reading, entertaining, woodworking, bicycling, hiking, kayaking and her granddaughter Danika.

Tony Keen is a retired mining engineer and an experienced photographer with an interest in landscape photography. No stranger to cold weather, having spent most of his professional career managing and consulting to mines in northern Canada and Greenland, he found snowshoeing a natural choice for a winter activity. In addition to photography he enjoys spending time with his family as well as kayaking, hiking, cooking, travel and watching rugby.